A Successful N…
Must … in Want
of a Sequel

Also by M. Carmen Gomez-Galisteo

The Wind Is Never Gone: Sequels, Parodies and Rewritings of Gone with the Wind (McFarland, 2011)

A Successful Novel Must Be in Want of a Sequel

Second Takes on Classics from The Scarlet Letter *to* Rebecca

M. Carmen Gomez-Galisteo

McFarland & Company, Inc., Publishers
Jefferson, North Carolina

ISBN (print) 978-1-4766-7282-3
ISBN (ebook) 978-1-4766-3327-5

Library of Congress cataloguing data are available

British Library cataloguing data are available

Printed in the United States of America

McFarland & Company, Inc., Publishers
Box 611, Jefferson, North Carolina 28640
www.mcfarlandpub.com

To Alejandro,
who is still too young to read this book,
but who inspires me every day,
and to Tiffani,
whose recent arrival merits mention

Table of Contents

Introduction

Once or Twice Upon a Time

She will read his little story to the end, and close the book very tenderly and smooth down the cover; and then, when he least expects it, she will toss it into the dusty limbo of her other romances. **Henry James: "Eugene Pickering" (1874)**[1]

What happened after Mr. Darcy and Elizabeth Bennet's wedding? Did they live happily ever after once he had conquered his pride and she had learned to control her tendency to jump to conclusions based on her prejudiced views? What were Mr. Darcy's thoughts during their unusual "courtship"? Did Elinor and Marianne Dashwood find happiness in their respective marriages? Was Marianne really able to settle for marriage to a much older man after having loved the dazzling Willoughby? What did little Adèle think of her new governess, Jane Eyre? Where did Heathcliff go after he left Wuthering Heights? Given the close relationship between *Wuthering Heights* and the Yorkshire moors where it is set, would Heathcliff's love for Catherine Earnshaw read differently if Wuthering Heights were a Caribbean plantation? What was Bertha Mason's life like before she married Rochester? Would Hester Prynne in twentieth-century America also suffer social ostracism for her adultery? And how would her husband take it—would he still plot revenge against his unfaithful wife? Would her lover be plagued by remorse and a guilty conscience? What could Mr. March's Civil War experiences have been, given that he largely failed to convey them in his letters home to his wife and his four little women? What happened after Manderley burned down? Where did Mr. and Mrs.

de Winter go next, their home lost to the fire? Was Rebecca de Winter as evil as her husband believed, or the angel Mrs. Danvers described?

Victorian novels ended with a section called a "wind-up" that summarized what happened next to the main characters so as to sate readers' curiosity about what the future had in store for them. Later books, for the most part, lack this section and therefore, to satisfy readers' inquisitive minds, sequel writers feel compelled to supply a whole, new novel filling this void and telling us how the characters wound up. This is especially true in the case of novels with inconclusive if not downright unhappy endings, which have prompted sequel writers to provide us with, as Henry James called it, the "love of a comfortable ending" that redresses the unhappiness of the original ending. Sequel writers have capitalized on endings deemed unsatisfactory by readers for a number of reasons: they do not provide a clear conclusion, they do not resolutely put at rest questions raised throughout the novel, or they are unhappy. Sequels spell out things half mentioned or half hidden, re-tell a well-known story in a different manner, from another point of view, or continue the action, long after the author writes "The end."[2]

Although feel-good works providing happy endings, such as romances, are routinely accused of reaching unreal or improbable conclusions, stretching credibility in the process, readers have been known to especially favor happy endings. So strong is this tendency that it has sometimes led to authors changing storylines. For instance, Charlotte Brontë was forced by her father, among others, to make the ending of *Villette* less bleak. Charles Dickens, who had written a rather pessimistic ending to *Great Expectations*, was persuaded by fellow writer Edward Bulwer Lytton to change it. As a result of his friend's plea, Dickens ended the novel with Pip and Estella resuming their friendship. Giving a story the happy ending its author deprived us of seems to be a valid and desirable reason for writing a sequel. However, the perceived necessity of having a sequel goes well beyond making amends and providing a happy ending, as evidenced by the fact that even novels with a happy ending have found a continuation in a sequel. Still, whereas even stories with happy endings may be resumed, not all disappointing or unhappy endings are likely to be rewritten and "redeemed" in readers' eyes. Some are past correcting—how could amends be made to reverse the finality of *Romeo and Juliet*?[3]

Upon the publication of *Good Wives*, the second part of *Little Women*, Louisa May Alcott wrote that "a sequel will be out early in April, & like all sequels will probably disappoint or disgust most readers, for publishers wont let authors finish up as they like but insist on having people married off in a wholesale manner which much afflicts me." While it is pretty clear why readers want a sequel to a novel with an unhappy ending, why are some happy-ending novels continued? The answer may well be that some happy endings disappoint because they strain readers' credulity in their pursuit of a happy or satisfactory ending. A happy ending, therefore, is no guarantee that a sequel will not be written if readers feel that the author has gone too far in securing a positive conclusion. Is it possible to believe that Elizabeth has completely suppressed her impulsiveness at hastily judging people and that Mr. Darcy has left behind his pride for good to live happily ever after? Can Marianne's broken heart be mended by Colonel Brandon? Will she be able to grow to truly love him after the disappointment caused by Willoughby? Is peace so easily restored in the March household as well as in Mr. March's mind after his Civil War experiences? With the ghost of Rebecca dispelled, can Maxim de Winter and his second wife have a new life, seemingly leaving all their problems behind? Is everybody so happy with Jane Eyre's marriage to Mr. Rochester?[4]

In *Slaughterhouse Five*, Kurt Vonnegut, Jr., expressed his admiration for the biblical Lot's wife, who became a pillar of salt after she looked back at the city of Sodom. Although she had been forewarned of the consequences, she still did it. For Vonnegut, Lot's wife's act of defiance was not an instance of religious disobedience (as it has usually been interpreted) but the human thing to do—"Lot's wife, of course, was told not to look back where all those people and their homes had been. But she *did* look back, and I love her for that, because it was so human." Writing back, rewriting a novel by a different author, is, in a way, the human thing to do. Ever since humans began telling stories, with each new re-telling, stories have changed. Stories are altered, with some details getting lost and others being added in the process, and some characters are aggrandized while others are belittled to fit new sensibilities, changing morals, audiences' tastes, or the storyteller's point of view or agenda in telling the story. If the necessity of telling stories is a very human need, changing, altering, adapting, transforming, and re-telling stories in a different way is another very human need, almost impossible to separate from the very process of storytelling. Yet, a sequel's mission is bound to be ultimately a failure, for "a sequel can never fully satisfy its readers' desire for repetition, however; its tragedy is that it cannot literally reconstitute its charismatic original. Readers know this; yet they are disappointed." Still, sequels continue being written and eagerly read because "the desire for a sequel is part of the impulse to hear stories and to tell them, the desire that they never come to a definitive end."[5]

The need to re-tell stories in a different manner is no new phenomenon. Already classical authors felt perfectly comfortable using one another as models. Ovid recreated in his *Heroides* the love letters between the fictional lovers Paris and Helen of Troy, using characters first introduced by Homer in *The Iliad*; thus, Paris and Helen, who in the Homeric play caused the War of Troy to ensue, came to the forefront in the Ovidian work. Miguel de Cervantes, the author of *Don Quixote*, got the unsavory surprise that his famous *hidalgo* was taken to new adventures without his consent by a mysterious Avellaneda. Cervantes, who had claimed in the preface to *Don Quixote* to be the translator of an Arabic work he had found, resuscitated his *hidalgo* to live new adventures in the second part of *Don Quixote*, even freely borrowing some elements from Avellaneda's version. He concluded his second work by killing off Don Quixote in order to prevent new versions without his consent or knowledge. Actually, there have been numerous adaptations and rewritings of *Don Quixote*, but no other sequel.

Some authors, afraid that others may attempt to continue their works without their authorization, decided to prevent this possibility by writing their own sequels, but these are rare. Except for the case of writers who write book series, usually centering on family sagas, not many authors have written a continuation of their own works. One of these few is Mark Twain, who wrote several sequels to *Tom Sawyer* (most notably, *The Adventures of Huckleberry Finn*) to extend his copyright period, as the forty-two-year copyright period that the law granted at the time was about to come to a close.[6] J. K. Rowling's concern that Harry Potter would be resuscitated in the future by other authors is well known. With the current legislation, Rowling and her heirs are safe until seventy-five years after Rowling's demise, but who knows if the twenty-second or twenty-third century will bring a new installment of the most famous teenage magicians ever?[7]

Contrary to the romance the protagonist of Henry James's "Eugene Pickering" reads, the seven novels analyzed in this book (*Sense and Sensibility, Pride and Prejudice, Jane Eyre, Wuthering Heights, The Scarlet Letter, Little Women* and *Rebecca*) have not been relegated to the dusty limbo of oblivion but taken as the starting point for producing new works. This book examines how the reading of sequels informs our understanding of the original novels; that is, can sequels be read apart from the original, as self-standing novels, or should we have some (even if not thorough) knowledge of the original work prior to enjoying and understanding the sequel? And why is there a sequel at all? As sequels are often accused of being a way to make a quick buck, this book explores some reasons behind the production of sequels, other than purely financial concerns, and advances theories as to why they continue to be written and read. It also explores what sequels contribute to our deeper and better understanding of the original novel. For clarity's sake, in terms of terminology, all the books based upon a previous work by another author will be referred to as sequels, regardless of whether they are rewritings (those works set in a different setting and a different period with different characters—although modeled after the original ones) or continuations (those which continue after the ending of the original work and which could be more or less smoothly incorporated into the original work). The current work does not intend to be an exhaustive study of all the authors who have used previous novels as inspiration for their own works; rather, it is a selection of seven well-known literary works that have had a sequel to them written. The purposes of these sequels will also be examined. Do they provide a happier ending to amend an unsatisfactory one in the original novel? And, if the original work had a happy ending (like Austen's novels), what do sequels contribute? Do they provide a better understanding of the main or secondary characters? Do they exploit previous plots merely hinted at but not fully developed? Do they stand in marked contrast to the original work in terms of style, plot, setting, and characterization, or, on the contrary, do they try to stay as true and close to the original as possible?

For Michel de Certeau, "readers are travellers; they move across lands belonging to someone else, like nomads poaching their way across fields they did not write, despoiling the wealth of Egypt to enjoy it themselves." Although Certeau spoke of readers, sequel writers also poach texts, aware that the potential readers of sequels are not so much interested in the literary merits of the sequel but in the continuation of an already well-known plot. According to Barthes, "a text consists of multiple writings, issuing from several cultures and entering into dialogue with each other, into parody, into contestation," sequels being one of these possible writings. Whereas medieval and Renaissance authors tried to convince their readers that they were merely transcribing (or translating) a manuscript they had found perchance, sequel writers have indeed found another author's ready-made text to modify for their own purposes. Writing a sequel is perceived by some as a piece of cake but it can be a rather challenging process, too. It is paradoxical that the closer a sequel is to the original, the more satisfying it will be as a sequel; on the other hand, the more innovative and the further it moves away from the original, the less it will meet the expectations of what a sequel should be like.[8]

The question of whether a sequel denotes a lack of creativity (since characters are already invented) on the part of the sequel writer or if sequel writing is rather a literary challenge (how to make characters already well-known come alive again in a credible manner) has been in the air for a while. That a text is offered different interpretations or is seen under a new light as time goes by and new critical schools appear is evidence of how each reader looks for something different in the same novel, bringing their own frame of mind into it. This is why sequels are especially telling of each period's respective values, morals, and interests. Reasons argued for the "easiness" of the task of sequel writing include that sequel writers have characters on a silver tray that have been offered by another writer for them to use with absolute freedom (except in the case of commissioned sequels). Sequel writers, however, reject that using another writer's characters makes it any easier to infuse them with life and a believable voice. They argue that one must find a voice of one's own but, in the meantime, that voice is constrained by the previous writer's work, restricting their literary freedom. Characters must still be truthful to the personality someone else gave them, must stay in the environment another writer designed, and sequel writers are compelled to accommodate their own chronology to the chronology of events previously narrated. Susan Hill, author of *Mrs. de Winter*, the first authorized sequel to Daphne du Maurier's *Rebecca*, explains that

> the fact that the characters come to a writer bearing something of their past life and doings with them makes no difference at all to the fact that the new writer has to give them a future, a new story and to develop their characters in new situations. In this respect it is no different from writing a novel as it were from scratch—except that actually it is possibly a little harder. You can begin your own new characters with a clean sheet and do exactly what you want with them. You have to obey the rules of the characters you inherit from another writer.[9]

Commissioned to write an authorized sequel or assuming this task voluntarily, all sequel authors had to revive and credibly recreate well-known characters that many readers remember and have cherished for years. Emma Tennant, author of some well-regarded novels, had a penchant for writing sequels. The heterogeneity of her literary production testifies to the different kinds of works she has continued—*The Austern Papers* by Henry James, *Sense and Sensibility* and *Pride and Prejudice* by Jane Austen (the latter with two sequels), *Dr. Jekyll and Mr. Hyde* by Robert Louis Stevenson, and *Jane Eyre* by Charlotte Brontë (continued with *Adele*, later revised and republished as *The French Dancer's Bastard*), among others.

One distinctive feature of literary texts (in contrast to scientific texts, for example) is that the reader's active participation is needed in order to give full meaning to the text. The sequel writer, in altering the original work from an authorial point of view, by becoming an author and not limiting their role to that of a mere reader, goes a step further. Yet, authors' approaches to sequel writing differ when it comes to determining to what extent to borrow from the original novel and how much to invent, add, and even replace. Geraldine Brooks, author of *March*, a sequel to *Little Women*, decided that "I would only go where Louisa May Alcott had chosen not to go." Accordingly, the only instance in which *March* overlaps with *Little Women* is the ending, where Brooks provides a different perspective to Alcott's depiction of the cheerful arrival of their father at Christmas. Other sequel authors continue the plot, forgetting about the original novel for the most part except when an explanation of an unresolved issue from the original comes in handy, such as Tennant.[10]

Sequels are born out of a perceived absence in the original work—a character left unexplored, an unsatisfactory or too open ending, plotlines not conveniently explained, characters' past lives being largely unknown. Sequel writing, in that it gives a voice to characters previously silent (or silenced), can therefore be regarded as an act of "literary ventriloquism." However, sequel writers reject that their work is limited to expanding a previously existing plot so as to make the characters live new adventures. For Hill, "a sequel is not simply a continuation of the plot—how dull that would be. The plot is always the least important part of any novel. A sequel is a valid novel by a novelist which takes over where the previous writer left off but then develops in very much its own way, its own style and has an existence entirely independent of its original." Yet, even sequel writers are often uncomfortable with the very label of sequel and its application to their works. Sally Beauman, author of *Rebecca's Tale*, the second authorized sequel to *Rebecca*, argues

> my book is linked to Daphne du Maurier's 1938 classic novel, *Rebecca*. But it is not, and was never intended to be, a sequel. On the whole, I dislike and distrust sequels, and those that I've read have always been pale shadows of the original. It can be read by those who know *Rebecca* intimately, and by those who have never read du Maurier's book (and for them, there's a treat in store). In other words, my novel is deeply indebted to du Maurier's but also, I hope, free and independent of it. We certainly return to Manderley, but we look at that dark and resonant fictional domain from a very different angle, and there are some surprises in store.[11]

Can sequels be read independently or do they depend on the original works for meaning and, ultimately, for their very existence? Can we enjoy or make sense of a sequel if we are unaware of the work it aims to continue? It is controversial if sequels can be read on their own or if they are absolutely dependent for their meaning, coherence, etc., on the original novels. For instance, Walter Allen read *Wide Sargasso Sea* as "a triumph of atmosphere [which] does not exist in its own right, as Mr. Rochester is almost as shadowy as Charlotte Brontë's Bertha Mason." The same applies to *The French Dancer's Bastard*—is it possible to like Jane Eyre after the utterly negative way in which she is characterized by Adèle? May *Mr. Darcy's Diary* read as the frustrated outpourings of a man whose love is unrequited? Would Mr. March deserve his own book if he were not the father of four well-known little women?[12]

Most sequels capitalize on endings that, for different reasons, are regarded as unsatisfactory. However, endings are meaningful because they bring the action to the end, and, moreover, they constitute the moment when characters reach their zenith. This is why "with the exception of preplanned sagas ... all sequels share the same problem. For the original story to be artistically satisfying, the central character must have exhausted her potential for development. At the end of her psychological odyssey, she will have nowhere to go—there'll be nothing to say in Part Deux." As a result, sequels are comfortable since readers know what awaits them in a number of aspects. Yet, they also defy the notion that a novel has an ending providing closure that is the finish line of the entire plot. What is then left for sequels to say? A minor character can be explored like Adèle or Bertha Mason or the past of a male protagonist like Mr. Darcy's or Heathcliff's or the story might be transplanted to a different setting. For Alexander Welsh, "endings are critical points for analysis in all examinations of plot; quite literally, any action is defined by its ending." Sequels, however, reject this, as they see the ending not as providing closure, but just the opposite—for opening up the possibility of a new work. Novelist and linguist Umberto Eco claimed that a text can be defined as open because "of its susceptibility to countless different interpretations." In sequels, the finality of the ending is open to reinterpretations and, therefore, rewritings. Sequels deny that endings are meaningful, that they provide closure or that they represent the conclusion of the novel. Endings are not written in stone and can be altered, reopened and expanded in a new novel-length work.[13]

For Suk, the popularity of sequels to famous and canonical texts in recent years is a result of the combination of three factors—the death of the author, the anxiety of influence, and marginality. Nevertheless, it is also worth noting that there is a strong economic component behind sequel writing up to the point that for some "a sequel is a creative decision made by an accountant" as "a sequel has an immediate market created by the popularity of the original work. In essence the sequel exists due to consumer demand." Judging by the number of sequels currently written, it has been said that "the journey between fast buck and sheer greed has a stopover called sequel." Because they already have a willing target audience (that of the original book), sequels are considered a sound financial venture in which "characters fully imagined by one author may be kidnapped by another, all in the irreproachable name of greed." On the other hand, while not mentioned often, sequels promote the sales of the original works. Sequel readers want to relive the pleasure they experienced through the reading of the original work—while learning more about their beloved characters. Sequels provide "the pleasure of repetition and nostalgia: something familiar, and something lost. For loss—or the memory trace that comes with the sense of something lacking—is itself, in this cultural realm, a kind of pleasure."[14]

Despite the economic revenue sequels are expected to reap, readers are not always enthusiastic. Readers' reactions to sequels (reactions made extensive to the authors of these sequels) have ranged from outrage to admiration. On the social networking site Facebook, the now extinct "The Society for the Promotion of the Assassination of Emma Tennant" group made of four members (one of them, curiously enough, being "Jane Austen," who complains that "I can't believe what this woman has done to my literature!!!") called for the capture—dead or alive—of Emma Tennant, as of June 2009. Moreover, despite the relative success sequels might have had in terms of sales, they have, for the most part, received scarce critical attention. Their contribution to the original work has also been questioned: "sequels—specifically sequels to classics by writers now dead—throw everything out of kilter. They elbow their way into our appreciation of the story like a bad architect's graceless in-the-style-of-addition to a fine old house. And they rattle with the wooden sounds of decisions made while eyeing the potential cash receipts." Critical interest in sequels has been reduced, more often than not, to the literary merits or lack thereof of the sequel in regards to its predecessor. Although this is understandable, it has also led to obscuring the aesthetic quality of some sequels, with authors of sequels remaining a largely ignored group. Their previous publishing record as well as their motivations for undertaking the task of writing a continuation to a popular novel are diverse, ranging from a rather unexpected commission by a deceased author's heirs to a personal predilection for a given work. In some cases, the nationality of the author has changed and, in the process, has brought about a colonial or postcolonial sensibility to the work, as it is the case with *Wide Sargasso Sea* or *Windward Heights*.[15]

Often sequels are penned by female authors, a reaction to the fact that "no male writer has written primarily or even largely for women, or with the sense of women's criticism as a consideration when he chooses his materials, his theme, his language. But to a lesser or greater extent, every woman writer has written for men even when, like Virginia Woolf, she was supposed to be addressing women." Because "the text's author is a father, a progenitor, a procreator, an aesthetic patriarch whose pen is an instrument of generative power," female sequel writers, through their exploration of scarcely sketched female characters in men's novels, challenge and disrupt this patriarchal order. Beloved and well-read novels which have provided women with entertainment and escape from their daily obligations and problems are, for feminist critics, a valuable object of study due to their accurate and minute depiction of a patriarchal society that kept women's options severely limited. Sequels are therefore needed to go beyond the stereotypes that have plagued the representation of women in novels. The feminist reinterpretation of canonical texts, offering a new reading and therefore proposing a new understanding of them, has for long been an academic practice: "re-vision—the act of looking back, of seeing with fresh eyes, of entering an old text from a new critical direction—is for women more than a chapter in cultural history: it is an act of survival.... Until we can understand the assumptions in which we are drenched we cannot know ourselves. And this drive to self-knowledge, for women, is more than a search for identity: it is part of our refusal of the self-destructiveness of male-dominated society." This need to see texts in a new light may then be the reason why so many sequels deal with the unexplored lives of female characters in the original novels, particularly of the female characters in novels penned by men.[16]

More unusual is that the character that was voiceless and is now brought to the forefront is male, as was the case with *March*. *Little Women* and sequels (*Good Wives*, *Jo's Boys* and *Little Men*) focused on the experiences of the four March girls while their father was serving as a chaplain for the Union army during the Civil War. A highly principled man who had succeeded in teaching his daughters the idea that it was better to be honest than rich, Mr. March in *Little Women* is absent because of war duties. Still, after his return from the war, he continues being in the background of the lives of those little women who "gave their hearts into their mother's keeping, their souls into their father's." *March* deals with Mr.

March but, also, with issues that did not appear in *Little Women*—for a novel set during the war that put an end to slavery, the novel does not deal with slavery, though, which is a flagrant omission. In contrast, *March* explores abolitionism as well as slavery conditions in the antebellum South.[17]

In some extraordinary cases, such as Austen's novels, the popularity of the original works has provoked an almost endless succession of sequels. The sequels to *Pride and Prejudice*, for instance, would in themselves fill an entire volume. When multiple sequels to a given novel exist, a selection has been made, choosing some while leaving others aside. The criteria for this selection has been, basically, the popularity of the sequels or of their authors and the thematic connection of the sequels to the original novel (and to other sequels, in some cases). The chapters in this book have been chronologically arranged according to the date of first publication of the original novel.

That Austen has a vast collection of admirers preying on anything related to her life and works (even if loosely related) is no news. Already in 1925, writer E. M. Forster was mocking those fans, calling them undiscerning and gullible, blinded by their admiration. Not surprisingly, her novels have been the object of an almost endless number of adaptations, both in print and cinema. The scarcity of Austen's literary production (six novels and the juvenilia writings) helps to explain the almost infinite number of sequels in print. The sequels to two Austen novels, *Sense and Sensibility* and *Pride and Prejudice*, are analyzed in this book while an introduction to the section briefly examines some of the characteristics common to the sequels to Austen's works.

"Elinor and Marianne," as drafted by Austen in 1795, was an epistolary novel recounting the life experiences of the two Dashwood sisters. Rewritten in the course of 1797–1798, it was given a new title, *Sense and Sensibility*, as well as a new form. Emma Tennant wondered what the novel would look like had Austen kept the epistolary form, and so chose letters to tell the story of Elinor and Marianne's lives after the end of the original novel. The complex world of family connections and social intrigue that is exposed in *Sense and Sensibility* could, for obvious reasons, be hardly conveyed by the personal correspondence between the two main characters, oblivious as they might be of certain incidents. Also, questions of moral propriety and sisterly affection might prevent Elinor and Marianne from informing each other of certain new developments. To overcome such shortcomings, Tennant did not limit herself to Elinor and Marianne's correspondence but also included letters from a varied assortment of characters that had peopled *Sense and Sensibility* to capture the milieu of upper-class English society at the time.

When Austen wrote *Pride and Prejudice,* she could hardly have foreseen the popularity not only of the novel itself but particularly of Mr. Darcy, its male protagonist, a man blinded by prejudice. Ever since the novel was written, thousands of females have fallen in love with the rude Mr. Darcy. Among the vast number of sequels to *Pride and Prejudice,* this chapter focuses on *Pemberley* by Emma Tennant, *Mr. Darcy's Diary* by Amanda Grange, *Pride and Prejudice and Zombies* by Seth Grahame-Smith, *Being Elizabeth Bennet* by Emma Campbell Webster and *Seducing Mr. Darcy* by Gwyn Cready. This chapter analyzes the developments that Tennant, Grange, Grahame-Smith, Webster and Cready introduce in regards to the action of *Pride and Prejudice,* paying special attention to their depiction of Mr. Darcy.

Literary sequels often explore minor characters that were ignored in the original work. In the sequels to Charlotte Brontë's *Jane Eyre,* not only are secondary characters brought to the forefront but, more importantly, disturbing events that were only slightly touched on in *Jane Eyre* are fully developed. Rochester's first marriage is too disturbing for Jane to learn much more about it other than the fact that his wife is still alive and presents an obstacle to her own happiness; accordingly, little is known about Bertha Mason—just that she comes from overseas and is crazy. Another disturbing event is that Rochester might be the father of Adèle Varens, a lovely though untamable girl, and, moreover, the illegitimate daughter of a French dancer. His reputation as a hero (regardless of his Gothic qualities such as his mysteriousness) and savior of Jane Eyre would be inevitably ruined had he an illegitimate child; readers (and Jane) are happier accepting his excuse that he might be Adèle's father or not, given her mother's many lovers. That Rochester had both a crazy wife and a bastard flew in the face of nineteenth-century Victorian morals and, accordingly, the novel, although presenting both possibilities, soon retreats from going further into the implications of the two events. The two sequels to *Jane Eyre* analyzed, *Wide Sargasso Sea* by Jean Rhys and *The French Dancer's Bastard* by Emma Tennant, explore the previous stories (what we might call "prequels") of these two characters who play a decisive role in Jane Eyre's life although they are left largely unexplored in *Jane Eyre.*

For a time, Heathcliff is gone from Wuthering Heights and Emily Brontë would not reveal much about his whereabouts. What did he do during those years? Where was he? All we know is that he returned a man of wealth. Lin Haire-Sargeant took upon herself the task of telling where the missing protagonist had been. *Heathcliff: Return to Wuthering Heights* tries to illuminate where Heathcliff was and what he did. *Wuthering Heights* is so closely associated in its readers' minds to the Yorkshire moors that the Brontës' home and its surroundings are a popular pilgrimage site for their many followers, a trend that began during Charlotte Brontë's lifetime. But can a setting so different as the Caribbean accommodate such an intense passion? If Catherine and Heathcliff's love is symbolized by the rocks in the area, what happens if the setting is not the rainy moor lands of northern England but a warmer, tropical location? Although the Brontës' novels have for long been considered the epitome of Englishness, postcolonial writers have found them to be universal and easily transplanted to the colonial world. If Jean Rhys recreated the life of Bertha Mason and Rochester in her native Dominica, author Marysé Conde imagined Heathcliff and Catherine's love story as taking place in Guadeloupe and Cuba.

In his "*Scarlet Letter* Trilogy," John Updike re-wrote Nathaniel Hawthorne's novel *The Scarlet Letter* in the twentieth century according to each of the three protagonists' point of view. In Updike's novels, Hester becomes a housewife bored with her lifestyle who decides to join a hippy commune (*S.*), Chillingworth is a professor whose wife cheats on him while he has an affair with his niece (*Roger's Version*), and the minister is sent to a sort of detention/rehab center in the desert because of his serial womanizing in his congregation (*A Month of Sundays*). The same topics that Hawthorne covered (adultery, jealousy, deceiving appearances) are still very much present in Updike's works, but transposed to the twentieth-century sensibility to explore how American society has changed since its Puritan origins.

The interrelationship between the American Civil War and literature has been present ever since President Abraham Lincoln allegedly referred to Harriet Beecher Stowe, author of *Uncle Tom's Cabin*, as the "little woman who wrote the book that made this great war." Stowe's depiction of the cruelties of slavery aroused the public's sympathy towards abolitionism in the pre-war days. Since Stowe's novel, the Civil War has occupied a prominent position in the fiction of women writers so it is not surprising that the two most famous literary depictions of this war that Stowe helped provoke are written by two women: Louisa May Alcott in *Little Women* when it comes to the Northern side of the war and Margaret Mitchell in *Gone with the Wind* in regards to the Southern defeat. During most of *Little Women*, the girls' father is absent, being an army chaplain. However, if in *Little Women* Mr. March's absence was justified, in the three other novels that Alcott wrote recounting the lives of the March sisters, Mr. March was repeatedly denied a prominent role. That he is such a small character was exploited by Geraldine Brooks, who wondered what Mr. March was doing in the front while Alcott was narrating the experiences and circumstances of his wife and four young daughters. *March* follows Mr. March to the front to deal with issues that, while vital for Alcott herself, are not mentioned in her most famous work, such as slavery, abolitionism, the women's movement and the war itself.

While most sequels are penned by authors who decide to continue a novel that has gone into the public domain, the sequels to *Rebecca* constitute a peculiar case, as they were commissioned by du Maurier's heirs. The two authors hired for the task, Susan Hill and Sally Beauman, approached their assignment differently. While Hill recounts where Maxim de Winter and his second wife went to after Manderley was devoured by the flames and follows them to their exile abroad and then back to England in *Mrs. de Winter*, Beauman recovers Rebecca's childhood and true story by having three first-person narrators, all of whom were heavily influenced by Rebecca's personality in *Rebecca's Tale*.

All in all, sequel writers go well beyond the end to contribute their own vision of the plot to well-known novels, as will be seen in the following chapters.

Chapter 1

Dear Elinor, Dear Marianne

Letter-Writing, Marriage Prospects and Women's Roles in *Sense and Sensibility* by Jane Austen and *Elinor and Marianne* by Emma Tennant

Elinor ... possessed a strength of understanding, and coolness of judgment, which qualified her, though only nineteen, to be the counsellor of her mother, and enabled her frequently to counteract, to the advantage of them all, that eagerness of mind in Mrs. Dashwood which must generally have led to imprudence. She had an excellent heart;—her disposition was affectionate, and her feelings were strong; but she knew how to govern them: it was a knowledge which her mother had yet to learn; and which one of her sisters had resolved never to be taught.

Marianne's abilities were, in many respects, quite equal to Elinor's. She was sensible and clever; but eager in everything: her sorrows, her joys, could have no moderation. She was generous, amiable, interesting: she was everything but prudent. **Jane Austen: *Sense and Sensibility* (1811)**

Mrs. Brandon has taken on airs at a fine speed ...—for it is well known that Colonel Brandon married her from pity of her condition after she made public an engagement that did not exist. It is a lesson to a young girl, to keep the state of her heart discreet—and it is no secret either that Mrs. Brandon rewards her husband by yawning in his face and going out, long after all the household is abed, to stand in the moonlight by the turnpike road. **Emma Tennant: *Elinor and Marianne* (1996)**

Jane Austen is one of the all-time favorite British novelists, with a vast collection of admirers suffering from "the Jane Austen syndrome" and who prey on anything related to her life and works (even if loosely related). Already in 1925, writer E. M. Forster was mocking those who, blinded by their admiration for the author, were undiscerning and gullible.[1] He characterized them in the following terms: "I am a Jane Austenite, and therefore slightly imbecile about Jane Austen.... She is my favourite author! I read and re-read, the mouth open and the mind closed. Shut up in measureless content, I greet her by the name of most kind hostess, while criticism slumbers. The Jane Austenite possesses little of the brightness he ascribes so freely to his idol. Like all regular churchgoers, he scarcely notices what is being said."[2]

Not surprisingly in light of this veneration (and its subsequent economic revenue), Austen's novels have been the object of an almost endless number of adaptations, both in print and cinema.[3] However, "despite the richness of the Austen film industry ... the handicap has always been that Austen wrote only six books, so source material is limited." This very scarcity of Austen's literary production might be a factor why "there is perhaps no other genre or author with as many prequels, sequels, and continuations as Jane Austen" that try to make up for this paucity. With Austen's sequels, "no minor character or plot line is left unturned." Another reason for this proliferation of Austen-related materials is that anyone feels entitled to use Austen, being endowed with a certain sense of ownership over the author on the grounds of their admiration. Ironically, it is "the slightly mawkish possessiveness some admirers feel about her" that has led to dozens of Austen-inspired books being written, causing in the process a certain sense of confusion about what Austen really intended. Austen's sequels could well constitute a genre on their own, since

> the AUSTENLIST itemizes sixty-eight Jane Austen literary "reversions" (including eight of *Pride and Prejudice*) written between 1850 and 2000. Most are sequels to the novels or a given novel's action seen from a minor character's point of view, but there are also such oddities as a re-creation of Austen's letters in rhyme royal, a postscript to *Persuasion* with a choice of endings à la *The French Lieutenant's Woman*, a play about Jane's mysterious seaside romance, a novel about "Antipods Jane" and her doings down under in Australia and, just in 1996, the first of three planned novels about Jane Austen, detective.

Just in the twentieth century, over sixty sequels to Austen's novels were published.[4]

Present-day novels are often inspired by Austen's nineteenth-century plots. Recent examples of such a trend are British novelist Helen Fielding's *Bridget Jones's Diary* (1996) and its own sequel, *Bridget Jones: The Edge of*

Reason (1999), both subsequently turned into cinematographic productions in 2001 and 2004.[5] While the plots of Fielding's works are intertextually related to *Pride and Prejudice* and *Persuasion,* respectively, often the connection is looser, being reduced to having Austen's name in the title to attract potential readers. The latter is the case of *Jane Austen in Boca* by Paula Marantz Cohen, *The Jane Austen Book Club* by Karen Joy Fowler, or *The Man Who Loved Jane Austen* by Sally Smith-O'Rourke.[6]

Additionally, Austen's works have been (with more or less success) adapted to new genres so as to bring her plots closer to the present time. For Bowman, this abundance of adaptations might be owing not to an updated, contemporary understanding of the validity of Austen's works in the twentieth-first century, but rather to a *mis*reading of Austen. There is fear that this crossing-over of Austen to other genres might blur the distinctive nineteenth-century Englishness of the original works, making us forget that Austen does belong to a certain historical and literary period. Because forgetting her novels' original setting and historical period entails the risk of having Austen become an author for all seasons and genres, there has been "a renewed awareness of the power of audiences to determine the status and meaning of literary works, to construct ... very different Austens." And yet, some genres have been more favored than others when it comes to rewriting Austen: while parodies are rare, most rewritings expand or recreate the romance aspect. Currently, the favorite genre for adapting Austen seems to be chick lit (or chick flicks), making Austen "the patron saint of chick lit." Evidence of this is that "'chick lit' tables are smothered with volumes boasting an Austen reference in a blurb on the back cover. Austen, it's been suggested, is the great-great-grandmother of chick lit—that exploding genre about upwardly mobile young women and their wayward travails through the world of modern courtship (and shopping), set mostly in the best neighborhoods in London or New York."[7]

This modern appropriation of the British author "suggests that Austen has been *pimped* [customized] by the many authors who have commodified her name and customized both Austen's body of work and her biography to accommodate niche markets." That Austen has become a commodity is, up to a certain extent, logical, given that, as Douglas McGrath, director of *Emma* (1996), put it, "she writes, you know, superb dialogue, she creates memorable characters, she has an extremely clever skill for plotting—and she's dead, which means, you know, there's none of that tiresome arguing over who gets the bigger bun at coffee time."

Emma Campbell Webster, author of *Being Elizabeth Bennet,* excuses her rewriting of *Pride and Prejudice* in similar terms: "I'd like to thank Jane Austen, very much, for being out of copyright."[8]

This process of adaptation has been far from innocuous, though, as Austen's works have been appropriated by a legion of groups (including but not limited to her fans, sentimentalists, feminists or politicizers) using her works to advance their own agendas or putting them at the service of their ideals, not necessarily matching Austen's own. In the words of Martin Amis, "Austen is weirdly capable of keeping everybody busy. The moralists, the Eros-and-Agape people, the Marxists, the Freudians, the Jungians, the semioticians, the deconstructors—all find an adventure playground in six samey novels about middle-class provincials." As a side-effect, the success of modern adaptations has made Austen books very popular among younger audiences, otherwise unlikely to approach Austen on their own. This, however, is a double-edged sword, as the realization that the original novels are thoroughly different from what these adaptations and sequels have misled us to believe may cause disappointment when "those who read as well as buy ... discover that the books are not harlequinized."[9]

Who owns Austen? Readers or scholars? Whose interpretation is valid and who is not entitled to have one? "The worry that Austen has been affected by the wrong sort of popularity seems a backhanded acknowledgement of the tenuousness of the boundaries between elite and popular culture," but, is it a genuine worry? It is paradoxical that the sequels to Austen's novels are enjoyed by many readers (with the exception of purist Austen fans) but almost universally despised by critics, a follow-up of "the history of Austen criticism [which] has created a tension in reading practices between the academy and the amateur or casual reader." Certainly, sequels are enjoyed by the kind of Austen readers scholars despise. Gwyn Cready in *Seducing Mr. Darcy* puts a finger on this situation in having her protagonist challenge an Austen scholar in the following manner[10]: "listen, Sigmund, just because you can quote the number of times the word pineapple or fanny appears in the text does not make you or anyone else an expert on Darcy's character. A character is more than the words on a page. A character's all the other stuff that's in a reader's head too."[11]

Further contributing to this negative view of Austen non-academic fans is the fact that the literary quality of Austen sequels is debatable. Not only are they frequently marred by anachronisms; more striking, sometimes they present information that contradicts the original work. Additionally, another recurrent flaw in Austen sequels is that "literal recapturing and repetitions of Austen's texts are not uncommon in sequels. They testify to the preference for repetition over rewriting," thus diminishing the creative input offered by the sequel. And if Austen has been often accused of having a restricted scope and limiting her novels to only plot, her sequels are guilty of the same. As their goal often is not to be faithful to Austen but to make her more attractive to present-day audiences, adherence to nineteenth-century mores is more often than not sacrificed.[12]

Many a romance or chick lit novel has reworked the *Pride and Prejudice* plot of the male and the female protagonists hating each other before realizing they have fallen in love, up to the point that it has become a rather frequent plotline for Silhouette and Harlequin romance novels. The same has happened with *Sense and Sensibility*—chick lit, romantic comedies, sitcoms, and many other cultural texts have repeatedly used the plot of *Sense and Sensibility* of a good girl being dumped by a Casanova of sorts only to later find a better, worthier love interest who has loved her all along. As a consequence of this repetitive homage of sorts, Austen has often been accused of using trite and well-known plotlines, when it is just the opposite. The plot of *Sense and Sensibility* was revolutionary in Austen's time, when literary conventions and social mores dictated that dumped women were undesirable and condemned to spinsterhood—if not to social censure and the subsequent ostracism. However, the fruitfulness of this plot and its many repetitions causes the negative and misleading impression that Austen wrote commonplace love stories. Austen's plots have been repeated over and over again, but she was highly original:

> did Austen actually invent any of these classic story-patterns? The only three patterns that I have been able to identify as having antecedents involve a heroine who is slighted like Cinderella, rescued from danger, or encouraged to develop an attachment by someone who is already engaged. If the other patterns she devised have been overlooked, it is because they are seen today as lowbrow, popular, or commercial. In Austen's time, however, they might very well have been regarded as distinctive or, at the very least, as providing ingenious solutions to one of the main problems not only of the courtship plot but of the novel in general: how to construct narratives that will postpone closure as long as possible.[13]

If many a sequel is written to bring together the protagonists who in the original work remained apart or to amend an unhappy ending, the reverse is often true when it comes to the Austen sequels. Where marriage was the end of all conflicts for Austen, for her sequel writers marriage is not an end but a beginning to start a new novel. Where Austen promised us a happy-ever-after marriage based on the recently completed growth process of the protagonist couple, sequels portray the difficulties in their married life, as in *Pemberley* or *Elinor and Marianne.* Is the marriage at the end of her novels Austen's endorsement of traditional social conventions? Brown reads marriage as an achievement of important consequences, given that "the increased freedom given to women in choosing a husband (one of the first freedoms women experienced) led to an emotional and sexual awakening in women, a sense of her own power and consequence, that fed into feminist politics and may have been a decisive internal force behind it, especially when we consider that among the early demands of feminists was economic equality under the law in marriage contracts."[14]

Offering an alternative point of view is a common and widely used technique in sequels. This might be the male protagonist's or of a minor and relatively unexplored secondary character. One of the problems of the sequels to Austen's novels told from the point of view of another character is that the final surprise of the happy ending is spoiled. Elizabeth Bennet is surprised by Mr. Darcy's unexpected first marriage proposal, but readers will fail to feel any kind of surprise after having been privy to Mr. Darcy's attempts to control his feelings for Elizabeth through the pages of *Mr. Darcy's Diary* by Amanda Grange. What could come as a surprise to readers of *Mr. Darcy's Diary,* however, might be Elizabeth's change of mind and her acceptance of his second proposal. Still, is it so important that the cat is out of the bag beforehand and the final surprise of the ending is spoiled? Is there really anyone who might read *Mr. Darcy's Diary* without having read (or watched) *Pride and Prejudice* first? Yet, because offering another character's point of view of the same events is rather restrictive, at other times sequel writers move the action forward so as to explore the lives of Austen's protagonists' offspring or their immediate kin such as unmarried sisters.[15]

* * *

When Jane Austen wrote the first draft of "Elinor and Marianne" in 1795, it was an epistolary novel recounting the experiences of the two homonymous Dashwood sisters. When it was rewritten in the course of 1797–1798, it was given a new form as well as a new title, *Sense and Sensibility,* which "perhaps too clearly [gives] the clue to its exploration of the limits of Romantic freedom." Further changes would be made when Austen again revised her manuscript during 1809–1810 before having it published out of her own pocket in November 1811. Reasons advanced to account for her decision to drop the epistolary style include that the genre was going out of fashion, her preference for an omniscient third-person narrator or her interest in presenting multiple voices and points of view, a diversity that the epistolary novel fails to convey, especially in regards to the aliveness of lengthy dialogues. Moreover, the complex world of family connections and social intrigue exposed in *Sense and Sensibility* could hardly be reproduced in the personal correspondence between the two main characters, as they might be oblivious to some incidents; furthermore, questions of moral propriety and sisterly affection might prevent Elinor and Marianne from informing each other of certain painful, new developments. Additionally, Austen's choice of having a third-person narrator implies a rejection of letters as the conventional mode for conveying female voices and instead gave Elinor the objectiveness traditionally reserved to third-person narrators.[16]

Because the destruction of the original manuscript of "Elinor and Marianne" makes it impossible to ascertain what remained from it in the published version, Emma Tennant wondered what the novel would have looked like had Austen kept the epistolary form. She chose to recount Elinor and Marianne's lives after the end of the original novel through the use of letters in *Elinor and Marianne*, recovering not only the use of letters but also the original title. To overcome the shortcomings of the epistolary novel, Tennant did not limit her scope to the Dashwood sisters' correspondence but also included letters from a varied assortment of characters that appeared in *Sense and Sensibility*—Mrs. Dashwood, Margaret Dashwood, John Dashwood, John Willoughby, Mrs. Jennings, Mrs. Ferrars, and Lucy Steele (now Mrs. Robert Ferrars), among others. Even Mrs. Jennings's daughter, Mrs. Thomas Palmer, has a say about events taking place in London and of which the protagonists are unaware. With this, Tennant offers a vast array of letters, with different styles, capturing the milieu of upper-class English society at the time.[17]

The need for a sequel to *Sense and Sensibility* comes, other than from readers' curiosity about what the future may hold for Elinor and Marianne, from the far-fetched conclusion of Austen's novel. Many critics have commented on the implausibility of the ending of *Sense and Sensibility*, with both sisters ending up quite happily married.[18] While Elinor's marriage to Edward was what she had hoped for all along, marriage to Colonel Brandon could not be further from Marianne's dreams at the start of the novel. Marianne having been seduced and then disposed of (as was the case for both Eliza, Colonel Brandon's youthful love interest, and the younger Eliza) would have been more in consonance with nineteenth-century novels' plots. Marriage to Colonel Brandon saves her from social ruin but Marianne's seeming contentedness with it has often been questioned, as

"Marianne, until brainwashed in the concluding chapters of *Sense and Sensibility*, is a firm believer in the impossibility of second attachments." Additionally, questions have also been raised about Elinor's marriage. Although it gives Elinor the happy ending her patience deserves, Robert Ferrars and Lucy Steele's sudden marriage has been considered hard to believe, as we only know about it in a reported manner, providing the perfect way out for Edward's engagement with Lucy. These starting points opened the door for Tennant to present an alternative version to Austen's happy ending.[19]

Tennant's continuation does not offer us a "happily ever after" once *Sense and Sensibility* finishes, but, rather, a troublesome continuation, plagued with even more problems than those posed by the original work. While other *Sense and Sensibility* sequels concentrate on Margaret, their younger sister, a minor character in *Sense and Sensibility*, Margaret remains largely absent in *Elinor and Marianne*, even though she follows in Marianne's footsteps. Margaret, as Mrs. Jennings tells her daughter, "has had her head filled with nonsense—she has taken leave of her senses by virtue of the charms of her seducer" and her role is limited to emphasizing the similarities existing between her and Marianne (and, in contrast, highlighting the differences between the two younger Dashwood girls and their eldest sister).[20] Margaret functions as an alter ego for Lydia Bennet from *Pride and Prejudice* since she gets involved with Willoughby, the former romantic interest of her eldest sister, just as Lydia married Wickham after his failed courtship of Elizabeth.[21]

Sense and Sensibility is a novel exploring what happens when two previously engaged men meet and fall in love with the two eldest Dashwood sisters. This "drama of prior commitment" does not prevent them from pursuing the objects of their affection, though, and hence the following conflict. The ways in which the two sisters behave and act upon their reciprocated feelings are dissimilar, as are the methods these two men use to show their affection. This starting point owed much to the literary momentum, for presenting characters with opposite values and behavior was a common feature of the didactic novels which were very fashionable in 1795–1796, when "Elinor and Marianne" was written. Austen also found inspiration in another very popular topic in the literary production of the period—unrestrained sensibility and its potentially harmful effects. *Sense and Sensibility* thus "engages with the cultural and intellectual fashions of the late eighteenth and early nineteenth century: the emergence of romanticism and its conflict both with the still persistent Enlightenment and the embryonic moralism which will characterise

English society in the nineteenth century." For Johnson, the problem at the core of the novel comes from "the eighteenth-century philosophical tradition, where the distinction between certainty and probability figures prominently."[22]

Because Marianne's independent spirit is all but quashed and Elinor's conventionality is rewarded, *Sense and Sensibility* has mostly been regarded as a conservative novel aiming at maintaining conventions and advocating for restraint in the face of the individual's romantic notions. Its longstanding reputation as a conservative work has prevented critics from perceiving the revolution that Marianne's character constituted at the time—instead of being punished for her moral and social transgressions with death, she is granted redemption. What is more, her rebelliousness against social mores is what makes of Marianne "one of the most interesting characters in Jane Austen's fiction. More than *Emma* even, she anticipates the tragically Quixotic heroines of the nineteenth-century novel, whose visions of existence can find no fulfilment within the limitations of their societies." Although Austen has been accused of cherishing or advocating for a system that constrained women to the domestic sphere, *Sense and Sensibility* condemns a patriarchal system that no longer worked. Despite the late Mr. Dashwood's dispositions for the financial well-being of his wife and daughters, his authority is not respected by his son and heir, therefore leaving the women in the family unprotected and the patriarchal order in shambles. Given that the system fails to protect or provide for women, "Austen's characterization of John and Fanny Dashwood gains power from a sense of bitter exasperation, that finer, more sensitive people should have to defer to people of their type, and be forced to choose between the indignity of accepting or expecting their charities and the hardship of doing without them." Even worse, those women who have acquired power, "overwhelmingly a male prerogative ... have internalized ... the patriarchal ethos" and become corrupted by it, as exemplified by Fanny Dashwood and Mrs. Ferrars or Catherine de Bourgh in *Pride and Prejudice*.[23]

Although *Sense and Sensibility* has often been read as a defense of sense and an indictment of sensibility, there are different grades of sense and of sensibility and neither is thoroughly embraced. Rather, in the novel, the answer is in moderation and decorum given that extreme sense comes under Austen's denunciation as well. While Elinor's moderate sense is cherished as the best possible course of action, extreme sense is represented by John and Fanny Dashwood; on the other hand, extreme sensibility is embodied by Mrs. Dashwood, who does not even have the excuse of young age, as is the case with Marianne.[24] If Marianne's youth is condemned because it almost leads to her total destruction, so are the flaws of the eldest, such as her half-brother John's selfishness and her mother's folly. Neither sense nor sensibility is necessarily better than the other when taken to extremes and, what is more, both can be as equally harmful—Willoughby is alternatively guided by sense or sensibility, but because he puts both at the service of his own, mercenary interests, he is no good example, as both sense and sensibility get corrupted by his selfishness and his self-interest.[25]

Even though Willoughby embraces sensibility too, *Sense and Sensibility* has been read as an attack on women's careless endorsement of sensibility and its pernicious effects. Yet, sensibility *per se* is not necessarily harmful—what is wrong is sensibility unchecked and, even worse, taking people's motivations at face-value. Because Elinor and Marianne ignore much about their love interests, *Sense and Sensibility* is full of secrets, which were particularly favored by Austen. Actually, "one of the most important truths about *Sense and Sensibility* is how much of the action depends upon ignorance, misconception, deception, and surprise." *Sense and Sensibility* is full of surprises—the surprise of Edward's secret engagement to Lucy Steele, Willoughby's involvement with the younger Eliza, Lucy's elopement with Robert Ferrars, and Willoughby's engagement to a rich heiress. In Austen's works, secrets and unspoken truths make it difficult to truly know people, to see if they really are who they seem to be, and only decorum can save characters from acting stupidly on rash judgments.[26]

While Marianne is willing to live according to sensibility (no matter the consequences, such as social censure of her too public display of her feelings for Willoughby without an engagement having been announced), not everybody is so willing to be totally overruled by feelings, particularly not Willoughby. Marianne misinterprets him in believing that, just as she can turn her back to society and conventions of propriety and decorum for his sake, he can forgo material riches and risk his inheritance and social position on the grounds of their love. Marianne, who is driven by sensibility and scorns sense, believes that Willoughby feels the same way, failing to realize that "Willoughby may want to support his life-style more than he will want to enter her view of affairs and sacrifice his worldly comforts to marry a woman in her financial situation." Marianne not only believes people to be transparent, she regards Willoughby as her double, or an extension of her own personality, a belief he uses for his own purposes. Because her mental image of Willoughby is proved to be incorrect,

Willoughby is, mostly, a fabrication of Marianne's vivid imagination, like Vronsky for Anna Karenina or Ashley Wilkes for Scarlett O'Hara; for Marianne, Willoughby's "person and air were equal to what her fancy had ever drawn for the hero of a favourite story."[27]

Mrs. Dashwood too, enthused by Willoughby, is ready to believe he and Marianne are engaged, despite nothing having been confirmed. This way, "at the beginning of the novel, Elinor is differentiated from her family not so much in terms of the power of her feelings as in terms of the powers of her understanding." In sharp contrast to Marianne and Mrs. Dashwood, Elinor does not rashly enter into conclusions: "'I want no proof of their affection,' said Elinor; 'but of their engagement I do.'" It is not only her restraint which marks Elinor as different from her sister and mother but also her deeper and more insightful understanding of human nature. While Marianne and Mrs. Dashwood rush to believe the best (and the purity of his intentions) from Willoughby, Elinor waits for proof to back up their optimism about the outcome of Willoughby and Marianne's relationship.[28]

Yet, Marianne and their mother's leaps of faith partly stem from the fact that, in courtship, women were to assume a passive role and wait for men to make a move, while wondering about their intentions: "women must observe their suitors' gestures, review their encouraging words, speculate about their intentions, and then wait." This uncertainty and the impossibility to act upon it planted the seeds for possible misunderstandings and thus "*Sense and Sensibility* ... dramatize[s] the view that women like Marianne are caught in a double-bind situation; they live in an inadequate reality from which they are unable to escape except through fantasies." Moreover, "Austen's novels assume from the outset that the courtship relation is spurious and misleading, distorting genuine human feelings and concealing important character traits. The passions generated by amatory gallantry are likely to be either transient and blind or, even worse, merely simulated." If in *Northanger Abbey* Catherine Morland had an overactive imagination, Elinor tries to keep sensibility in check even in the face of events that seem to defy sense and which would be better interpreted using sensibility such as "her sister's dramatic rescue by a dashing stranger, the unexpected appearance of several people, bizarre revelations of character and circumstance, unanticipated complications in her love-life." Elinor is able to keep sense even when reality seems to defy it to favor instead an interpretation according to sensibility. Because Marianne is wrong, Austen uses her to warn women of the dangers they expose themselves to if they try to interpret real life according to romantic ideas found in novels.[29]

Although Marianne stops short of engaging in a sexual affair with Willoughby (which saves her from eventually enduring the same fate as the second Eliza), Austen shows that for a woman's reputation behaving in such a restless manner can be almost as damaging. Whereas Willoughby can make a good marriage despite having already been disinherited by his aunt, her careless behavior costs Marianne her health and almost her social reputation. Marianne comes to realize that "I have been too much at my ease, too happy, too frank. I have erred against every commonplace notion of decorum; I have been open and sincere where I ought to have been reserved, spiritless, dull, and deceitful."[30]

In her relationship with Edward, Elinor, too, is forced to wait but her behavior is diametrically different from Marianne's and their mother's. She does not rush to conclusions. Even though she must hope for the better and the whole situation escapes from her control, Elinor can command her own feelings. Therefore, Elinor "felt that Edward stood very high in her opinion. She believed the regard to be mutual; but she required greater certainty of it to make Marianne's conviction of their attachment agreeable to her. She knew that what Marianne and her mother conjectured one moment, they believed the next—that with them, to wish was to hope, and to hope was to expect." Whereas Marianne sees her engagement to Willoughby as certain (and suffers because of his sudden indifference), Elinor does not let herself believe that it is possible for her to get married to Edward. Instead, she has to wait for others to work things out (namely, for Edward to stand up for her against his mother and get out of his previous engagement)—despite the unlikelihood of this happening, if we take into account Edward's shyness and mild character.[31]

Elinor is not the only one patiently waiting—where Willoughby acts (although rashly and unwisely), Edward waits, just as women do, leaving the impression of his feminine character. This makes Marianne especially critical: "she began almost to feel a dislike of Edward; and it ended, as every feeling must end with her, by carrying back her thoughts to Willoughby, whose manners formed a contrast sufficiently striking to those of his brother elect." Because they wait rather than act, Elinor and Edward's relationship is far less appealing to readers than the whirlwind romance of Willoughby and Marianne, which resounds with echoes to romantic novels. Readers tend to side with Marianne, for whom "the meeting between Edward and her sister was but a continuation of that unaccountable coldness which she had often observed at Norland in their mutual behavior. On Edward's side, more particularly, there was a deficiency of all that a lover ought to look and say on such an occasion."[32]

Further contributing to cause this impression, Edward's own personality and physical appearance do him no favor in the light of Willoughby's vitality and more charismatic personality. In contrast to Willoughby's "manly beauty and more than common gracefulness ... [whose] person and air were equal to what her fancy had ever drawn for the hero of a favourite story," Edward's appeal comes from Elinor's appreciation of his qualities rather than from his own, personal characteristics. Because "Edward Ferrars's attractions are not external," most readers have failed to be fond of him or appreciate his charm—at least until Hugh Grant was cast as Edward in *Sense and Sensibility*,[33] the 1995 cinematographic adaptation.[34]

Willoughby and Marianne's romance is at odds with "Edward's proposal to Elinor, reported by the narrator in a brisk, somewhat hurried fashion." In common with other Austen novels, Edward's marriage proposal to Elinor goes unrecorded and left to readers' imagination:

> why these specifics "need not be particularly told" can be explained by Edward's earlier romantic folly: his premature engagement to Lucy nearly earns him a life of boredom and frustration. The narrator kindly spares the reader the embarrassment of witnessing Edward's declaration of love, a declaration which might risk a "here we go again" from the reader. One presumes that Edward's proposal to Elinor, though undoubtedly warm, is nevertheless circumspect in the light of his past.

In Austen, ardent marriage proposals or intense courtships are fake and help mask, through their passionate outlook, a lack of genuine feelings. Selfish motivations (such as Willoughby's) or an imperfect and inaccurate knowledge of the other's needs and aspirations (like Mr. Darcy's first proposal or Mr. Collins's in *Pride and Prejudice*) drive these apparently passionate suitors. True suitors, attuned to their beloved's mind and speaking out of love and not of worldly concerns, in contrast, do not need the author to transcribe their proposal (like Mr. Darcy's second proposal or Edward's).[35]

Nevertheless, despite Edward's apparent coldness, his lack of dashing looks or an attractive personality to commend him, for Austen, the relationships that are socially appropriate and, therefore, more likely to succeed are those like Edward and Elinor's—based on love but also restrained within the conventions of propriety and social manners, as well as being grounded on a realistic perception of the world and the demands their status, social condition, and class impose upon them. Edward and Elinor know an elopement or rushing into an engagement is not proper (partly because Edward already made that mistake with Lucy Steele); instead, they bide their time and wait in silence, without overtly expressing their inner feelings because no formal relationship has yet been established between them. Willoughby and Marianne, instead, engage in public displays of familiarity and affection that their current situation (they are not engaged yet) does not allow. Furthermore, Willoughby and Marianne's perception of the world is unrealistic, as they believe that their love gives them *carte blanche* not to respect and follow the rigid conventions of courtship. Their behavior is flawed, as Marianne comes to realize once things go wrong—since she had tried to live in a society solely composed of Willoughby and herself, without him, she is totally alone in the world and, moreover, is bound to face harsh criticisms because of her socially unacceptable past behavior.[36]

Marianne's open display of her feelings makes it seem as if she is the one suffering the most when, actually, she expresses her sensibility "according to convention and is actually selfish and superficial. Simply put, Elinor feels more than Marianne. It is Elinor who controls her own disappointment." Marianne's sleeplessness when Willoughby goes away is but a pose, as she is expected to act so:

> Marianne would have thought herself very inexcusable had she been able to sleep at all the first night after parting from Willoughby. She would have been ashamed to look her family in the face the next morning, had she not risen from her bed in more need of repose than when she lay down in it. But the feelings which made such composure a disgrace, left her in no danger of incurring it. She was awake the whole night, and she wept the greatest part of it. She got up with a headache, was unable to talk, and unwilling to take any nourishment; giving pain every moment to her mother and sisters, and forbidding all attempt at consolation from either. Her sensibility was potent enough!

Marianne's determination that "I must feel—I must be wretched" shows her feelings (or at least their outward display) to be quite conventional. Meanwhile, Elinor's restraint may read like coldness, if not lack of feelings, and even if Marianne and their mother regard her as unfeeling, the truth is that her suffering matches Marianne's. Also, because Marianne's very public involvement and subsequent breakup with Willoughby make her the talk of town, Austen indicts such careless behavior, instead pointing out Elinor's (similar to Austen's sister, Cassandra's reaction after the death of her fiancé) as the example to follow. While she suffers as much as Marianne or even more (Edward was never so open in his attentions as Willoughby was to Marianne, which might lead to uncertainty on Elinor's part in regards to Edward's actual feelings), she presents a cool façade. Both Elinor and Marianne lack sufficient information about their love interests but while the latter rushes to see in Willoughby an alter ego with motivations as pure as her own, Elinor waits and sees.[37] But because the story is seen through Elinor's perspective, we fail to see her sufferings while worrying over Marianne's.

More than between sense and sensibility,

> the true opposition in the novel is between selfishness and selflessness. Marianne's relationship with Willoughby errs, not in its warmth, but in its self-centeredness. In public they have words and glances only for each other. Their imprudent display of attachment, their lack of reserve in company and between themselves comes from belief in a personal morality which cuts them off from the rest of the world. Their relationship flourishes for their own pleasure, independent of the demands of society and family.... Their love is exclusive and smugly self-centered.... [Edward and Elinor's] behavior is decorous and inoffensive.

Because Elinor loves and suffers for love too, Austen indicts not feelings but their excess, against which Samuel Johnson and William Cowper, her favorite writers, had already written. Yet, Elinor is not infallible and she makes the mistake to interpret Edward's conduct according to her preconceived ideas; accordingly, she assumes that Edward's hair ring is hers (when it is actually Lucy's) or puts the blame for his strange behavior on his mother (when it is due to his uneasiness about his engagement to Lucy), as Elinor is unaware of Lucy's very existence. Because both Elinor and Marianne have to judge their situation "on the basis of partial evidence," mistakes are bound to happen. Still, Elinor is able to regard all judgments as tentative, which enables her to change her mind when new information is provided. Different from Marianne and Mrs. Dashwood, who continue hoping for the best even when faced by the evidence of Willoughby's desertion and subsequent silence, Elinor can act according to new evidence.[38]

While "Elinor's major activity throughout the novel is doubting—resisting eager or premature assent" and patiently waiting (in regards to both Willoughby's and Edward's intentions), Marianne sees her hopes of a marriage proposal from Willoughby as all but a *fait accompli*. Marianne's world is a secure, simple place where people are transparent, which leads her to make wrong decisions with potentially catastrophic results. Because she tries to force the world to conform to her wishes, "the major limitations of Marianne's sensibility ... are that it places excessive faith in the self's inner ability to reach moral decision intuitively and rejects entirely the need for living within conventional limits." Her belief that people are who they seem to be also leads her to misjudge others, such as Mrs. Jennings or Colonel Brandon.[39]

Apparently, *Sense and Sensibility* makes for a gloomy picture—if women are impotent when it comes to marriage and courtship and, moreover, they are to remain passive if they do not want to face social rejection and potential ostracism, this situation is necessarily frustrating. However, Austen saves her female characters from frustration or even downright desperation by securing them happy endings through chance. Despite the fact that her heroines cannot direct their own matrimonial choices and depend on men's decisions, unexpected events ruled by chance will provide them with a happy ending—as long as they do not ruin their chances by their impulsiveness or defying of social rules. Criticisms of the novel on the grounds of securing happy marriages for the protagonists miss the point that "her consistent use of economic language to talk about human relations and her many portraits of unsatisfactory marriages prevent us from dismissing her novels as romantic love stories in which Austen succumbs uncritically to the 'rewards' her culture allotted women." While men had "access to work that paid, access to inheritance and preference, and access to the independence, the personal power, that belonged to being prosperous and male," women with no means or fortune such as the Dashwood sisters had to seek a wealthy husband to provide for them and their families. However, their poverty represented an obstacle to marry well, with their individual qualities and virtues going unnoticed because of their lack of money.[40]

Austen attacks "the instability of inheritance as a result of personal whim," making of *Sense and Sensibility* "Austen's sourest look at the oppression of women through marriage, property and family." Because Marianne and Elinor are powerless in the face of a materialistic society where family connections or economic power are valued over the individual's worth or qualities, they are dependent on their male relatives for financial support—or almost charity, as Fanny Dashwood intends, with her husband's acquiescence. Failing to understand this, as Mrs. Dashwood does, is nearly a fatal mistake. In contrast to Elinor's sound and realistic assessment of the world and their own circumstances as penniless young women, for her mother "it was contrary to every doctrine of her's, that difference of fortune should keep any couple asunder who were attracted by resemblance of disposition." To believe this is to risk getting badly hurt, though.[41]

Chance is vital in the novel, as "one's happiness must in some measure be always at the mercy of chance." With so many obstacles in their way, Elinor and Edward's marriage is a question of sheer chance (only because Lucy manages to ensnare Robert Ferrars and elope with him) and true love or Elinor's inner qualities do nothing to change the ending the novel's course led to (Edward honoring his promise to marry Lucy despite his love for Elinor). It is merely chance that leads to their happy ending because in *Sense and Sensibility*, "chance plays an important role ... unobservable causes continually reverse expectations and unfold misleading prospects or doubtful retrospects in order to demonstrate the 'shortness of our views.'" Since true affection or one's worth is of no avail, Austen resorts to the incident of Lucy and Robert's marriage, of which there had been no previous hint. It is so unexpected that, in spite of its securing the desired conclusion by removing the main obstacle for Edward to marry Eleanor, it "seems mere literary sleight-of-hand which Austen employs to bring her novel to a close. Its preposterousness even stumps Elinor." As it stands, "Lucy's marriage is a puzzle, but one which is of a piece with all the other unforeseeable twists in this novel that baffle the reason and judgment." This, however, is Austen's only option to deliver a happy ending. Elinor's poverty could not be miraculously solved and Austen, not resorting to divine providence, had to rely just on coincidences. Whereas "previous novelists equate virtue and happiness, but always with a nod towards heaven, either in terms of explicit theology or providential plot-devices. *Sense and Sensibility* might contain odd coincidences, but they are never referred back to God. The norms she derives are this-worldly and depend for their determination on human experience, not divine revelation."[42]

The lesson to be learned at the end of *Sense and Sensibility* is that sense will be rewarded whereas sensibility is harmful and dangerous. Marianne's illness is a recovery from extreme sensibility and in contrast to her potentially disastrous embrace of sensibility, "Elinor's marriage plot should convince readers that recognizing reality and accommodating oneself to it honorably can lead to happiness in ways that Marianne's approach cannot." *Sense and Sensibility* advocates for a combination of love and reason, so that affection must be balanced by a good head for a relationship to be successful.[43]

Weddings are usually presented as the culmination of a growing process on the part of the heroine, who is then rewarded with a good marriage to a worthy husband. But is it so for Marianne? Elinor's sensibility and restraint are rewarded with marriage to the man she has loved all along, while Marianne marries Colonel Brandon, a good catch especially in the light of Marianne's less-than-perfect reputation after her involvement with Willoughby. For Austen, "marriage [works] as a metaphor for self-knowledge, the overcoming of egoism and the mark of psychic development" and *Sense and Sensibility* conforms to this pattern, as Marianne has indeed learned that an excess of sensibility is dangerous and likely to expose a woman to moral ruin. However, it is not so certain that she has thoroughly changed or that her marriage has tempered her character. Very tellingly, "the tone ... makes it difficult to see the wedding as a reward. The sarcasm and exaggeration make the passage come across as an authorial sneer mocking Marianne and reveling in her having had to relinquish her romantic illusions." Because this is a far less promising marriage than the ones Austen usually gives her female protagonists, Tennant explored its outcome in *Elinor and Marianne.*[44]

For Tennant, Marianne is far from being happy in her marriage to Colonel Brandon. Moreover, the doubts she had about their considerable age difference return to her mind now that she is expecting a child—"is not Colonel Brandon's age against him, when it comes to fathering a child? Are not his advancing years a reason for me to fear my pregnancy? I have a freak within me, Sister, who prefers not to be born and be seen to be the offspring of an old man.... Oh, Elinor, my heart is filled with dread and every possible fear." From this starting point, in *Elinor and Marianne* Tennant offers a feminist reading of *Sense and Sensibility*, including such postmodernist features as metafiction, parody, intertextuality, and dialogism-polyphony. Offering letters written by different narrators advances the postmodernist notion that there is not a single truth, but that the truth is a construction largely dependent on the teller. Unfortunately, in choosing to recover Austen's original idea of an epistolary novel and sacrificing the third-person narrator in the process, Tennant at times loses depth in portraying characters. While we read Elinor's pleads for her sister to find conjugal happiness with Colonel Brandon or are privy to Edward's exhortations to Elinor to return home with him, we are largely ignorant of their inner thoughts or those feelings they may not dare to disclose in their correspondence.[45]

Although *Sense and Sensibility* ended with two apparently happy marriages, *Elinor and Marianne* opens just a few months later with two marriages that are undergoing serious difficulties, as the sisters reveal to each other in their correspondence. *Sense and Sensibility* deals with hope and disappointment but *Elinor and Marianne* primarily focuses on the restrictive roles reserved for women in nineteenth-century England and whether rebelling against them and defying social conventions is feasible. This is a marked departure from Austen's novels, whose protagonists, while trying to make the most of their circumstances, never revolt against the status quo. Elizabeth Bennet in *Pride and Prejudice* might feel slighted because of her lack of a fortune and Emma Woodhouse in *Emma* tries to have Harriet Smith socially accepted as an equal despite her humble origins, but in Austen's world women live and behave according to their station, never denying social order or going against moral conventions of propriety.[46] To do so would imply becoming an outcast and a pariah. In contrast to other romantic protagonists, "Austen's heroines themselves desire the kind of equality denied to the eighteenth-century woman, and they demand romantic love as well. Marriage must be prudent, dignified, and romantic. In brief, these clear eyed girls stand as virtuous individuals with assertive rights" but they never go so far as to alienate society and risk social banishment or moral censure.[47]

Sense and Sensibility offered as happy an ending as the patriarchal society in which Marianne and Elinor lived could afford. For Austen, marriage plots were solved at the end of her novels with the heroine's finding true love and getting to know herself better, conquering her flaws in the process. Yet, maybe because Marianne's transgressions were more serious that Elizabeth Bennet's rushing to prejudiced conclusions or Emma's cruelty to an impoverished spinster lady, it is not so clear if Marianne could learn to see Colonel Brandon as her true love. Similar to Elizabeth, Marianne undergoes an introspective process of self-knowledge that leads to her marriage to an honorable man.

Yet, we do not quite believe Marianne's future marital happiness, contrary to what we expect at the end of *Pride and Prejudice* given that "the reader is told that in Marianne's new relationship with Brandon, 'Marianne found her happiness in forming his'; their relationship is a hierarchy in which Marianne derives happiness apparently only from serving her mate." That the independent Marianne, who wished to live in her own society of two outside social rules, should be so conventional and submissive to her aging husband remains hard to believe. For all these reasons, "it is thus logical to expect that her marital relationship will be a reversal of her relationship with Willoughby. There should be no surprise then, that the relationship entails her giving up her desire for an attractive lover, along with her desire to be empowered and to garner recognition of her importance for her own sake." While Emma, Elizabeth or Elinor are entitled to entirely happy marriages, this is denied to Marianne because of her past transgressions of social codes. Elinor, who has been the sensible one, can marry for love while Marianne must resign herself to a sensible marriage that might eventually lead to love. However, Tennant did not believe that she was so ready to give up romantic love (or Willoughby, for that matter).[48]

In *Elinor and Marianne* Marianne turns out to be a nagging wife complaining about her husband's imminent trip to Wales and his frequent absences. In *Sense and Sensibility* the rumors about Colonel Brandon's illegitimate daughter by the elder Eliza were put to rest with the assurance that he had not fathered her and he was just a good person helping out a friend in disgrace. For Tennant, however, Colonel is the father of the younger Eliza and now that she has followed in her mother's footsteps and been seduced by Willoughby, Colonel Brandon intends to give her a nice stay in London before having her removed out of proper society for good. *Elinor and Marianne* also continues *Sense and Sensibility*'s indictment of the system of inheritances that played such a crucial role in nineteenth-century England. Mrs. Ferrars's preference for Robert (to the detriment of Edward) is shown not only as unfair but as a mistake, as Robert leads her to bankruptcy and then flees to Africa to take part in an expedition that will finally bring about his death as the object of a cannibal ritual. This, then, helps further advance the fierce criticism of wills and inheritances of *Sense and Sensibility*—as the system is unfair, worthy heirs might be dispossessed in favor of less respectable or less wise heirs.[49]

Elinor and Marianne's relationship in Tennant's novel is radically different from the one they had in Austen's. In *Sense and Sensibility* their relationship was largely modeled after the writer's own with her sister Cassandra, whom she deeply admired. None of them ever married, and they remained very close all their lives. Maybe because of this, all of Austen's literary production deals, to some extent or another, with the relationships between siblings, which she considered of utmost importance and to be cherished. In *Mansfield Park*, she wrote that "children of the same family, the same blood, with the same first associations and habits, have some means of enjoyment in their power, which no subsequent connections can supply; and it must be by a long and unnatural estrangement, by a divorce which no subsequent connection can justify, if such precious remains of the earliest attachment are ever outlived."[50]

In contrast to her sobriety and sparingness in presenting love declarations, Austen dwells on the feelings of siblings at length, advancing the idea that romantic love should mirror fraternal love since ideal sisters and ideal husbands share a number of characteristics. The relationship between sisters transcends the family realm and is tinged with larger resonances; thus, "Austen treats divisions between sisters as catastrophic, since these disunions destroy the harmony of family life, which is analogous to the stability and peace of society." While Austen is not the only author who emphasizes cherishing the family, she gives the bonds between sisters a special importance. Whereas Austen's Elinor tries to guide her sister and prevent her from making a fatal mistake, Elinor for Tennant no longer embodies sense or caution against rash judgments. Instead, Elinor helps enforce patriarchal, traditional values that suffocate women's freedom.

Marianne, in turn, is a symbol for women's limited opportunities in contemporary England and for their thirst for a more egalitarian society—ambitions that, as we see at the end of the novel, are ultimately quashed.[51]

While Austen's novels have repeatedly been accused of staying too much at home and therefore ignoring current political matters or international affairs, Tennant has Willoughby and Marianne planning to found a utopian community in America. America, home for dissenters, has been, ever since the sixteenth century, a place reformers and utopian thinkers have made their destination to put into practice their revolutionary ideas and create a new, better society. In her sequel, Tennant combined feminist vindications with utopian pursuits, all of them to be ideally carried out in America given the constraints women and freethinkers alike experienced in England then.

Because America has long been a shelter for unconventional people who felt at odds living in society for a number of reasons (religious ideas, political theories, revolutionary notions of social organization, and many others), Willoughby and Marianne, whose unconventional character and open nature clashed with the rigidity of social norms in nineteenth-century England, entertain ideas of a utopian sort that they plan to put into practice in America in Tennant's take. While in *Sense and Sensibility* the attraction of Willoughby was largely due to his playing the role of romantic hero (aided by Marianne and Mrs. Dashwood's vivid imaginations), in *Elinor and Marianne*, if he becomes so appealing to Marianne it is because he sees her as an individual (the only man in the book to do so), with even Elinor urging her to adjust to the role of wife and mother. In the face of the limits nineteenth-century England imposed on women and social reformers, *Elinor and Marianne* presents America as the perfect solution for all types of social dissenters and discontents. However, because Marianne never makes it to America, it remains an unfulfilled promise.[52]

Willoughby, who seemed so much at ease moving in the upper circles of English society, now longs for a utopian society in the New World. He is given a somewhat more respectable role than that of the careless, selfish seducer he was in *Sense and Sensibility*—for Tennant, Willoughby's previous mercenary view of marriage and human relationships is redeemed now, as he becomes a utopian reformer and prospective founder of an ideal community. How Willoughby, who recklessly toyed with young, naive women's hearts (when not downright ruining their lives) and only sought his material well-being, grew disillusioned with society and careless about money matters is not convincingly explained, though. Why this sudden change of heart in the course of a mere few months? What brought about this epiphany of sorts? Why a man so attached to worldly luxuries and his own comfort that he can trample on a woman's heart suddenly dreams of founding society anew far from social rules and hierarchical order? It is not explained if, just as he made Marianne's opinions his own in *Sense and Sensibility*, now he has also taken on somebody else's utopian ideals. Willoughby, although still very much a seducer, is given a coat of "respectability" in his becoming a utopian reformer of sorts instead of the selfish rake seducing and abandoning women in his path before marrying into money. Yet, he appears as a seducer several times—not only does he lure Marianne into his trap again, but young Margaret also falls prey to his charm and flees with them, in addition to his seduction of the second Eliza, who bears him a daughter. Just as Colonel Brandon saved Marianne from social ruin, this time around their half-brother John rescues Margaret, although he makes quite an unlikely rescuer, as he had not shown too much interest in any of his half-sisters' well-being before.[53]

Critics spared no insult for *Elinor and Marianne*. For Rolf Breuer, "the silliness of the plot has its counterpart in the significance of the style.... Sometimes Austen's sequel is so absurd that one is unable to suspend disbelief." Among the flaws of *Elinor and Marianne* figures Tennant's mixing-up priests and clergymen and her calling Marianne's newest musical instrument a harp or a harpsichord alternatively. Tennant is also too bold in having Elinor and Marianne openly broach fertility problems in their letters.[54]

In *Sense and Sensibility*, Marianne might have desired a society of two without having to live by social standards. Her rejection of rules to instead follow her own placed her in danger of becoming a social pariah. However, the error in her ways is eventually ascribed to an excess of sensibility and Willoughby's deceit and she is redeemed by her marriage to Colonel Brandon. In contrast, Tennant's characters become outcasts in their search for happiness. Just as Willoughby's change of heart is not convincingly explained, neither are Marianne's fears about her husband's age in relation to her pregnancy, as it was not uncommon in England at the time for men (especially widowers with young children) to marry much younger women. Motherhood, instead of pacifying Marianne, seems to be the source of her unrest to a great extent, for she fears the notable age gap between her and Colonel Brandon (he is just five years younger than Mrs. Dashwood) will lead to "a progeny of monsters."[55]

At the same time, Colonel Brandon and Elinor are presented as patriarchal figures preventing the individual from enjoying freedom and self-development—Colonel Brandon being the patriarch himself while Elinor makes a good example of the way in which women help men repress other women in order to keep the patriarchal order, siding with the oppressor instead of with their fellow women. Elinor is more worried about having "the whole county gloating and smacking their lips" over Marianne's disappearance than about her sister's well-being or happiness. However, it is interesting to note that, for once, Mrs. Dashwood sides with Elinor's assessment of the situation instead of with Marianne's dreams of a new life in the New World. Elinor, who in *Sense and Sensibility* was the voice of reason and good sense (although it was mostly ignored by both Marianne and Mrs. Dashwood) only gets an unsympathetic and negative portrayal from Tennant, who has her as a perpetuator and enforcer of the patriarchal system's evils, calling for Marianne's submission and passivity. Where Elinor in *Sense and Sensibility* cautioned her sister not to put her good name at risk by openly displaying her closeness to Willoughby as long as there was no firm marriage commitment, in *Elinor and Marianne* she restrains Marianne from fulfilling her needs and desires, trying to clip her wings and keep her trapped into a loveless marriage, all for appearances' sake or social approval: "be of good cheer, Sister: Colonel Brandon loves you, and you him; even if you doubt at times, the sanctity of the marriage vows cannot be betrayed." Whereas for Austen Elinor was "a dutiful elder sister, a teller of polite lies," here she becomes her sister's oppressor as much as Colonel Brandon. Tennant thus takes the view of *Sense and Sensibility* as "a conservative book, a defense of control and regulation against the threat of romantic individualism," going a step further in characterizing Elinor and nineteenth-century society as restricting and suppressing individualism in general and women's freedom in particular.[56]

For Poovey, "romantic relationships ... cannot provide women with more than the kind of temporary and imaginative consolation that serves to defuse criticism of the very institutions that make such consolation necessary." While some have criticized Austen's apparent contentment with marriage as the only venue for women's success instead of further exploring other, more radical possibilities, we should bear in mind that, in her times, protofeminist vindications focused on women's freedom to marry for choice and equality on marriage, not on the abolition (or even the questioning) of marriage itself. Tennant, not marred by these historical considerations, jumps at the chance of Marianne rebelling against the established social order again and takes Austen's happy ending as a temporary mirage.[57]

Another character who gets a different treatment from Tennant is Edward, who pens a few of the letters in the book. In *Sense and Sensibility* he was presented as a man scared of love because of the unfortunate situation in which he finds himself as a result of juvenile folly (engaged to an inappropriate woman he has long ceased to love and unable to pursue a more serious relationship with Elinor). He is certainly mildly appealing and is shown as a sensible man and a love match for Elinor. In *Elinor and Marianne* he comes across as a weak man, a nonentity, who is still unable to stand up to his mother. Even worse, in his reluctance to do so, he fails to defend his wife, his love declarations to the contrary. His only redeeming feature could be that, in contrast to his coldness in *Sense and Sensibility*, here he openly writes to Elinor loving declarations, such as "oh my Beloved, if you could only know how much I dream of returning to your side."[58]

In *Sense and Sensibility*, knowing so little about Edward and because of his discretion, when others offer their opinions of him, we learn more about these people than about Edward himself. In *Elinor and Marianne*, Edward, in contrast, pens his own letters but his failure to side with his wife in her disputes with his mother alienates him from both Elinor and the readers. If Elinor and Edward's relationship in *Sense and Sensibility* was marked by his dependence on his mother for his financial survival and his previous engagement, in *Elinor and Marianne* their relationship is equally fraught with problems brought about by these two women. Mrs. Ferrars, a terrible mother-in-law, has lost her mind and moves in with Edward and Elinor and accuses both Mrs. Dashwood and Elinor of stealing her property. Once Elinor leaves the house, Lucy moves in purportedly to take care of Mrs. Ferrars, with whom she is in connivance to try to trap Edward again and who seems to consider Lucy now the lesser of two evils for a daughter-in-law. Eleanor's being snubbed by her sister-in-law in *Sense and Sensibility* here becomes a chronicle of Elinor's strained relationship with her mother-in-law. Austen's tale of how a worthy young woman might win the object of her love despite her poverty and low social standing becomes for Tennant the typical story of enmity/rivalry between daughter- and mother-in-law with an indecisive husband not too willing (or, alternatively, too weak) to take his wife's side and stand up to his mother. The growth process he experienced in the course of *Sense and Sensibility* and which gave him confidence is thus totally reversed. Once more, Marianne is callous to Elinor and fails to see the depth of Elinor's feelings, too self-centered on her own problems—"I have understood the meaning of tender love, Elinor. You cannot know it with Edward (though I fear to say this) if you castigate me for my actions." Another inconsistent point in *Elinor and Marianne* stems from the fact that Mrs. Ferrars is bent on having a cottage built for herself on the estate of Colonel Brandon, who is but loosely related to her, when it would make more sense to have her move in with her daughter (or build a cottage on the Dashwoods' property, Norland).[59]

For Tennant, the ending of *Sense and Sensibility* offers an idealized vision of Elinor's and Marianne's respective marriages, which she dismantles in her sequel. But just as Tennant problematized Austen's ending, it is not clear at the end of *Elinor and Marianne* if Marianne's return to her husband means that she has learned to truly appreciate him or if, as at the beginning of the novel, her resignation to her marriage is not to last for long. It is also unclear if she returns home out of love for Colonel Brandon or out of disappointment after Willoughby's plans to go to America have been frustrated. Although for Lara Rallo what Tennant was doing was "providing a similarly quick and artificial ending to her own novel [that] ... lays bare the conventionality of the conclusion of *Sense and Sensibility*," in my opinion, Tennant's ending strains readers' credulity unbearably. While Austen gave Marianne an ending which was far more charitable and happier than she could have expected from other nineteenth-century authors, and we might try and believe that she could grow to love her husband, it is hard to believe that at the end of *Elinor and Marianne* Marianne would willingly return home—or be taken back by her husband after such a well-publicized scandal.[60]

CHAPTER 2

Looking for Mr. ~~Right~~ Darcy

Pride and Prejudice by Jane Austen and Its Multiple Rewritings

It is a truth universally acknowledged that every man in possession of a fortune must be in want of a wife. **Jane Austen: *Pride and Prejudice* (1813)**

It is a truth universally acknowledged, that a married man in possession of a good fortune must be in want of a son and heir. **Emma Tennant: *Pemberley* (1993)**

It is a truth universally acknowledged that a young Austen heroine must be in want of a husband, and you are no exception. **Emma Campbell Webster: *Being Elizabeth Bennet* (2007)**

It is a truth universally acknowledged that a zombie in possession of brains must be in want of more brains. **Jane Austen and Seth Grahame-Smith: *Pride and Prejudice and Zombies* (2009)**

We have been to the Meryton assembly, and it was even worse than I had expected. We had not been there five minutes before I heard one woman—I hesitate to call her a lady—whispering to another that I had ten thousand a year. It is of all things the one I hate the most, to be courted for my wealth. **Amanda Grange: *Mr. Darcy's Diary* (2005)**

Not that she did not enjoy Darcy and Lizzy's long, fitful submission into love. It was like waiting for two strongly repelling magnets to flip over and snap together with a bang. But given her own current state of carnal deprivation—two years, three months, one week and 2,437 laps in the YMCA pool, but who was counting?—what she really needed from her reading material was not a flight of imagination, but an intricately detailed charter excursion into cool sheets, silky boxers, and the snap of panty under insistent fingers. **Gwyn Cready: *Seducing Mr. Darcy* (2008)**

When Jane Austen began writing "First Impressions," whether she wrote it in the manner that the 2007 movie *Becoming Jane* claims or not, she could not have possibly foreseen the popularity not only of the novel itself but especially that of Mr. Darcy, its male protagonist, a man blinded by prejudice. Written roughly at the same time that she was working on "Elinor and Marianne," both were epistolary novels, and would be published in different form and under new titles—*Pride and Prejudice* and *Sense and Sensibility*, respectively. The chronology of the composition of the novel was, according to her sister Cassandra, as follows: "*First Impressions* begun in October 1796. Finished in August 1797. Published afterwards, with alterations and contractions, under the title of *Pride and Prejudice*." Shortly after completion, "First Impressions" was offered by Austen's father, the Reverend Austen, to a publisher who rejected it without even reading it, resulting in the loss of the original manuscript. It would be in the course of 1811–1812 that Austen put aside the manuscript on which she was then at work, *Mansfield Park*, to rework her earlier "First Impressions."[1]

In its final form and title, all rights to *Pride and Prejudice* would be sold for £110 and published in 1813. Austen's changes were significant to our understanding of the novel, for they

> enabled Austen to advance a kind of writing that showed the interconnectedness between the growth processes of her thinking, feeling protagonists. Thus, the narrative form of *Pride and Prejudice* supports the depiction of the development into maturity of both Elizabeth Bennet and Darcy.... This intricacy of novelistic construction thus prevents either character from being reduced to a one-dimensional, moral representative of human fallibility ("pride" versus "prejudice") and from functioning merely as a foil to the other's education, as had frequently been the case in epistolary novels.... Although the novel itself presents a firm rejection of the epistolary tradition, its turning point hinges on a letter. It is Darcy's letter that changes not only Elizabeth [*sic*] opinion about him, but her idea of herself, breaking down the barrier of her prejudice against him by appealing to her pride.

Pride and Prejudice became immediately favored by a multitude of readers, including the Prince Regent, who endorsed the novel—much to Austen's chagrin, since she was hardly an admirer of his lifestyle. Since then, *Pride and Prejudice* has become a must on every list of the most widely read and beloved novels in English and in nineteenth-century English literature curricula.[2]

Ever since her nephew James Edward Austen-Leigh famously asserted in his *Memoir of Jane Austen* that "of events her life was singularly barren: few changes and no great crisis ever broke the smooth current of its course," Austen's biographers and *aficionados* have tried to find any record, no matter how tenuous, of a love affair in Austen's life that would explain the mastery of her novels or the writer's block she seemed to suffer from after completing "First Impressions" in 1797 until she resumed her literary production in 1811 with *Mansfield Park*. Although Virginia Woolf wrote that "here was a woman about the year 1800 writing without hate, without bitterness, without protest, without preaching," twenty-first-century representations of Austen now tend to portray her as a spinster wistfully thinking about her one lost chance at a happy marriage. Moreover, this lonely Jane finds solace in her writings, as suggested in *Becoming Jane*, which presents Austen's literary career as a replacement for her failed romance with Tom Lefroy.[3]

Becoming Jane is loosely based on Jon Spence's *Becoming Jane Austen* (2003), which claims that Austen had two important love relationships in her life: one with her future sister-in-law Eliza de Feuillide, and the other with Tom Lefroy, the former very conveniently omitted from the movie, which has Eliza solely as Austen's brother's love interest. While Spence was careful to stress that, based upon his evidence (three letters sent by Austen to Cassandra during the Christmas season of 1795), he was taking a leap of faith, the movie presents Lefroy's role in inspiring *Pride and Prejudice* as a *fait accompli*. It also reinterprets Austen's life under the light of *Pride and Prejudice*, giving to real-life people many of the attributes and traits of *Pride and Prejudice* characters: thus, Mr. Darcy is almost an alter ego for Mr. Wisley while Austen's parents remind us of Mr. and Mrs. Bennet, among other changes.[4]

Scholars and moviemakers are divided when it comes to Lefroy's influence on Austen's literary career. Carroll sees *Becoming Jane* as part of a current trend of disliking Austen's single status (in contrast to the enthusiasm it generated in earlier generations of admirers) and "a symptom of anti-feminist backlash." In contrast, for *Becoming Jane* producer Douglas Rae, "her story is as real and romantic as any of her greatest novels" whereas scholar Deirdre Le Faye disagrees: "it's nonsense." For Le Faye, "she'd obviously been flirting with him. And it does rather sound like for a time, Jane was regretting his absence, but that is all there is to it.... It's like saying Shakespeare murdered people to give him enough information to write Macbeth.... She'd have been a good writer in any circumstances."[5] Were Lefroy's role so vital or not, the fact remains that there were certain parallelisms between his life and the novel—as in the Bennet family, Lefroy had five sisters and his mother's maiden name was Gardiner.[6]

It is often the case that sequels are born from a perceived need to clarify a vague or ambiguous ending or to amend an unsatisfactory one. *Pride and Prejudice* proves that, happy and unequivocal as an ending may be, there is still room for a sequel. Because the conclusion of *Pride and Prejudice* shows that "although they have each learned to defer to the other's perspective, neither is prepared to yield completely," it has opened the door wide open for sequel authors to dwell further into the "marital bliss" of the newly-wed Mr. and Mrs. Fitzwilliam Darcy. Because of the vast number of sequels to *Pride and Prejudice*, in this chapter I limit my study to *Pemberley* (1993) by Emma Tennant, *Mr. Darcy's Diary* (2005) by Amanda Grange,[7] *Being Elizabeth Bennet* (2007) by Emma Campbell Webster,[8] *Seducing Mr. Darcy* (2008) by Gwyn Cready, and *Pride and Prejudice and Zombies* (2009) by Jane Austen and Seth Grahame-Smith. This chapter analyzes the developments that Tennant, Grange, Webster, Cready and Grahame-Smith introduce in regards to the action of *Pride and Prejudice*, paying special attention to the depiction of Mr. Darcy.[9]

At first glance, Austen's novels, being distinctively nineteenth-century products, with their rigid social class rules and their lengthy discussions about appropriate marriages and annual rents, are not easily extrapolated into a twentieth-century setting. Austen's scope is certainly a restricted one, which has had the negative side effect of Austen having been seen as a "limited" writer. However, her plotlines, dealing with human relationships, particularly love ones, can be transferred anywhere—even to present-day India for a Bollywood production, *Bride and Prejudice* (2004). There have been several movies that have put Elizabeth and Mr. Darcy into flesh and bone, beginning with Greer Garson and Laurence Olivier in the 1940 film version (the first Austen cinematographic adaptation). The famous 1995 BBC miniseries had Colin Firth and Jennifer Ehle in the main roles while its (up to now) last cinematographic adaptation, *Pride & Prejudice* (2005), had Keira Knightley and Matthew Macfadyen as the protagonist couple.[10]

Although Austen's novels are certainly not romances, "*Pride and Prejudice* is a classic love story because it set the pattern for a modern popular love story, the story in which an independent-minded and fascinating woman is loved by a remote, powerful man. The attraction between the two of them is exhibited as hostility.... It is the pattern imitated by three-quarters of the romance novels on the shelves." Austen's plot was not conventional at the time but later, popular romances exploited this storyline of a hero and a heroine at odds only to eventually discover they are really madly in love with each other. Nowadays, if we may see the plot of *Pride and Prejudice* as predictable or even trite, it is because in pulp romance and TV soap operas we can see it reworked over and over again up to the point that it has become "one of the models for the late twentieth-century mass-market romance." This borrowing is deliberate and often acknowledged; for instance, for her *Bridget Jones's Diary*, Helen Fielding had no qualms in admitting that "I shamelessly stole the plot from *Pride and Prejudice*.... I thought it had been very well market-researched over a number of centuries and she probably wouldn't mind."[11]

Part of the enduring popularity of *Pride and Prejudice* comes from the depiction of its male hero. Ever since the novel was first published, thousands of females have fallen in love with the rude Mr. Darcy, both in England and elsewhere. For example, Bridget Jones fell for him, playing over and over the scene in the BBC miniseries in which Mr. Darcy gets out of the lake, completely wet. Voted in a British Channel 4 poll as one of the *Top 100 TV Moments*, it generated lots of attention, including political talk on BBC1's program *Question Time*. The scene, reflecting miniseries producer Sue Birtwistle's view that "the real subjects of the novel ... [are] sex and money," is totally missing from the novel, to the distress of those who only turned to read the novel after having watched the miniseries, although "who knows, perhaps one day in the far future, Darcy's plunge into the Pemberley lake will, like Maid Marian in the Robin Hood stories, become accepted as canon." The causes for Mr. Darcy's enduring success and popularity with women worldwide would well deserve a volume-long study on their own. Why is the surly Mr. Darcy, with his coldness and bad manners, so attractive even in the twenty-first century?[12]

Pride and Prejudice is often defined as a novel about falling in love, somewhat against one's will. It is debatable whether Austen herself would be satisfied with such a characterization because, paradoxically enough, in *Pride and Prejudice* passionate love, as in other Austen novels, is presented as dangerous, insensible and risky. Examples of such are Lydia Bennet's ending up rushing into a most disadvantageous marriage and Mr. Bennet's hasty marriage to a woman who turned out to be unsuitable. For Austen, "the courtship relation is spurious and misleading, distorting genuine human feelings and concealing important character traits. The passions generated by amatory gallantry are likely to be either transient and blind or, even worse, merely simulated." Courtship in Austen is relegated to "subordinate plots—in the flattering attentions that Robert Bingley pays to Jane Bennet, in Mr. Elton's fatuous address to Emma" but not in Mr. Darcy and Elizabeth's relationship. Actually, "more of the action of *Pride and Prejudice* can be accounted for as a tale of love which violates the traditions of romance."[13]

For Austen, true love is the kind that happens when nobody is looking (or listening), the kind that goes unspoken or at least unrecorded by the narrator. While she had no pains in writing unsuccessful marriage proposals (Mr. Collins's to Elizabeth or Mr. Darcy's first proposal), in her novels she omitted successful marriage proposals (Mr. Darcy's second proposal, or Edward Ferrars's to Elinor Dashwood in *Sense and Sensibility*). This absence of a successful proposal shows that *Pride and Prejudice* is not a romance story and Austen is not primarily interested in the love story itself but in morality, social values, behavior, virtue, punishment, reward and vice.[14]

It is commonplace to accuse Austen of paying scarce attention (when not outright indifference) to love scenes and marriage proposals. Her denying readers an ardent love declaration or a passionate acknowledgment of the heroine's feelings "has caused readers to regard Austen as being unduly reserved, even cold, either ignorant or afraid of strong emotion." Many *Pride and Prejudice* readers are disappointed when they realize that, after Elizabeth and Mr. Darcy's verbal fights, his second and successful proposal is rendered indirectly, by the author's narration (as she did in her six novels). Austen's dislike for sentimentality, of which her correspondence bears proof, gave G. H. Lewes cause to complain that "she has little or no sympathy with what is picturesque and passionate. This prevents her from painting what the popular eye can see, and the popular heart can feel." Similarly, Charlotte Brontë confided in a letter her opinion on Austen's works: "what throbs fast and full, though hidden, what the blood rushes through, what is the unseen seat of Life and the sentient target of death—*this* Miss Austen ignores; she no more, with her mind's eye, beholds the heart of her race than each man, with bodily vision, sees the heart in his heaving breast. Jane Austen was a complete and most sensible lady, but a very incomplete, and rather insensible (*not senseless*) woman, if this is heresy—I cannot help it."[15]

Austen's silence, however, far from evidencing a lack of literary skills or tact, stems from her belief that language cannot convey heart-felt emotions adequately, that language fails to express one's most private thoughts and strongest feelings. In marked contrast, conventional love declarations have been lightly used so often that they have been rendered void of any true feeling: "but that expression of 'violently in love' is so hackneyed, so doubtful, so indefinite, that it gives me very little idea. It is as often applied to feelings which arise from a half-hour's acquaintance, as to a real, strong attachment. Pray, how *violent was* Mr. Bingley's love?" Actually, "many of Austen's finest characters—Darcy, Fanny Price, Elinor Dashwood, Anne Elliot, Jane Fairfax, Mr. Knightley, Jane Bennet—struggle not to express but to hide their emotions." Only after repressing his feelings for a long time is Mr. Darcy able to acknowledge that "in vain I have struggled. It will not do. My feelings will not be repressed. You must allow me to tell you how ardently I admire and love you."[16]

It is only those who are not truly in love who can be articulate when they talk about love, as exemplified by Mr. Collins's proposal to Elizabeth. Mr. Collins, who does not truly love (or even know) Elizabeth and merely considers that she would make an appropriate wife, can offer a long marriage proposal that evidences his "complete self-absorption and ignorance of Elizabeth's own needs and desires." Shallow characters such as Harriet Smith, Lydia Bennet, Wickham, or Lucy Steele, among others, show an "emotional transparency [which] springs from an essential vulgarity and light-mindedness" whereas those characters who really love remain silent, as "Austen's characteristic practice ... is to suspend the dramatized presentation of events leading up to the romantic climax, a presentation developed largely through close-grained dialogue, and to shift instead to indirect discourse or, more often, narrative summary." Austen's speechless proposals allow readers to imagine them without embarrassing the characters. This way, "instead of ending with a 'clinch,' Jane writes that Mr. Darcy 'expressed himself as a man violently in love is supposed to do.' What is meant by 'expressed himself?' For some of us, that means a confession of love, the exchange of intimate vows. For others, it is a passionate embrace. Jane left it up to us to decide. She left it up to us to fill in the scene." Because the actual proposal is left out, language is not so important, not even the proposal itself—this marriage is not an achievement of Mr. Darcy's persuasiveness or eloquence but the result of the growth processes both he and Elizabeth have undergone.[17]

Although the two eldest Bennet sisters marry into wealthy families, *Pride and Prejudice* makes it clear that the main motivation on entering those marriages is not money, distinguishing between mercenary marriages (as would have been the case had Elizabeth first accepted Mr. Darcy) and prudent ones, such as when Elizabeth finally accepts Mr. Darcy. Prudence and common sense go hand in hand, for "prudence is not only the practical wisdom of moral conduct; it is also what we might define as acting in one's own interest in accordance with virtue, but with a realistic appraisal of the limits and difficulties life presents." If Elizabeth first rejects Mr. Darcy it is because she finds him a disagreeable man and a prospective unpleasant and tyrannical husband, regardless of his £10,000 a year. This is not to deny the importance of economic issues, given that the author herself wrote in a letter (dated March 13, 1817) to her niece Fanny that "single women have a dreadful propensity for being poor—which is one very strong argument in favor of Matrimony." Certainly, Elizabeth does regret not being the mistress of Pemberley after having turned down Mr. Darcy's first marriage offer, with which "Austen exposes the fundamental discrepancy in her society between its avowed ideology of love and its implicit economic motivation." What is more, this situation affects men as well, as exemplified by Colonel Fitzwilliam, "the younger son of an earl.... Though attracted to Elizabeth he is not at liberty to woo her. Younger sons of noblemen were not free to follow their own hearts.... To marry for money was crass: to marry without it was folly."[18]

Despite Austen's well-known assertion that "a single man in possession of a good fortune, must be in want of a wife," men did not feel the need to get married in the nineteenth century as acutely as women did. While men certainly weighed women's accomplishments and their family connections, as Mr. Darcy and Mr. Collins admit, for a woman's future, her prospective husband's connections and fortune were vital, given that "for women, marriage and its effects permeated every aspect of their daily existence and shifted the focus of their emotional and social contacts." It is therefore understandable that Mrs. Bennet, mother of five daughters, is so anxious.[19]

Austen, single and dependent on her brothers, knew first-hand how hard it was for a single woman without means to survive financially, as her letters testify. What is more, rich women also felt compelled to find a husband, as illustrated by Miss Bingley and Anne de Bourgh. Even though her heroines make good marriages, Austen is careful to stress that they are not solely driven by financial concerns. It is common to agree with Charlotte's view that happy marriages in Austen's novels depend on chance—yet, that Austen's heroines will have a happy marriage is not a closed affair from the beginning and her protagonists are uncertain as to the result (as in the case of Elinor Dashwood), when they are not positive that any such marriage will ever take place, as in the case of Elizabeth. For Austen, marital felicity is not a matter of chance but of being prudent enough so as not to rush into an unwise marriage one will later probably regret.[20]

Although Austen dwells at length with the unpleasant consequences of inappropriate marriages, her novels do not offer many models for good marriages. Therefore, a reason why Austen's novels, despite their happy endings, have made such a popular starting point for sequels is that these deal with "an area of life untouched by Austen herself, whose loving couples are rarely able to rise above conventional dialogues." In *Pride and*

Prejudice Elizabeth "wondered ... that she would learn to lose her propensity to prejudice" and Emma Tennant shows us in her sequel, *Pemberley,* that, despite having been proven wrong in *Pride and Prejudice,* old habits die hard and Elizabeth is still a rather prejudiced woman. Her tendency to make rushed assumptions (causing trouble in the process) continues in Tennant's novel, where we have "a virtual replay of the pattern of *Pride and Prejudice,* at least with respect of Elizabeth's talent for misinterpretation." This, however, brings *Pemberley*'s Elizabeth closer to Emma Woodhouse's mismatch-making skills in *Emma* than to *Pride and Prejudice*'s Elizabeth.[21]

The ending of *Pride and Prejudice* has generally been considered a satisfactory one, as Elizabeth marries a man she loves (and with £10,000 a year) who has loved her all along; as Mr. Bennet puts it, "I have given him my consent.... I know your disposition, Lizzy. I know that you could be neither happy nor respectable, unless you truly esteemed your husband; unless you looked up to him as a superior. Your lively talents would place you in the greatest danger in an unequal marriage. You could scarcely escape discredit and misery." However, for some it is an anticlimax, as the woman who was so fiercely independent submits to marrying a man she has for so long resisted. This view does not take into account the evolution of both of them, though. Elizabeth and Mr. Darcy's happy marriage is far from being the conventional ending of the heroine being subdued by the hero. Rather, it was revolutionary in that "everything about Elizabeth—her poverty, her inferior social position, the behavior of her family, her initial preference for Wickham, and her refusal of Darcy's first offer of marriage ... ideologically should lead if not to death, at best to genteel poverty and spinsterhood. Instead Austen has her marry despite her violations of these accepted norms of female behavior." More importantly, "in the earlier [Austen] novels only Darcy learns to regard his future wife as his intellectual equal."[22]

In the same manner that the subsequent repetition of the *Pride and Prejudice* plotline in hundreds of popular culture texts might make us fail to appreciate the originality of Austen's creation, the change in social standards of propriety and women's role in society might make us not realize how revolutionary and bold Elizabeth's words were in the nineteenth century. Mr. Darcy and Elizabeth, now taken for many readers as typical nineteenth-century lovers, are far from being characteristic of the period, and were "developed in critical antithesis to the conventional heroes and heroines of romance." Whereas "her society taught men and women to manage oral disagreements along disparate gender lines; women learned to back away from verbal conflict with men, remain meek, and avoid speaking up," Austen offers us "pivotal scenes of verbal conflict between the sexes."[23]

For Tennant, Austen's ending is but the prelude to many subsequent problems. *Pemberley* opens with the "they lived together merrily ever after" that the ending of *Pride and Prejudice* suggested, with Elizabeth getting everything she wants from her husband—"Mr. Darcy was generous in his love as well as in his gifts; and the more he showered on his wife, the less she felt able to ask for further kindnesses." However, Elizabeth fears that problems might be on the way—"there was nothing that Elizabeth Darcy wanted that would ever be refused to her, and this sometimes made her fear that her fortune was too great to last."[24]

If in *Pride and Prejudice* Mr. Darcy was looking for a wife, in *Pemberley* he is looking for a male descendant that will inherit Pemberley. This need for a son and heir is the most peremptory because his only sibling is Miss Georgiana, and Pemberley, like the Bennets' estate, is entailed and cannot possibly be inherited by a female relative. To highlight the urgency for this, Mr. Bennet has just died and Longbourn has already passed to their odious cousin, Mr. Collins, a fate which could well apply to Pemberley. Because "Mr. Bennet, like most fathers in Jane Austen's fiction, is ineffective. He is unable to check the follies of his wife and daughters since he never takes direct responsibility for his family," significantly enough, he is dead in Tennant's book and, therefore, responsible for his wife and single daughters' dire financial situation.[25]

Because Jane is the happy mother of a one-year-old daughter and pregnant, as is Charlotte Collins, and there are already four little Wickhams under the age of four, Elizabeth frets over her inability to conceive a baby a year after her wedding.[26] Jane's soothing words to Elizabeth cannot prevent her from worrying that she will never give Mr. Darcy a child—"was he as content as he seemed, with the love he so frequently and ardently announced to her? Was being a wife enough, for him and for Pemberley? Was she not already a failed mother?" The approaching Christmas festivities is the excuse Tennant uses to bring the Darcys, the Bennets, the Wickhams, the Bingleys, as well as Lady Catherine de Bourgh and her daughter, together at Pemberley. That Bingley's sister, who pursued Darcy's love, also shows up does not help either. To follow with the subplots paralleling those in *Pride and Prejudice*, the newly widowed Mrs. Bennet has a suitor, a colonel Kitchiner who turns out to be a fraud and a fortune-seeker, very much in the fashion of Wickham.[27]

If Elizabeth continues to jump to conclusions, Mr. Darcy is still proud.

As Jane warns her sister, "he has his pride still, and all favour of his office, and fawning courtiers in anyone he meets, to keep him proud." Elizabeth is shown as a good influence helping Mr. Darcy control his pride whereas marriage to Miss Bingley would have only made him even prouder. This Mr. Darcy continues being moody, but only occasionally, while new aspects of his personality are revealed due to his love for Elizabeth. He is shown as a devoted husband[28]:

> anyone who wished could enter her own or Mr. Darcy's rooms and see the evidence of their devotion and faithful love to each other—for Elizabeth's room bore all the marks of his constant occupancy, and his room was as bare as a bedchamber allocated to a bachelor guest before his arrival to stay. Whether at Pemberley or in the lodge in Yorkshire, this was invariably the case; and Elizabeth knew Mr. Darcy's manservant had at first been surprised to find his master so seldom in his own quarters. But the truth was there for all to see: Mr. Darcy used his room as a dressing-room only, and there were few couples even in these enlightened times who could say as much for the harmony of their conjugal relations.

At the same time, Tennant brings in a new dimension to Mr. Darcy's character as a prospective father.[29]

Because his bad temper is considered an intrinsic feature of his personality, Mr. Darcy in *Pemberley* is as cross as ever: "Mr. Darcy ... could as little evade the dark, thunderous looks that sometimes crossed his face and lingered there as he could sidestep his position as master of Pemberley." His bad mood, though, is not necessarily a negative trait or even a disadvantage; just the opposite, given that "in Austen's time, an eager desire to please had begun to signal danger much more than it counted as an asset." Mr. Darcy, who dares to be ill-tempered, shows that he is unwilling to betray his true feelings to please others. Still, he has changed a bit: "Mr. Darcy, for whom she had set out to soften, was certainly more approachable, less harsh, and a good deal less proud than he had shown himself before they wed."[30]

To make matters worse, the sudden appearance of Thomas Roper, a distant cousin who is, for the time being, Mr. Darcy's heir, only comes to disrupt the already tense atmosphere. Property and inheritance laws that occupy a prominent role in *Pride and Prejudice* (or *Sense and Sensibility*) are again a source of distress for Elizabeth in *Pemberley* with the arrival of Roper, whose existence had been previously unmentioned. The entail or strict settlement, which was widely used in a number of British novels, was a legal practice that constituted a means to preserve a family inheritance from possible creditors since the estate was used by the current incumbent while belonging to future generations (more often than not, the grandson). *Pride and Prejudice*, however, presents the entail as something alien to Mr. Bennet, when, actually, it "is not a state of affairs simply imposed on the Bennet family out of nowhere, or nature, or history, the product of some impersonal and implacable determining force.... [T]he exclusion of his daughters from the entail is an arrangement to which Mr. Bennet *agreed*, in exchange for the short term benefit of an income on which he (and perhaps a young wife) could survive." If in *Pride and Prejudice* the entail illustrates women's powerlessness and the necessity for them to get married, in *Pemberley* it points out the urgent need to produce an heir, consistent with the fact that "the theme of disinheritance loomed large in Jane Austen's thoughts, some critics see it as the axis her world rotates on."[31]

Gradually, ruining her happy marriage, Elizabeth begins to suspect that Mr. Darcy might have an illegitimate son by a French woman living in a nearby cottage and her fears are only increased by Georgiana's puzzling statement that "my brother has sins to atone for." Upset that her husband might have a bastard, Elizabeth leaves Pemberley and wants to put an end to her marriage, a most radical notion in nineteenth-century England that would have made her a social pariah. Nonetheless, the recently deceased French woman turns out to have been Bingley's lover, not Mr. Darcy's, and the reason why Mr. Darcy did not want his friend to marry Jane was because he feared that Bingley was still in love with her and in mourning. Elizabeth and her husband's reunion and the subsequent happy ending are sealed with the discovery that there is a baby on the way, ending the novel in a rather hurried way: "just as *Pemberley* is starting to get under way, everything is resolved in a sudden flurry, as if Tennant had suddenly repented of her temerity in attempting the work at all (or her publisher had only contracted for 180 pages)."[32]

An interesting aspect of *Pemberley* is that it reveals that Mr. Darcy had been a spy during the French-English War, adding a heroic dimension to his character. It also covers a gap, for many critics have complained that the war is notably absent from Austen's work (mainly, because she wrote it before the war, although it was published much later): "Austen took little account of war. No one would guess from her novels that she lived through the most perilous time Great Britain endured until 1940.... Miss Austen neglected war; and, in return, war has passed her by. Not only are her homes unharmed, but the very streets through which her characters moved on their morning walks are little touched." Because of Tennant's inklings for rewriting well-known British novels, *Pemberley* has for many been considered the true sequel to *Pride and Prejudice*, along with her own continuation to *Pemberley, An Unequal Marriage*. For Grudin,

"Tennant's narrative is made uncomfortably compelling by her utter mastery of Jane Austen's style. In its pace and sensibility, the text virtually breathes Jane Austen." Yet, Tennant was accused of significantly departing from Austen and instead having created characters modeled after mid-nineteenth-century British authors such as Dickens. Also, there are a few mistakes, most notably stating that Wickham did abduct Georgiana, which in *Pride and Prejudice* had been prevented by Mr. Darcy's unexpected arrival and Georgiana blurting out her plans to elope with him. Tennant found critical acclaim for her two *Pride and Prejudice* sequels but was not so successful in terms of sales, selling around 20,000 copies of each.[33]

If Tennant had a penchant for writing sequels, so does Amanda Grange, who has cemented her literary career writing the diaries of a number of male characters off Austen's novels, including not only Mr. Darcy's but also *Captain Wentworth's Diary, Mr. Knightley's Diary, Edmund Bertram's Diary* and *Colonel Brandon's Diary*. More recently she has published *Mr. Darcy, Vampyre*, a reworking of Mr. Darcy in the light of the vampire fad begun with Stephenie Meyer's Twilight series.

Different from *Pemberley*, which sees Mr. Darcy as a husband, Grange centers on him as a caring brother, most concerned for Georgiana and displaying a paternalistic attitude because of their age difference and the death of their parents. Because "Darcy becomes an even better prospect as a husband when he demonstrates his excellence as a brother to Georgiana," *Mr. Darcy's Diary* shows him as a doting brother. In contrast to the less than flattering way in which he is portrayed in *Pride and Prejudice*, colored by Elizabeth's negative opinion of him, in *Mr. Darcy's Diary* we have a far more positive portrayal. Bingley certainly remains more easygoing than his friend, but Mr. Darcy is a true and responsible master, who knows how to handle things and successfully manage an estate whereas Bingley, who does not have one of his own yet, does not know how to do it—"I was glad he had taken my advice. If not, he would have arrived at the same time as his servants, and then wondered why there was no dinner waiting for him." His role as a mentor towards Bingley is representative of the new type of men on the rise in English society at the time:

> England must now establish new models of male social identity and begin training non-aristocratic men to assume greater civic responsibilities.... Mr. Bingley and Mr. Gardiner ... have benefited from the successes of the trade class in the early nineteenth century, and each receives important guidance in proper masculinity from Darcy; moreover, the special attention that Darcy devotes to Bingley, whose family has risen from the trade industry, suggests that landed men are concerned enough about the future of the nation's masculinity to mentor men of new money.[34]

In this novel, Mr. Darcy does not come out as rude as he was in *Pride and Prejudice*—at the Meryton assembly he did not intend for Elizabeth to overhear his unfortunate comment, contrary to what Elizabeth thinks. It is at this point that we begin to see the divergence between Elizabeth's point of view as conveyed in *Pride and Prejudice* and Mr. Darcy's true feelings, for he soon realizes that Elizabeth is better looking than he first gave her credit for and begins to feel attracted to her, much to his chagrin. Gone is his self-confidence of *Pride and Prejudice*; instead, he suffers because of Elizabeth's obvious preference for Wickham—"I could not bear the thought of him being her favourite, or the thought of my being valued at nothing by his side." Her predilection for his old enemy in contrast to her distaste for himself tortures Mr. Darcy:

> Wickham, in Meryton! It has robbed my visit of its pleasure. Even worse, I am haunted by a glimpse of memory, something so slight I can hardly be sure if it is real. But it will not leave me, and fills my dreams. It is this: when I rode up to the ladies yesterday, I thought I saw an expression of admiration on Elizabeth's face as she looked at Wickham. Surely she cannot prefer him to me! What am I saying? Her feelings for me are unimportant. As are her feelings for George Wickham. If she wishes to admire him, it is her concern. I cannot believe she will still admire him when she finds him out, and find him out she will. He has not changed. He is still the wastrel he has always been, and she is too intelligent to be deceived for long.

Because of this, he resolves never to see Wickham again, in contrast to Tennant's novel, which presents an obsequious Wickham admitted back into Pemberley for the Christmas celebrations and trying to win Mr. Darcy's favor back.[35]

Mr. Darcy remains a proud man indeed: "would Elizabeth have changed since the autumn? Would she be surprised to see me? No. She knew of my visit. Would she be pleased or otherwise? Pleased, of course. To reacquaint herself with a man of my standing must be desirable for her." Nevertheless, he is well aware that his pride is serving him ill: "it is small wonder she had been so angry with me at the parsonage. I only wonder now that she was not even angrier. I begin to see clearly why she refused me. And to see that, through my own pride, arrogance and folly, I have lost the woman I love." His displays of bad temper are, along with his pride, one of his distinctive features and are shown throughout Grange's book. Still, he is also ready to change and redeem himself by making amends for his past behavior: "I cannot believe I was ever so proud!" Moreover, the emotional inarticulateness that plagues Austen's male protagonists is made manifest in his diary, as he is at a loss for words when in Elizabeth's presence—"I tried to think of something to say, but I found that I was speechless. It surprised me. I have never been at a loss before. To be sure, I do not always find it easy to talk to those I do not know very well, but I can generally think of at least a pleasantry. I believe the hostility I felt coming from Elizabeth robbed me of my sense."[36]

The topic of Mr. Darcy and Elizabeth's future children, which is recurrent in *Pride and Prejudice* sequels, also appears here: "little had I known when I had returned to Pemberley that it would hold so much of interest for me. It would soon have a new mistress, I hoped. I looked across the sweeping lawns and pictured my sons going down to the river to fish. I looked to the house and saw my daughters returning from a walk." He even longs to become a father: "the nurse brought Elinor [Collins]. I have never seen any attraction in babies, but Elizabeth was delighted with the little girl, and took her from the nurse. As she cradled the infant in her arms, she looked at me in a way that made my heart stand still, and suddenly babies became the most interesting thing in the world." Grange offers a hint at the happiness of their future married life, as they share the same opinions: "in this, Elizabeth and I are one." Sex between the newly-married couple is insinuated in several instances: "she looked so beautiful that I gave in to the urge to kiss her. She was surprised at first, but then responded warmly, and I knew our marriage would be a happy one in every way" or "I am looking forward to this evening. After dinner, our true marriage will begin."[37]

Yet, the problem with reading Mr. Darcy's private thoughts as transcribed in his personal diary has the negative side-effect that no surprise is in store concerning his feelings for Elizabeth. The appeal of secrets to explain a novel's lastingness has been used to explain the never-ending popularity of *Gone with the Wind*, the biggest one being Rhett Butler's love for Scarlett O'Hara. Readers' fondness for secrets might also be applied to *Pride and Prejudice*, as the novel is based upon the existence and subsequent revelation of secrets: before "the novel's central episode—Darcy's proposal, his letter the next morning, and Elizabeth's ensuing reflections.... Darcy and Elizabeth are separated by secrets; after this point, secrets unite them." These secrets are Jane's hidden feelings for Bingley, Wickham's true character, that Mr. Darcy prevented Bingley from learning that Jane was in London, Mr. Darcy's love for Elizabeth, and Elizabeth's gradual falling in love with Mr. Darcy. In *Mr. Darcy's Diary*, his feelings for Elizabeth are in the open, therefore spoiling the surprises Austen reserved for her readers.[38]

In *Seducing Mr. Darcy*, Gwyn Cready, RITA award winner, recreates an encounter between a twenty-first-century divorced ornithologist, Philippa "Flip" Allison, and Mr. Darcy, "the most famous man in literature except maybe Hamlet." Cready, an author who specializes in time-traveling romance novels, has her female protagonist travel to nineteenth-century England to become Lady Philippa Quillan and meet Mr. Darcy before he meets Elizabeth. Her ensuing relationship with Mr. Darcy turns out to be a very intimate one, for he obliges her by impregnating her when her husband refuses to, as Lord Quillan intends to secure the rights of his nephew (who is actually his illegitimate son by his brother's wife) as his only heir at the expense of the children he deprives his wife of.[39]

Although most sequels aspire to critical recognition, this is not the case with Cready's novel. As one reviewer pointed out: "*Pride and Prejudice* purists may want to reach for their smelling salts, but there's sexy fun to be had in Gwyn Cready's time-traveling take on Jane Austen's classic tale in *Seducing Mr. Darcy.*" Cready defends her novel arguing that "Austen will survive a minor alteration or two" and that "*I'm* sure Austen would allow for changing interpretations in a changing world." *Seducing Mr. Darcy* plays on the idea of lucid dreaming, a very popular trend as of late, judging by the sheer number of movies and books devoted to the topic. In a state of lucid dreaming one is aware of being in a dream and can manipulate and direct the course of the dream according to one's wishes.[40]

Whereas one of the charges leveled against Austen is that we do not have Mr. Darcy's thoughts but solely Elizabeth's point of view, it is recurrent in *Pride and Prejudice* sequels that we learn more about Mr. Darcy's inner thoughts and personal turmoil. Another frequent cause of dissatisfaction among Austen's readers is her lack of detailed descriptions when it comes to emotions, especially love. Cready's twentieth-first-century female characters voice the same opinion and so, in *Seducing Mr. Darcy,* her protagonist, after meeting Mr. Darcy, realizes that "there was a realness to this man she had never found in the pages of *Pride and Prejudice.*"[41]

Cready acknowledges the influence of the BBC miniseries on modern readers of the novel, too. Even though *Pride and Prejudice* is well-loved by women all over the world, this popularity has not gone down all that well with the academic world in general and with Austen scholars in particular. Cready addresses purists' negative reaction to modern-day adaptations or rewritings of *Pride and Prejudice* in having as her male protagonist a nineteenth-century literary scholar, who decries that "the damned BBC should have had their license revoked for reducing a complex socioliterary masterpiece into a pantalooned version of When Darcy Met Lizzy." To enhance the Austen referentiality, his name, Magnus Knightley, is a reference to *Emma*'s Mr. Knightley. Cready contrasts the learned versus popular views of *Pride and Prejudice* by means of her two protagonists' differing opinions. Whereas Magnus accuses Flip of being "the worst sort of reader. The one who will see only what she wishes. *Pride and Prejudice* is a love story only to the most unsophisticated. It is a story of manners and change," Flip argues that "it is a story of desire—fulfilled and unfulfilled." Magnus represents the academic view that adaptations and rewritings of Austen just adulterate her works. If "Darcy will never behave against one's expectations.... That, my dear, is the sublime beauty of Austen's prose. Darcy is a man of his times, a perfect man of his times," as he contends, many Austen women readers' wishes that he might behave differently are made true with Cready's novel.[42]

Just as rewritings and sequels may change our understanding of Austen, Flip's intrusion into the *Pride and Prejudice* world is far from innocuous and sets a series of changes in motion. Thus, Mr. Darcy's bastard by Lady Quillan is one of the reasons why Elizabeth turns him down when he first proposes: "I have every reason in the world to think ill of you. Even were I to forgive you that, your intemperate conduct this past year would utterly preclude it." More than updating *Pride and Prejudice,* as *Seducing Mr. Darcy* has a twenty-first-century woman transplanted to Austen's novel, Cready sexes up *Pride and Prejudice.* Sex-related changes include Sir William Lucas and a maid having an affair, Mr. Bingley and Jane having sex before their wedding or Elizabeth's strange determination to lose her virginity, an incongruous idea in the nineteenth century unless a woman was aiming at becoming a social outcast or a prostitute (actually, Elizabeth gets pregnant by Wickham and ends up becoming a pariah). It is also significant that the present-day protagonist gets into *Pride and Prejudice* but not as Elizabeth Bennet, a common point with other Austen-inspired works such as Alexandra Potter's *Me and Mr. Darcy* (2007) or Shannon Hale's *Austenland* (2007), whose protagonists meet and fall in love with Mr. Darcy as themselves, without usurping Elizabeth's identity.[43]

In *Seducing Mr. Darcy,* mock is always readily available at the expense of anything. Because of the nineteenth-century trend to address men solely by their last names, Mr. Darcy's very first name is a matter of mockery—"Whatever-His-First-Name-Is Darcy?" The anachronisms that frequently mar Austen's sequels are here exploited and enjoyed—the delight is in the anachronism, not in historical accuracy or socio-cultural plausibility. However, mistakes also occur and Mr. Darcy and "Bingley's horrible sister Louisa" are engaged when Caroline Bingley was the one who pursued him.[44]

Being Elizabeth Bennet by Emma Campbell Webster, despite its title, builds on *Pride and Prejudice* as well as on all of Austen's literary production and the author's life in order to offer readers the possibility of choosing their own development and ending. Readers are offered a number of options regarding what path they think Elizabeth Bennet should take. Depending on readers' choices and preferences, Elizabeth may marry Henry Crawford (*Mansfield Park*) just to be scandalously abandoned by him in favor of Mrs. Hurst and end up working as a governess; die of a broken neck slipping on ice when leaving the Netherfield ball in a hurry; marry Mr. Collins, almost die of boredom and kill him, trying to make it pass as a natural death; meet Henry Tilney (*Northanger Abbey*), become a fan of Gothic literature, be caught while trying to solve the 'mystery' of Mrs. Tilney's death, and be expelled from the house in disgrace; find Fanny Price's secret room at the Tilneys' and be imprisoned to death; marry Mr. Darcy after his first proposal, be miserable, have an affair with a farmer and be banished as a result of the subsequent scandal, to later commit suicide; accept Colonel Fitzwilliam's marriage proposal, which causes a duel between him and Mr. Darcy, and ultimately leads to Lady Catherine de Bourgh killing Elizabeth whereas Mr. Darcy kills both his aunt and cousin before killing himself; die a spinster; expose Wickham, who reforms and woos Elizabeth until she accepts to marry him, to discover that it was just a ploy to get his revenge on her and die of a broken heart; meet Mr. Knightley and Frank Churchill (*Emma*) and play matchmaking; marry Mr. Knightley and be unhappy because of their constant arguments; marry Mr. Knightley and be content enough although Mr. Darcy's marriage to Miss Bingley fills her with jealousy; kill Mr. Elton (*Emma*) with her carriage horses in a freak accident and be imprisoned for his death; be run over and killed by Miss Bingley's carriage; decide not to tell Mr. Darcy about Wickham and Lydia, who ends up pregnant and abandoned by Wickham, causing Mr. Bennet's death and the Bennet women being expelled from Longbourn by Mr. Collins so that Elizabeth eventually ends up in the debtor's prison; go to Bath and meet Captain Wentworth (*Persuasion*); marry Captain Wentworth and have an average life; turn down Captain Wentworth twice; meet an estranged Bennet cousin and fall for him, marrying him just to discover that he is a sham and just married her for her money; accept Mr. Darcy and have a happy ending; accept Mr. Darcy's marriage offer and realize that her life is over and there will be no interest, no fun, no excitement, flee to London to avoid this and become an author; be rescued by Willoughby (*Sense and Sensibility*), fall in love with him, and elope with him to Gretna Green after his fiancée is killed by a carriage; be bereft by Willoughby's murder, become an actress, retire and die alone in poverty; marry Colonel Brandon (*Sense and Sensibility*) and have a happy marriage; marry Colonel Brandon and have an unhappy marriage; or fall for Tom Lefroy.[45]

By offering the possibility of marrying Lefroy or becoming an author, Webster follows the trend of seeing Elizabeth Bennet as a barely distinguished alter ego for Jane Austen. Apart from the non-linear structure of *Being Elizabeth Bennet,* it differs from more conventional narratives in that the reader can score points in a number of categories (Confidence, Intelligence, Accomplishments, Connections and Fortune) that denote the reader's eligibility and desirability as a prospective bride in nineteenth-century English society.

Pride and Prejudice and Zombies is a rewriting of *Pride and Prejudice* by Seth Grahame-Smith keeping 85 percent of *Pride and Prejudice* while adding 15 percent of Grahame-Smith's work. Grahame-Smith's novel deals with an England plagued by "present difficulties," namely, a zombie invasion that has to be repelled. Women's main (if not sole) concern in *Pride and Prejudice* was marrying well, which in *Pride and Prejudice and Zombies* is scorned, as Mr. Bennet holds revolutionary ideas about women's role in society: "I would much prefer their minds be engaged in the deadly arts than clouded with dreams of marriage and fortune." Women's role is not limited to spinsterhood or marriage and because of the entail, "Jane and Elizabeth tried to explain that all five of them were capable of fending for themselves; that they could make tolerable fortunes as bodyguards, assassins, or mercenaries if need be." Elizabeth finds pride in being a student of Shaolin and master of the seven-starred fist and all the Bennet sisters, who have studied in China, are brave warriors. Jane "is a warrior first, and a woman second"; actually, "Jane was a fine killer, but a deficient judge of character."[46]

Other than her dowry, family connections or personal qualities, a woman's desirability in the marriage market is determined by her zombie-killing ability and "no sooner had he [Mr. Darcy] made it clear to himself and his friends that she hardly had a good feature in her face, than he began to find it was rendered uncommonly intelligent by the beautiful expression of her dark eyes, and her uncommon skill with a blade." Elizabeth's zombie-killing skills play an important part in Mr. Darcy's attraction to her: "Darcy had never been so bewitched by any woman as he was by her. He really believed, that were it not for the inferiority of her connections, he should be in some danger of falling in love, and were it not for his considerable skill in the deadly arts, that he should be in danger of being bested by hers for never had he seen a lady more gifted in the ways of vanquishing the undead."[47]

Being a warrior is another one of the many accomplishments a woman must possess and Georgiana Darcy "is not only master of the female arts, but the deadly as well." Although Lady Catherine de Bourgh also has a reputation as a brave zombie slayer, her daughter's poor health prevents her from following in her mother's footsteps. Despite the fact that Grahame-Smith's introduction of women's zombie-killing skills opens up a professional career for nineteenth-century women, this has not been appreciated by critics. For Halford, "the book effectively undermines the seriousness of, in the original, the Bennet sisters' matrimonial quest by suggesting a non-linear positive correlation between the number of zombies present during courtship and the degree of difficulty in obtaining a husband." This is an England dominated by violence and Elizabeth thinks, after Miss Bingley's affront, that Jane's "honour demands she be slain." Daily life is permeated by notions of fighting and, therefore, "after breakfast, the girls retired to the dojo and attended to their mid-week musket disassembly and cleaning." The book continues with Austen's rejection of sentimentality, for it blurs a fighter's vision and good judgment: "you *forget* yourself, Jane—you have allowed your feelings for Mr. Bingley to soften the instincts bestowed by our Oriental master."[48]

In regards to Mr. Darcy, his desirability as a prospective husband does not merely come from his £10,000 a year, for "the report which was in general circulation within five minutes after his entrance, of his having slaughtered more than a thousand unmentionables since the fall of Cambridge" makes him equally appealing. Because a man's value is to a large extent determined by his ability to fight, Mr. Bennet sides with Elizabeth's rejecting Mr. Collins's marriage proposal: "I shall not have my best warrior resigned to the service of a man who is fatter than Buddha and duller than the edge of a learning sword."[49]

"Critics have commented that recent adaptations ... foreground heterosexual romance at the expense of feminist critique" but in *Pride and Prejudice and Zombies*, thanks to their fighting skills, the Bennet sisters attain the professional validation Austen denies her heroines and which is stressed in recent cinematographic adaptations of Austen's works such as *Clueless* (1995), *Kandukondain Kandukondain* (2000), *Bridget Jones's Diary* (2001), *Bride and Prejudice* (2004) and *Pride & Prejudice* (2005). For example, "Pidduck has identified the country walk as a recurrent motif of Austen films, a motif that suggests the possibility of women overcoming the limitations on 'mobility and aspiration' placed on them in Austen's age, limits symbolized by interior spaces." In *Pride and Prejudice and Zombies*, these country walks constitute a chance for the Bennet girls to display their fighting abilities as they are attacked by zombies whenever they dare to venture beyond Longbourn. If a good marriage in Austen is a match of similar minds, for Grahame-Smith a good marriage brings together two good zombie killers: "if the female slays a zombie in the presence of a male during courtship, the difficulty is reduced somewhat by an upsurge in the male's lust." Because women are offered a professional career, *Pride and Prejudice and Zombies* presents a more egalitarian society, more attuned to twenty-first-century social mores than the original novel.[50]

Negative critical reception and best-selling figures aside, *Pride and Prejudice and Zombies* opened the way for "the canonical literature/monster mash-up subgenre," a subgenre characterized by "a form of vital and original popular postmodern interaction with and appropriation of the existing literary canon" in "an attempt to move beyond previous ideological attacks on the literary canon and into a popular interaction with the existing literary canon." Chretien reads *Pride and Prejudice and Zombies* as a feminist version of *Pride and Prejudice*, resulting in "a coauthored, hybridized text, written across two centuries, with a complex and occasionally contradictory purpose and function." Grahame-Smith's addition of violence points a finger to the paradox that, despite living in one of the most convoluted periods of English history, Austen failed to register this social and political turmoil, merely hinting at it. Just like in *Pemberley* it is revealed that Mr. Darcy and Bingley had fought in France, in *Pride and Prejudice and Zombies* the violence of the zombie invasion and subsequent fight to repel them brings attention to the unstable historical period of Austen's lifetime, only mentioned in passing in Austen's *opus*.[51]

For Chretien, the fears that plagued Austen's contemporaries (the loss of the truly British character, a revolution of the lower social classes, and the anxieties about a French invasion), and which are absent from her works (and, therefore, unknown by later Austen readers not too familiar with the historical background depicted in the novels) are made obvious with the addition of zombies, which highlight the uncertainty of Austen's times. Thus, "in a purely Marxist reading, zombies represent the threat of the masses rising up and overthrowing the ruling classes. As zombies, individuals no longer have any social rank or distinction." While some have located the appeal of Austen's novels on the fact that "they supposedly show us men and women who engage in romantic relationships devoid of angst or crisis in a world free of conflict, controversy, and uncertainty," her novels are not so turmoil-free as one might think at first. Grahame-Smith, with his violence-ridden world, brings this turmoil to the forefront.[52]

Whatever the take that the authors of the various *Pride and Prejudice* sequels adopt, one salient feature common to all of them is the special attention they pay to the characterization of Mr. Darcy. The sequels to *Pride and Prejudice* analyzed in this chapter are of a very different sort—a parallel novel (*Mr. Darcy's Diary*), a continuation (*Pemberley*), a time-traveling romance (*Seducing Mr. Darcy*), a rewriting with zombies (*Pride and Prejudice and Zombies*), or a choose-your-own-ending rewriting (*Being Elizabeth Bennet*). But, where does this need to focus on Mr. Darcy come from? Because "Darcy, albeit a humanized and fallible version of Richardson's paragon of masculinity, remains rather inaccessible to the reader who is tempted to rely on Elizabeth's own reading of him for information," we need other versions of *Pride and Prejudice* from which we can learn more about him.[53]

It is sometimes the case that a literary character's fame transcends that of the corresponding literary work and becomes a fixture of popular culture. This has happened to Mr. Darcy, transformed and updated for the twentieth century into Bridget Jones's Mark Darcy. Yet, although Mark Darcy is a twentieth-century reworking of Mr. Darcy, it is possible to find twentieth-century versions of Mr. Darcy as well without having to invent a brand-new character. These newer versions are due to our own, personal reading of Austen and, illustrating this trend, "Bridget's Austen fixation centers on lusting after Colin Firth, as she finds particular satisfaction in the film's now-famous pond scene.... Bridget is primarily enthralled with 'Austen' rather than Austen." Therefore, "our" Mr. Darcy does not necessarily have to be the same as Austen's Mr. Darcy. We should wonder if, although *Pride and Prejudice* sequels help revitalize the original, with so many sequels, we are creating "other" Austens, some versions having little (if at all) in common with the original one. Our *Pride and Prejudice* is not necessarily the genuine *Pride and Prejudice*; for example, "watching *Pride and Prejudice* is a communal event in Fielding's novels.... Bridget and her friends are not interested in enacting Austenian manners or courtship codes; rather, Austen creates a space that enables therapeutic discourse."[54]

But why do present-day women sigh for nineteenth-century Mr. Darcy instead of being attracted to present-day male characters found in print, cinema or TV nowadays? Why is he still evoked as women's favorite heartthrob? It seems that Mr. Darcy offers women consolation from modern dating practices, and "for Bridget, watching Colin Firth as Darcy is escapist and therapeutic: the 1995 BBC TV series provides a fantasy that allows her to leave the chaos of her romantic life behind." Penny Gay wondered where the need to adapt an Austen novel came from:

> the simplest answer has to be that she provides many of the ingredients that have traditionally engaged audiences: a narrative that centres on the coming to maturity of a young person; a love story; moral and ethical dilemmas satisfyingly resolved. All of this takes place among people who are recognisably like ourselves in their psychological make-up, supported by a cast of lesser characters who fill a range from the gently comic to the grotesque. Austen's world, despite the manifest differences in social structure, is that of the literate middle-class which her readers still inhabit.

The same applies to sequel writing. Screenwriter Robin Swicord, who wrote and directed *The Jane Austen Book Club* (2007), based on Karen Joy Fowler's homonymous novel (2004), admitted that "I want Austen to be an antidote to our fractured, busy lives."[55]

Sometimes, reality aims to be modeled after literature and one can find online tutorials on how to find Mr. Darcy in real life. Thus, the wikiHow "How to Find a Modern Day Mr. Darcy" gives single women "tips on seeking your modern-day Mr. Darcy, along with some advice on not making things too hard on yourself or your suitors." This list of tips, however, is careful to warn prospective Elizabeth Bennets that "loving an idea can lead to sadness and frustration." It also cautions readers not to "expect to get 'Mr. Darcy' gift-wrapped in a box! *Pride and Prejudice* is a great book but nothing is *ever* fairytale-perfect in real life." In the search for Mr. Darcy, *Pride and Prejudice* is also used to encourage women to lead Christian lives. Just as Elizabeth won Mr. Darcy's heart without her noticing his feelings for her or doing anything about them, Christian women will attract men (Mr. Darcy-like men, of course) who will recognize their virtues. While some have deplored Austen for being a sex-free author, "Austen's popularity as a default-relationship advisor may even stem from the absence of sexual desire in her novels' concluding marriages. Modern society desperately wants marriage to be cleansed of the messiness of sex and desire." Christian women's books and guides do this in using Austen to advance their own agendas of sexual chastity.[56]

But where does Mr. Darcy's appeal come from? Why does such a rude character continue to appeal to legions of contemporary women? After all, "women's favourite fictional icon is a dominant patriarchal male." Just like our Austen is not the genuine Austen, the version of Mr. Darcy we may cherish is not an exact replica of the one found in *Pride and Prejudice*; since "twenty-first-century women want Austen's heroes with a difference ... adapters are selective in the aspects they copy or rewrite." The sequels to Austen's novels, just the same as cinematographic adaptations (including loosely inspired films such as *The Lake House* [2006]), emphasize "both increasing male sensibility and contemporary women's greater opportunities and more active role in society." Not only is the man present-day women have chosen as their masculine ideal long gone; even more tellingly, this type of man was already on the verge of disappearing as Austen herself was writing: "Darcy as an exemplar of a vanishing type of man; he is a resplendent figure who is at once chivalric, rational, and romantic, and I argue that his status as an ostensibly impeccable man highlights his uniqueness. The aristocratic tradition that Darcy embodies and Pemberley institutionalizes is waning, and while it is still greatly admired in the novel, its representatives are dwindling," while modern men such as Bingley were on the rise.[57]

Mr. Darcy's sexuality has repeatedly been overstressed in the sequels. Beginning with the BBC miniseries that showed a soaking wet Mr. Darcy coming out of a lake, "one of the main characteristics of the recent spate of Austen adaptations in the 1990s seems to be their emphasis on the body, through the attention to sensuous period details or to the desire relationships between the characters." As a result of this, Mr. Darcy has become the object of desire for the female gaze. Since "the vulgar signalling of things sexual which Davies inserted into *Pride and Prejudice* via Darcy's watery exploits," a number of sequels have taken upon themselves to expose Mr. Darcy's sexual side. His physical attributes, despite Austen's scant physical description of her hero, have been emphasized: "for the Hero, well, Miss Austen, for once in her short life, held nothing back: tall, dark, handsome, brooding, clever, noble, and uninhibitedly rich." Sequels in turn have enhanced his physical attributes; in view of her silence, "what she does provide is a perfect blank screen on to which Darcy's admirers, by identifying with Elizabeth Bennet, can project that most archetypal of all female fantasies—that they will be the one and only woman to discover the key to unlocking a man's tortured soul, thus setting free his hidden passions."[58]

Because "Austen's novel betrays nothing of Darcy's actual sexuality or lack of it," the sequels come in to solve this omission. For example, to bring in an explicit sexual dimension, in *Seducing Mr. Darcy* he enjoys a sexual encounter with a sex-deprived divorced ornithologist. But interestingly enough, we never see a sex scene between Mr. Darcy and Elizabeth, which seems to be closed territory for any sequel writer. The racy *Seducing Mr. Darcy*, which cannot be accused of prudishness, does not have qualms in presenting Lady Quillan (the nineteenth-century identity of her twenty-first-century protagonist) having sex with Mr. Darcy, but stops short of having Elizabeth and Mr. Darcy in bed and respects the couple's privacy instead.[59]

Austen dealt with the adjustments English society had to face in order to become a modern, industrial nation as well as the adjustments expected from men in such a new society. Those were changing times and "Austen's men respond to a variety of cultural directives for proper masculinity, and they acclimate themselves to the needs of a changing society." Sexuality also plays a role in this adjustment and "Austen repeatedly represents men who monitor their sexualities as part of their larger civic duty, and their self-management allows them to participate more fully in a modernizing culture." In *Seducing Mr. Darcy* Mr. Darcy's failure to restrain his sexuality leads to trouble and almost prevents his marrying Elizabeth, as she despises his affair with a married woman. The French woman hidden in *Pemberley* is also evidence of Englishmen's lack of (sexual) restraint—they have been corrupted by French mores and women. Even worse, the discovery of this woman's existence leads to chaos (Elizabeth's flight).[60]

Mr. Darcy is much more than a literary character or a fantasy for female readers, as evidenced by the fact that "according to a recent poll conducted by the Orange Prize for Fiction, 1,900 women ... voted for Mr. Darcy as the man they would most like to go on a date with. He was also the fictional character women would most like to invite to a dinner party." So extended is his appeal that a sexual pheromone present in male mice urine that attracts female mice was named Darcin after him. However, this attraction can be negative and potentially harmful when taken too seriously or into real life. To Carole Welch, associate publishing director of Sceptre, "it encouraged me to fall for moody, charismatic, seemingly unattainable men, with unfortunately less happy results than for Jane Austen's heroine." "The dark side of the Darcy syndrome" involves "that dark, smouldering, moody, charismatic, arrogant Darcy types, whom we hate at first sight and then later find ourselves falling in love with, often—particularly after we have married them—turn out to be rigid, dominating and controlling." An additional risk is the improbability of finding a real man that lives up to this fantasy, as happens to the protagonist of *Me and Mr. Darcy*: "Why aren't men today like the men in books? ... Just imagine being in a world where men didn't steal your cab, cheat on you or have an addiction to Internet porn, but were chivalrous, devoted and honorable." In the novel, the protagonist shies away from the real world and real men to find shelter among the pages of *Pride and Prejudice*, finding succor and deriving hope (and surrogate love) from the characterization of Mr. Darcy. Austen-inspired sequels have problematized this obsession and "more recently, authors have depicted Austen's modern devotees in a less flattering light: as obsessive, escapist readers, for whom Austen becomes the source of their romantic problems." For Rodríguez Martín, the anti–Janeite phenomenon comes not from a dislike of Austen's works, but from a dislike of the irrational admiration she causes.[61]

"The pious and vigilant Janeite looks on, ever ready to be scandalized by the merest breach of decorum" but sequels continue being written. Sequels to Austen's novels revealing the future of her characters or retelling the same story from another character's point of view have given way to more loosely inspired works such as *Seducing Mr. Darcy, Being Elizabeth Bennet, Pride and Prejudice and Zombies* or *Me and Mr. Darcy.* This phenomenon has been seen as a consequence of the exhaustion of Austen: "cleverly, the movie and television people mainly responsible for feeding the Austen media behemoth have realised they can't simply recycle the same six similar novels for ever." Just like the film "adaptations of Jane Austen's novels respond to both trends in popular culture and industry practices of the time of production," Austen sequels owe a great deal to the literary momentum of their publication, being greatly influenced by the demands of the publishing market. This is why it is likely that, as times and customs change, more *Pride and Prejudice* sequels are due to be written.[62]

The sequels to *Pride and Prejudice* and *Sense and Sensibility* are but a few of the sequels analyzed in chapter 1 are but a few of the sequels Austen has been subjected to. The many rewritings, sequels and adaptations of Austen (not to mention their cinematographic counterparts) make that nowadays "we live in a Jane Austen universe." Putting aside the potential confusion as to which the real Austen is, there are those who celebrate Austen's prominence: "purists can criticise, but imitation keeps the original in our minds and enables a celebration of Austen's text for today." However, because "the sequel that adequately combines the atmosphere of Jane Austen's novels with a full-scale historical novel, however, has yet to be written," we may well anticipate more sequels to come.[63]

Chapter 3

The Madwoman in the Attic and Other Family Secrets

Jane Eyre by Charlotte Brontë, *Wide Sargasso Sea* by Jean Rhys and *The French Dancer's Bastard* by Emma Tennant

You may think of her as dead and buried—or rather, you need not think of her at all. **Charlotte Brontë: *Jane Eyre* (1847)**

Names matter, like when he wouldn't call me Antoinette, and I saw Antoinette drifting out of the window with her scents, her pretty clothes and her looking-glass. **Jean Rhys: *Wide Sargasso Sea* (1966)**

Not my own child—a French dancer's bastard? **Charlotte Brontë: *Jane Eyre* (1847)**

As I really am, a child in need of company, a budding actress who desires an audience for the lovesick ballads she was taught to sing at her mother's knee. **Emma Tennant: *The French Dancer's Bastard* (2006)**

Literary sequels often explore minor characters that were largely unexplored in the original work. In the sequels to *Jane Eyre*, not only are secondary characters brought to the forefront but, more importantly, disturbing events that are only lightly touched on in *Jane Eyre* are analyzed to their fullest extent. Rochester's first marriage is too disturbing for Jane to learn more about other than the fact that his wife is still alive and poses an obstacle to her own happiness. Little is known about Bertha Rochester—only that she comes from overseas and is crazy. Another disturbing event is that Rochester might be the father of Adèle Varens, a lovely though untamable girl, and the illegitimate daughter of a French dancer (an ill-reputed profession in the nineteenth century, when actresses and dancers were just a step above prostitutes and all three professions were almost synonymous). Rochester's reputation as a hero would be inevitably ruined had he fathered an illegitimate child; readers and Jane alike are happier accepting his excuse that he might be Adèle's father or not, given her mother's deceiving nature.

That Rochester had both a crazy wife and a bastard flew in the face of nineteenth-century Victorian morals and, accordingly, the novel presented both possibilities, only to soon retreat from going further into the implications of these two events: Rochester's wife is left in the background, little information is provided about her and she is eventually killed off. As Jean Rhys remarked,

> the Creole in Charlotte Brontë's novel is a lay figure.... She's necessary to the plot, but always she shrieks, howls, laughs horribly, attacks all and sundry—*off stage*. For me ... she must be right *on stage*. She must be at least plausible with a past, the *reason* why Mr. Rochester treats her so abominably and feels justified, the *reason* why he thinks she is mad and why of course she goes mad, even the *reason* why she tries to set everything on fire, and eventually succeeds.

About Adèle, her paternity could well be attributed to any of her mother's other lovers, including the one with whom Rochester surprised her just a few months after Adèle's birth.[1]

The two sequels to *Jane Eyre* analyzed in this chapter, *Wide Sargasso Sea* by Jean Rhys and *The French Dancer's Bastard* by Emma Tennant, explore the previous stories of two characters who play a decisive role in Jane Eyre's life though they are ignored for the most part in *Jane Eyre*—Bertha Mason and Adèle Varens.[2] Rhys conceived *Wide Sargasso Sea* not only as a sequel or a companion text to Brontë's but as a challenge to the literary canon and free-standing on its own, a mother text for *Jane Eyre*. As the events in *Wide Sargasso Sea* take place prior to Jane's meeting Rochester, we could call it a prequel. *The French Dancer's Bastard*, on the other hand, is a parallel novel, for it recreates most of the events taking place in *Jane Eyre* from another perspective, that of ten-year-old Adèle, but also includes the perspectives of Rochester, Bertha's guardian Grace Poole, and Mrs. Fairfax. The addition of the last two is significant because their study has been neglected in the vast majority of critical analyses of *Jane Eyre*, deeming both characters too irrelevant or uninteresting for comment. In the preface, Tennant acknowledged that she wanted to tell the story of Adèle, about whom we learn little from Jane's description of her later life. This made Tennant wonder if "perhaps, as is often found in the lives of girls as they grow into women, it was all a little more complicated than that."[3]

Jean Rhys brought her postcolonial sensibility to her rewriting of the story of Bertha Mason Rochester. Born in Dominica at a time when there were only three hundred white inhabitants out of a population of 30,000, Rhys, the daughter of an Englishman and a white Creole, moved to England when she was seventeen years old to go to boarding school. She would not return home except for a brief visit in 1936, during which she felt utterly uncomfortable because of racial unrest. Rhys, who never forgot her colonial background and did not feel English, found it easy to identify with Mr. Rochester's first wife, who also came from overseas.[4]

Rhys had in mind the idea of writing a novel with Bertha Mason as the protagonist for years and confided to a friend that "that unfortunate death of a Creole! I'm fighting mad to write *her* story." However, dissatisfied with the way in which her novel, then titled *Le Revenant*, was turning out, she abandoned the project and only resumed its writing in the sixties, when she was virtually a literary recluse. By then the literary popularity she had enjoyed after World War I had long vanished, her novels had gone out of print (they were only republished after the success of *Wide Sargasso Sea*) and it was generally assumed that she must have died. In rewriting the story of Rochester's wife, Rhys allowed herself some poetic license in order to include some events that she deemed important in regards to Dominica, even if it meant altering the chronology. Also, although Bertha Mason was born in Jamaica (a British colony) and her mother Annette was from French Martinique, Rhys blended the two places together. Additionally, in Rhys's version, Richard Mason is not Bertha's brother but her stepbrother.[5]

Jane Eyre is far from being the "plain tale with few pretensions" that Charlotte Brontë claimed it was. Autobiographical echoes can be perceived in all of her novels and in *Jane Eyre*, she especially conveyed the anxieties, concerns, dreams and hopes that had filled her mind during the writing process. Charlotte was desperately in love with Monsieur Heger, principal of the Brussels school she and her sister Emily had attended, but his marriage to Madame Heger, owner of the school, prevented Charlotte's chances at happiness, even though she (but not Heger) contemplated adultery as a possibility.[6] Because the Heger marriage seemed happy and Monsieur Heger never replied to any of Brontë's passionate love letters, she transformed the wife in *Jane Eyre* into a monster locked in the attic. Brontë also found inspiration in a real case: while she was employed as a governess for the Sigdwick family, she learned that in a neighboring house a madwoman had been kept in the attic for years.[7]

Biographical parallelisms between Brontë and her heroine do not end here. Brontë was always painfully aware of her own plainness, which was a source of constant distress her whole life. She thought that this would be compensated if Heger were to be absolutely dependent on her. In having her male protagonist crippled, she recreated her father's greatest terror—a house fire. Because characters in Brontë's novels were often based on people she knew, a great deal of attention has been devoted to speculating over the inspiration for her works. Playing on her own limited life experience (reviewers and critics have often marveled at how it was possible for the Brontës, who hardly ever left Yorkshire, to describe human passions so vividly with so scarce worldly contact), Jane's refusal of St. John's marriage proposal was inspired by the proposal Brontë had received from Henry Nussey, brother of her life-long friend Ellen. Nussey, very much like St. John to Jane, delineated to Charlotte the qualities he sought in a wife. Brontë claimed that Jane's being summoned by Rochester's voice came from another real-life experience; Bertha's drunkenness and Rochester's blindness are directly related to her brother Branwell's alcoholism and her father's cataracts, respectively (it was during his convalescence from surgery to remove them, during which she was nursing him, that Brontë began writing *Jane Eyre*).[8]

Brontë experienced first-hand and then explored in her novels how young women of intelligence but without financial means found it difficult to find a husband in the marriage market and the same can be said of Rhys's female protagonists. While she was living in London, Rhys suffered from poverty, illness, and alcoholism, providing her with an insight into the toll of being a single woman in a patriarchal world. Her first four novels, *Postures, After Leaving Mr. Mackenzie, Voyage in the Dark,* and *Good Morning, Midnight* are largely autobiographical, with heroines who are social pariahs alienated from society. The humiliation and victimization of her female characters is one of the main topics in Rhys's fiction, their isolation being largely due to their colonial backgrounds.[9]

The fear of becoming the madwoman in the attic is one of the literary tropes that has had a most pervasive bearing both in highbrow and lowbrow cultural manifestations of all sorts. The lucid and innocent young woman who is driven crazy by a mysterious force and is put (or threatened to be put) in an asylum, with nobody believing that she is the innocent victim of a scheme, is the basic plot of numberless plays, novels, short stories, and, more recently, also made-for-TV movies and soap operas. Whereas most of these texts expose how a woman is deluded and falls prey to schemers' tricks, presenting the decoys that make her even doubt her own sanity, *Jane Eyre* presents the madwoman in the attic as a *fait accompli.* By the time her existence is discovered, this woman is irremediably lost to society and sanity. How she got to that point is retold by others, while her own side of the story remains forever lost because of her madness. For Jane, Bertha, her fiancé's very much alive wife, is no more than an impediment for her marriage, an obstacle for her happiness, which she will only achieve once Bertha is dead. Bertha's insignificance (she is just a problem, a stone in Jane's already stony path to happiness) is marked by her otherness—a Creole from overseas, different from her husband and Jane, ill-fitting in cold England, without a friend or relative to comfort or take care of her, with a paid companion as her sole help.

Jane's position as a governess involves teaching "but one pupil, a little girl, under ten years of age," who is introduced to her by Mrs. Fairfax as Mr. Rochester's ward. From Adèle herself, Jane learns that "I lived long ago with mamma; but she is gone to the Holy Virgin. Mamma used to teach me to dance and sign, and to say verses. A great many gentlemen and ladies came to see mamma, and I used to dance before them, or sit on their knees and sing to them: I liked it," although Jane later learns that her mother had abandoned Adèle. Jane begins to dislike Adèle's background when Adèle sings a song about a woman deserted by her lover—"the subject seemed strangely chosen for an infant singer; but I suppose the point of the exhibition lay in hearing the notes of love and jealousy warbled with the lisp of childhood, and in very bad taste that point was—at least I thought so." Critics have noted that despite Jane's rebellious childhood that causes her to be sent to Lowood by Aunt Reed, Jane wants Adèle to be docile. Whereas Jane sees herself as fully justified in her rebellion against Aunt Reed's tyrannical ways, Adèle is to be tamed and her natural will crushed so as to make her forget her French upbringing, which Jane considers improper.[10]

Meanwhile, Rochester considers Adèle "not bright, she has no talents; yet in a short time she has made much improvement" thanks to Jane's efforts. For him, rather than an object of affection, Adèle is a subject of study, when not the target of his scorn:

> my Spring is gone, however, but it has left me that French floweret on my hands, which, in some moods, I would fain to be rid of. Not valuing now the root whence it sprang; having found that it was a sort which nothing but gold dust could manure, I have but half a liking to the blossom, especially when it looks so artificial as that now. I keep it and rear it on the Roman Catholic principle of expiating numerous sins, great or small, by one good work.

Despite Rochester's claims that he is not her father ("not my own child—a French dancer's bastard?"), Jane describes Adèle's talents and shortcomings and tries to find some resemblance. In her novel, Tennant further explores the issue of illegitimacy. As in *Jane Eyre*, Rochester doubts his paternity and, what is more, he considers Adèle a monstrosity: "the child sent by the devil," "the child's wickedness may be the natural and inevitable consequences of an upbringing that can barely be described as such," "Adèle Varens, at eight years old, is already wedded to the devil and beyond conversion or repair," "this thieving Jacobin guttersnipe," "Céline's diabolical daughter."[11]

Rochester has often been linked to Bluebeard, the man who killed his wives, in a number of scholarly studies. This association is repeatedly made more explicit in *The French Dancer's Bastard*, where upon first seeing a picture of Rochester, Adèle comments on "the angry, darkly shadowed face—which reminded me of nothing so much as the illustration for Bluebeard, in my book of Perrault's fairy tales." Tennant builds up on the echoes of fairy tales found in *Jane Eyre* and, thus, Rochester is a figure who fills Adèle up with dread: for her, he is "the ogre," "he might chase me right up the stairs and kill me like Bluebeard before locking me in a secret room," "none with a physiognomy as vile, as clear a transcription of evil, as Papa," "the man I must love with filial devotion is a Bluebeard, and his castle, I have little doubt, has locked and forbidden rooms." Eventually, after she finds him crying, she pities him and begins to appreciate him in a different light—"up close he was no more frightening than the Beast in 'Beauty and the Beast,'" "I know that this monster of male selfishness and arrogance is not a murderer," "*Pauvre* Papa: who loved me far better than Maman did, all along."[12]

Adèle also offers an alternative version of Jane and, in her view, she is not the sweet governess who tries to improve her pupil's education. Adèle even suspects that Jane may have hidden motives in trying to educate her: "that she had affection for me, I cannot gainsay, but I had been for her a conduit to the greater profit of her master's love, and little more." Her negative view of Jane leads Adèle to reject her: "my absolute refusal to the knowledge that there was only one person in the world [Jane] who would show a human heart at work, when it came to caring for the bastard of a French opera dancer" while she still longs for Jane to realize she is not like her mother—"I wish only for purity and happiness." It is only late in the novel that Adèle realizes Jane's love towards her: "do I hate the poor little governess so much, who has tried from the very beginning to instil modesty, education and decency into the *fillete* to whom Monsieur Rochester was more inclined to deny paternity than to love?"[13]

Running away from school only to discover that Jane has become her father's wife, she again flees, afraid of "the future that dear 'Miss Eyre' certainly has in mind for me: as carer for her children with her husband, Monsieur Rochester, somewhere between a nursemaid and a companion; and, if I persist in my studies, eventually a governess to the daughter for whom Jane inevitably pines?" After a brief period in Paris, Adèle becomes ready to return to England because she has now learned to appreciate Jane. "The family at T. Hall lived happily ever after" and Adéle takes on an invitation to train as an actress.[14]

Tennant sought to imitate the polyphonic structure of *Wide Sargasso Sea*, in which we hear the story narrated by both Bertha and Rochester. Tennant replicated the voices of Adéle, Rochester, Grace Poole and Mrs. Fairfax. In Tennant's version, Adéle shares with Bertha the same dread that Rochester inspires in her as well as the dislike for England and soon becomes friends with her. Tennant offers an alternative explanation to the novel's ending too—according to *The French Dancer's Bastard*, Adèle set accidentally fire to Thornfield with a magnifying glass and Mrs. Fairfax killed Bertha.[15]

About Grace Poole, she resents her own, forced captivity while feeling sorry for "the wretched Creole," with whom she has a love-hate relationship, pitying her at the same time that she sometimes resents the airs that Bertha puts on. Bitter because of her own imprisonment, Grace kidnaps Bertha and hides her away as part of a scheme to blackmail Rochester. Grace also offers yet another vision of Jane, whom she does not regard as Rochester's equal—"Mr. Rochester can go after his governess, with her yes, sirs and no, sirs, but he can't get a true equal like the Frenchwoman to agree to live by his side." In Grace's view, the true freedom is to choose to love, not Jane's final submission to Rochester at the end of the novel. In regards to Mrs. Fairfax, she is presented as a dutiful and loyal servant, even after she is sent away to Scotland to live with relatives after the destruction of Thornfield, almost a caricature of the good servant. Her loyalty goes so far that she denies that Rochester ever had his wife locked up in the attic. However, eventually it is discovered that she killed Bertha, giving another insight into her character.[16]

Rochester is presented in a light far from becoming and he is no patriarchal figure at all. He appears doubtful, remorseful about his past behavior with Adèle's mother, Céline, and afraid of being condemned as a murderer under French law for having killed her lover in a duel. He is a man bought by £30,000 by the Mason family in exchange to agree to marry Bertha and willing to engage in yet another mercenary marriage with Blanche Ingram. Still, he has some redeeming points, for he cares about Bertha's well-being. However, Tennant makes a mistake in her description of Rochester's reunion with Jane, for Jane states in *Jane Eyre* that she will never tell him about the supernatural summons she heard but in *The French Dancer's Bastard* he does know about it.[17]

During her decade-long rewritings to her original manuscript, Rhys sought to present Bertha as a real person, with her own motivations, state of mind, ideas, and thoughts, far from the stereotype of the madwoman. As Rhys explained, "I've never believed in Charlotte's lunatic, that's why I wrote this book." In *Jane Eyre* Bertha can be seen as Jane's double, the one who plays out Jane's repressed anger. In a way, it is necessary that Bertha exists for Jane to be able to properly live in society. Victorians were horrified by Jane's anger, far more dangerous than unrepressed sexuality so any time that Jane has to repress her anger, Bertha acts out on it, allowing a release that Jane could not have had otherwise. Bertha becomes "a substitute self who realizes and suffers for all the dangerous potentials of the protagonist's character." However, because Bertha is a colonial woman whereas she is an Englishwoman, Jane fails to identify Bertha as her double. Bertha, as portrayed by Rhys, is much more than a mere double for Jane and she herself has two doubles in *Wide Sargasso Sea*—Tia and Christophine. If Bertha acts out Jane's wrath, so does Tia for Antoinette (Bertha's real name). Bertha is a woman who fights patriarchy and in her failure, she finds in her madness a way to escape from patriarchy. In *Wide Sargasso Sea* Bertha can also be a double for Rochester regarding his repressed anger for his arranged marriage, especially once he feels trapped by his wife and the lies about her family.[18]

Bertha is deprived by Brontë of humanity as a result of her desire, which has masculinized and animalized her, making her subhuman. Bertha becomes less of a real person or less of a well-rounded character to become a stereotype of the madwoman. Madness has long being considered an outcome for sexual excesses, especially for women given that it was one of the symptoms of the last stage of syphilis. In *Jane Eyre*, madness can also be interpreted as a malady resulting from the individual's inability to conform to social standards and moral rules: Englishness, whiteness, moderation and propriety. Thus, Bertha's madness is her way to escape from her harsh realities, to escape from her imprisonment, almost "the inevitable result of situating a sexually voracious, independent-minded and wealthy woman within the confines of a white, Protestant, nineteenth-century *Bildungsroman*." This is a danger Jane also faces but she does learn to control her emotions in the course of the novel. Jane's rebellious attitude causes her to make decisions going against religious zeal and society but without ever going so far as to turn her back on either religion or society.[19]

In Brontë's rendering, Bertha lacks manners, sanity, verbal capacity, a motivation or even a dissenting voice, since her story is told by Rochester, Jane and even her guardian. Brontë was conscious that she had not thoroughly analyzed Bertha, as she acknowledged in a letter to a friend: "it is true that profound pity ought to be the only sentiment elicited by the view of such degradation, and equally true is it that I have not sufficiently dwelt on that feeling: I have erred in making *horror* too predominant. Mrs. Rochester, indeed, lived a sinful life before she was insane, but sin is itself a species of insanity—the truly good behold and compassionate it as such."[20]

Bertha's characterization as a madwoman owes a great deal to racial considerations. She is the Other—overtly sexual and prone to sin and madness. Race is a central concern in determining Bertha's personality and moral deficiencies. Rochester sees his marriage to her in racial terms, tinged with connotations of miscegenation: "her family wished to secure me, because I was of a good race." Rochester lives in fear that Bertha might not be white and "even before Daniel Cosway's letter informs him of old Cosway's sexual profligacy with black women and of Annette's madness, he harnesses racism to misogyny in order to justify his colonization of Antoinette, thereby reducing her—albeit metaphorically—to the status of a slave concubine." Rochester voices this in *The French Dancer's Bastard*: "Antoinette may be white—but she bears the marks of the slavery I imposed on her, and of my own cruel repudiation of her, too."[21]

Slavery and sexuality are closely connected in *Jane Eyre*: "hiring a mistress is the next worse thing to buying a slave: both are often by nature, and always by position, inferior: and to live familiarly with inferiors is degrading." Tennant plays with this connection in her novel, exploring the relationship of Rochester with one of his willing "slaves," Céline. Although he does perceive her as a sort of slave ("if the slave trade in which my late father dealt so profitably has now been ruled unlawful, then the women of Europe are well prepared to make up the deficit"), their relationship is different from how it was portrayed in *Jane Eyre* and Céline is presented as Rochester's great love: "I will never hear her again, or hold in my arms the daughter of freedom who taught me to love slavery."[22]

In this discourse of slavery, naming is an important sign of who is in charge and who has power to name and, in turn, who is powerless and must accept others' actions, even when it means their own name. In *Wide*

Sargasso Sea we learn that Mrs. Rochester's real name was Antoinette, but Rochester calls her Bertha, a name she rejects because "Bertha is not my name. You are trying to make me into someone else, calling me by another name." This change of name reflects his failure to understand his wife at all. For Rhys, the heart of the problem lies not so much in Bertha's questionable madness but in a lack of understanding. As Bertha/Antoinette complains to her husband—"you don't know anything about me" and he agrees that "the woman is a stranger. Her pleading expression annoys me."[23]

Bertha's "madness triggers the plot and moves it forward to its climax." Consequently, for Rochester to portray himself as the hero of *Jane Eyre*, a man worthy of the protagonist's innocent purity, he has to distance himself as much as possible from Bertha by presenting her as a mad, corrupted woman. To disassociate himself, at least in his mind, from his "infernal union" with "a nature the most gross, impure, depraved I ever saw, [that] was associated with mine," he has to resort to "the creation of a series of roles which Rochester attributes to Antoinette but which in fact effectively echoes the gamut of male projections of woman throughout history." He tries to sever all connections with Bertha, denying any kinship: "I played the part I was expected to play. She never had anything to do with me at all" so as to distance himself from "Bertha Mason, the true daughter of an infamous mother, [who] dragged me through all the hideous and degrading agonies which must attend a man bound to a wife at once intemperate and unchaste."[24]

Obscuring the racial overtones Bertha brings into the novel, the paperback Penguin edition proclaims that "*Jane Eyre* is a love story with a happy ending, rare in its time for its sympathetic portrayal of the love of a married man for another woman," thus obscuring Jane's growth process. A main concern in *Jane Eyre* is Jane's sense of her own worth. Self-worth, she claims, is not to be found in one's occupation, not even in one's social status or wealth; rather, personal worth is to be found in one's moral qualities, allowing her to be equal to Rochester and even superior to him at times. In this inner power struggle, control is a central component in Jane's relationship both towards Rochester and towards St. John later. However, in Jane and Rochester's relationship the power is held by both; Rochester admits that "you master me.... I am influenced—conquered; and the influence is sweeter than I can express; and the conquest I undergo has a witchery beyond any triumph I can win." In contrast, St. John threatens to exert absolute control over Jane, denying her any agency. Still, both Rochester and St. John are subsequently punished for their attempts to control Jane although the latter receives the harsher punishment for trying to lure Jane to an early death in India; he is the one who dies abroad. Significantly, while patriarchal attempts to subjugate Jane are punished in the narrative, Rochester goes unpunished for his cruel treatment of Bertha.[25]

Nonetheless, although Jane and Bertha are victims of the oppression exerted by a patriarchal social order, the identification of Rochester with a strong patriarch is difficult, even in *Jane Eyre*. To begin with, Thornfield Hall is not the repository of stability and patriarchal power a manorial house should be, for the tale is told from the point of view of the outside gaze of the governess. Also, Jane has personal characteristics that, while serving her well enough to achieve her own ends, are not appropriate or fitting for the hostess of a manorial house, as is made patent when Jane and Rochester later retreat to Ferndean, with no public role whatsoever. In *Wide Sargasso Sea*, he becomes less of a symbol of patriarchy and the enforcer of its values, and rather another victim of patriarchy. His maleness does not prevent him from being a victim of a system in which he has been sold in the marriage market. *Wide Sargasso Sea* shows that the picture of patriarchy is even more complicated, since for both Creole women forced to comply with metropolitan standards, and British men sent to the Caribbean, the process of adjustment is equally traumatic (and impossible).[26]

Rochester's blindness has generally been regarded as a symbolic castration given that in Freudian terms the male gaze is a symbol for desire. Other, alternative interpretations reject this possibility, for Jane wants an equal, not a castrated lover and if she flees from him, it is because she is afraid not of sexuality but of becoming a kept woman like Rochester's past lovers. It is only once Rochester becomes dependent on her that he proclaims, "I love you better now, when I can really be useful to you, than I did in your state of proud independence, when you disdained every part but that of the giver and protector." Now when he can no longer pose a threat as a patriarch to Jane's autonomy, "there was no harassing restraint, no repressing of glee and vivacity with him; for with him I was at perfect ease, because I knew I suited him." With this, Jane's personal progress is not cut short by her marriage.[27]

Still, there are some problems with the ending. That it is a happy ending is questionable, for brave, independent Jane *dies* in favor of becoming a doting wife, a criticism also leveled against the ending of *Pride and Prejudice*: "I will be your neighbour, your nurse, your housekeeper. I find you lonely: I will be your companion—to read to you, to walk with you, to sit with you, to wait on you, to be eyes and hands to you." Ferndean is an isolated space where Rochester no longer fulfills a public function and they are detached from society. While this is the realization of Rochester's previous dream, "I wish I were in a quiet island with only you; and trouble, and danger, and hideous recollections removed from me," the ending of *Jane Eyre*, for Tennant, is not so happy, for Rochester is very much aware of their isolation—"we were no painting of a landowner and his wife, prosperous and contented, a past and future of respect from neighbours, family, and friends written on our countenances; we were, though my darling wife did not know it yet, pariahs and outcasts forever in the country."[28]

Yet, these two sequels do not challenge the ending—they are a prequel and a parallel novel and therefore seem to regard *Jane Eyre*'s ending as fitting. Rochester is a man troubled by his West Indian experiences and even though Adèle's upbringing might have been more complicated than Brontë gave it credit for, in these two sequels Jane's ending remains the same.[29]

Chapter 4

Beyond Wuthering Heights

Emily Brontë's *Wuthering Heights*, *Windward Heights* by Maryse Condé and *Heathcliff: The Return to Wuthering Heights* by Lin Haire-Sargeant

> We crowded round, and over Miss Cathy's head I had a peep at a dirty, ragged, black-haired child; big enough both to walk and talk: indeed, its face looked older than Catherine's; yet when it was set on its feet, it only stared round, and repeated over and over again some gibberish that nobody could understand. **Emily Brontë: *Wuthering Heights* (1847)**

> Nobody could say exactly when Razyé had arrived in Havana nor where he had come from. They only knew him by this odd name, as if his parents had not bothered to give him a saint's name. **Maryse Condé: *Windward Heights* (1995)**

> I did not spring from the festering river mud like a toad; I had had a human father and mother, however low, and it was growing in my mind that I would claim my birthright. I knew from Nelly's tales that the city where your father had found me was Liverpool, and to Liverpool I would go. **Lin Haire-Sargeant: *Heathcliff: The Return to Wuthering Heights* (1992)**

"This is a strange book," was the damning remark that *Wuthering Heights* merited in the opinion of the *Examiner* reviewer on January 8, 1848, and since then, many a reader has experienced the same feelings upon approaching the book, including Emily Brontë's eldest sister, Charlotte. This comment, however, ranked among the mildest that it received after being first published. Reviewers found it especially hard to tolerate the apparent void of moral laws in which the protagonists of Brontë's only novel lived, with no clear punishment for her malefactor by the close of the book. In the years after its publication, *Wuthering Heights* has defied classification and baffled readers, who are left wondering about its meaning or moral—if it had any. *Wuthering Heights* defies categorizations, readers, critics, and genre classifications. Reviewers, in general, did not understand it and neither did Charlotte, whose doubts delayed the publication of the second (posthumous) edition.[1]

Already Charlotte's work *Jane Eyre* had been criticized by reviewers for its apparent defiance of conventional morality. Jane Eyre's bold claim that "I am a free human being with an independent will," was almost universally disapproved, while her apparent but not full conformity to Victorian gender roles shocked readers and reviewers alike. Anne Mozley expressed in 1853 her conviction that *Jane Eyre* must have been authored by "an alien ... from society [who was] amenable to none of its laws." Charlotte herself was aware that her novel flew in the face of conventional morals, with which the Brontës, because of their extensive reading of foreign and past literature and isolated lives, were not too familiar with.[2]

This defiance of society and its norms present in *Jane Eyre* went further in *Wuthering Heights*. If *Jane Eyre* shocked many, *Wuthering Heights* scandalized many more. That "the conduct of Mr. Rochester on the one hand, and Heathcliff and Catherine on the other, is not painted as particularly reprehensible," at a time when readers wanted wrongdoers' punishments to be hard and clearly spelled out, was outraging. An example of this is the *Eclectic Review* in 1851, which called *Wuthering Heights* "one of the most repellent books we ever read." The *Graham's Lady's Magazine* reviewer in July 1848 asserted that "how a human being could have attempted such a book as the present without committing suicide before he had finished a dozen chapters, is a mystery. It is a compound of vulgar depravity and unnatural horrors." On these grounds, Emily earned a reputation as a largely unusual writer who, in her strangeness, had produced only one novel, whose moral content or even its literary worth was questionable. That it took quite a while for the second edition to appear also contributed to the snubbing of Emily in literary and academic circles. In contrast, *Jane Eyre* was more widely read although, as time has gone by, the critical evaluation of both novels has taken different directions and "*Jane Eyre* in the first half of the twentieth century still had a popular appeal, especially among children, but among academic critics tended to be dismissed as melodramatic, romantic and incoherent. Meanwhile Emily Brontë's reputation rose." It would not be until the end of the century that *Wuthering Heights*'s literary worth began to be vindicated.[3]

The unconventionality of *Jane Eyre* and *Wuthering Heights* misled numerous early readers and critics to believe that both, although published under the pseudonyms of Currer Bell and Ellis Bell, respectively, were the work of the same author, as was *Agnes Grey*, written by their sister Anne using the pseudonym of Acton Bell. Contributing to this confusion of literary identities, Thomas Newby, the editor of the joint volume including *Wuthering Heights* and *Agnes Grey*, which had come out a few months before *Jane Eyre*, "was clearly dishonest since, when Currer Bell's work was a success, he did not hesitate to advertise the works of Ellis and Acton as being by the same author. This was in a way counter-productive since, so far from the good reputation of *Jane Eyre* helping to sell the novels of Newby, the reputation of *Wuthering Heights* for coarseness helped to damn *Jane Eyre* for the same fault." The reviewer for *Paterson's Magazine*, however, drew a distinction and urged readers to "read *Jane Eyre* ... but burn *Wuthering Heights*."[4]

As is often the case with works that have sparked sequels, the ending of *Wuthering Heights* became a source of disappointment and caused numerous criticisms. Its "ending ... is in accordance with the examples of Victorian novel. The happy ending achieved through the union of Hareton and Cathy accords with the Victorian attitude to life," but not with the perceived need of having transgressors appropriately punished. Many expressed their shock at the crudity and violence that permeated *Wuthering Heights*; for the *Atlas* reviewer, "we know nothing in the whole range of our fictitious literature which presents such shocking pictures of the worst forms of humanity." *Paterson's Magazine* stated that "we rise from the perusal of *Wuthering Heights* as if we had come fresh from a pest-house" while others were mesmerized by its bizarre appeal. The character of Heathcliff was irresistibly enthralling to many and thus, in the *Westminster Review* Angus Mackay, an admirer of Emily's, wrote that Heathcliff "fascinated the imagination, and in some scenes almost paralyses us with horror, and yet that subtle human touch is added which wrings from us pity and almost respect."[5]

Appalled by such dismaying comments about her late sister's only work, when Charlotte finally allowed the publication of the second edition, she felt compelled to include the "Biographical Notice of Ellis and Acton Bell" and the "Editor's Preface to the New Edition of *Wuthering Heights*" offering an explanation and an apology to account for *Wuthering Heights*' "strangeness." Charlotte, who admitted that "*Wuthering Heights* must appear a rude and strange production," was puzzled by Heathcliff's portrayal and tried to absolve Emily by emphasizing other worthy characters in the novel, writing that "for a specimen of true benevolence and homely fidelity, look at the character of Nelly Dean." Well-aware that the portrayal of Heathcliff was frequently the target of critics' rejection, she argued that "Heathcliff betrays one solitary human feeling, and that is *not* his love for Catherine.... No; the single link that connects Heathcliff with humanity is his rudely confessed regard for Hareton Earnshaw...; and then his half-implied esteem for Nelly Dean." She justified the extremely negative reactions that *Wuthering Heights* caused by arguing that "an interpreter ought always to have stood between her [Emily] and the world."[6]

The sequels to *Wuthering Heights* have approached Heathcliff in different ways. One way has been by explaining Heathcliff's mysterious origins. For a period of time, he is gone from Wuthering Heights. What did he do in the meantime? What were his experiences during his absence? Where was he during those years? These are crucial questions, which, however, remained unanswered at the end of *Wuthering Heights*, as Brontë "does not explain mysteries away—in the fashion of Ann Radcliffe or Jane Austen." All we know is that he returned a changed man:

> Now, fully revealed by the fire and candlelight, I was amazed, more than ever, to behold the transformation of Heathcliff. He had grown a tall, athletic, well-formed man; beside whom my master seemed quite slender and youth-like. His upright carriage suggested the idea of his having been in the army. His countenance was much older in expression and decision of feature than Mr. Linton's; it looked intelligent, and retained no marks of former degradation. A half-civilised ferocity lurked yet in the depressed brows and eyes full of black fire, but it was subdued; and his manner was even dignified: quite divested of roughness, though stern for grace.

Despite the fact that we never learn what really happened to Heathcliff, this is not to deny its centrality to the plot of the novel, for "the known span and compass of Heathcliff's life at Wuthering Heights is the span and compass of the novel. When he is not there, there is no story.... Heathcliff is, therefore, the structure of the story." Heathcliff may have abandoned Wuthering Heights but only physically, not spiritually.[7]

Moreover, with Heathcliff gone, life at Wuthering Heights seems to be in a suspended state, in a lethargy it will only awaken from with Heathcliff's return, as "Heathcliff *is* the story. He not only acts and suffers, but causes others to act and suffer; his strength permeates the story; his power for good and for evil shocks and surprises the reader; his deeds and his reactions from the ghastly beginning to the pastoral close make a coherent whole out of what might have been a chaotic heap." And yet, Heathcliff's life does not seem to be of any interest if Cathy is not part of it, as both his years before arriving to Wuthering Heights and the years during which he is absent are given no space. While Cathy is able to live an independent life without Heathcliff, Heathcliff's life is shaped by his relationship with Cathy and cannot exist without her, up to the point that "Heathcliff's personality begins to disintegrate when he allows himself to become obsessed by a physical passion for Catherine and deliberately fosters this passion to the point of mania. He sacrifices every other part of his personality to the satisfaction of his passion, until by its very violence it destroys its own object."[8]

While the orphan was a recurrent character in Victorian novels, their origins were always explained in the course of the novel; not so in *Wuthering Heights*, where Heathcliff makes two mysterious acts of appearance—as a child and as a gentleman, both of which are unexplained. Because we remain ignorant of Heathcliff's whereabouts or how he became a man of fortune, Lin Haire-Sargeant devoted herself to the task of finding out where the missing protagonist had been during his years away. *Heathcliff: The Return to Wuthering Heights* tries to illuminate where Heathcliff was and what he did. Haire-Sargeant resolved that "I would take a stab at solving that mystery.... I began planning a conventional academic analysis, but it somehow didn't jell; Heathcliff's voice kept breaking through. Finally I just let him talk."[9]

A different take on *Wuthering Heights* has been moving the novel's plot to the West Indies, reproducing the same story in a different setting; a setting, moreover, marked by racial and postcolonial concerns. Even though the novels by the Brontës are closely connected to their native Yorkshire, postcolonial writers have found them to be universal. Just like Dominica-born Jean Rhys imagined the prequel to *Jane Eyre* in Bertha Mason's native Jamaica, Guadeloupean Maryse Condé imagined what *Wuthering Heights* would have read like had it been set in Guadeloupe and Cuba in *Windward Heights*. For writer V. S. Pritchett, *Wuthering Heights* offers "the most realistic statement about the Yorkshire people of the isolated moorland and dales that I have ever read" and, according to Gérin, "no book was more rooted in its native soil, more conditioned by the local background of its author, than *Wuthering Heights.*" However, Condé transplanted it to her native West Indies. Can a setting so different from England as the Caribbean accommodate such an intense passion? If Catherine and Heathcliff's love is identified with the rocks in the area, what happens if the setting is not the rainy, harsh moorlands of northern England but a warmer, tropical location?[10]

Wuthering Heights owed a great deal to Emily's close relationship with her only brother, Branwell, who died at the age of thirty-one as an unpublished author, a failed portraitist and an alcoholic tortured by despair following the end of his love affair with the mother of his former tutee, and the subsequent loss of his job. Despite his regular promises to reform, Branwell kept to his life of dissoluteness, much to his family's misery. Heathcliff's depiction is largely due to Emily's intense love for her brother, in spite of his failings and his self-destruction—evil as Heathcliff might be, she refuses to censor him or pass any kind of moral judgment. That Heathcliff hails from Liverpool (or, at least, he was found there) owes much to Branwell's own stay in the city. At the time, when Ireland was undergoing the potato famine of 1845, the city was full of Irish immigrants sailing from Liverpool to a better future in America, which Branwell witnessed and later reported to his sisters. Building on this connection, some critics have identified Heathcliff with the situation in Ireland and, for Terry Eagleton, Heathcliff is "'a fragment of the Famine.' To this extent, Heathcliff's destitution, insurgency and ferocious desire (or 'hunger') can be read as a buried political or revolutionary metaphor for a subjugated nation starving and aspiring on the doorstep of its colonial master."[11]

Heathcliff's coloring, which is often commented upon by the other characters, is fundamental to his description. Actually, his dark looks are the only piece of information or clue regarding his origins. It is significant, especially in light of the many references to Heathcliff's dark skin, that "the native Irish, ... in the nineteenth century were often thought to be descended from early pre–European Iberians, and were not considered fully 'European' anyway." Another connection to Heathcliff's dark looks is that Liverpool was a central outpost for the burgeoning slave trade back then. Heathcliff's ethnicity is often discussed when talking about his uncertain origins and dubious parentage. His dark looks and his having been found as an orphan in the streets of Liverpool make him an enigma and might even insinuate a mixed ancestry with colonial roots; he represents

> the sign of a colonial repressed; and, as a figure of vengeance, of the revolutionary *return* of that repressed. Heathcliff's darkness of complexion is mentioned throughout the novel, and there is a sense in which his "gipsy" swarthiness exoticizes and demonises him on broader colonial level ... his phylogenetic indeterminacy renders him all the more powerful as a figure of *otherness* in general, of that which is excluded from the constituted structures of civility, ideology and nationality in the novel but that enters irresistibly to disrupt or "wuther" the equanimity of these categories.[12]

But when all of the characters of *Wuthering Heights* are of an ethnic origin, how is Heathcliff's difference to be marked? In *Windward Heights*, the female protagonist herself is the daughter of a Creole and a native woman. With her characterization of Cathy as a mulatta, Condé was connecting her novel to the North American literary tradition of the "tragic mulatto": a figure that simultaneously causes repulsion and fascination, and, more often than not, encounters disaster. The fear of miscegenation lurking in *Wuthering Heights* is made more explicit in *Windward Heights*, where Condé's Heathcliff, Rayzé, is black. The racial undercurrents in Brontë's characterization of Heathcliff are, therefore, fully played out in *Windward Heights* (in contrast, *Heathcliff* refrains from the implications of miscegenation by denying Heathcliff any black origins).

Some have ventured that Heathcliff might even come from America, a hypothesis supported by the fact that he stages a revolution of sorts, as he turns the former hierarchical and class order at Wuthering Heights and Thrushcross Grange upside down. That the American Revolution took place in roughly the same period of time as the novel has helped to give validity to this hypothesis. With its realization of the common man overthrowing a powerful empire, the American Revolution resounds in Heathcliff's story of how a man with no means eventually gets control over the most important houses in the neighborhood at the expense of the true heirs. Alternatively, Heathcliff can be seen as embodying class struggle, as he rises from the most abject poverty to get control of the two manors.

Because Heathcliff's evil is proved beyond a doubt at the end of *Wuthering Heights*, neither Haire-Sargeant nor Condé try to atone for his many sins or even redeem him; instead, they offer a new perspective. This is possible because Heathcliff is a mystery figure on whom the reader's own ideas and feelings may be projected. Just like Lockwood, with his "blind metropolitan assumptions," attributes to Heathcliff his own qualities, Heathcliff can be whatever the reader—or the sequel writer—wishes. While Condé does not delude herself and makes no excuses for her Heathcliff character's appalling behavior, Haire-Sergeant tries to explain Heathcliff's revenge partially on Edgar Linton's deviousness during Heathcliff's years away, when they met. His bad deeds being far too numerous to justify, Condé resorts to present a darker-skinned Heathcliff overseas but just as evil as the original one while Haire-Sargeant presents his years away in an attempt to make us feel sympathy for the man he was before he turned evil.

But where does Heathcliff's evil emanate from? Part of the answer might be that

> Heathcliff can in some ways be seen as a victim of social prejudice, fighting against concepts such as breed and gentry, concepts that were linked to high social classes at that time.... The Industrial Revolution made men like Heathcliff capable of earning

the title "a gentleman" through money. Heathcliff does not use his newfound wealth for good purposes, which can be seen as Brontë's portrayal of the corrupted side of the new aristocracy.

While in *Pride and Prejudice* Mr. Gardiner and Mr. Bingley rise from modest origins, Heathcliff's new wealth only coarsens and debases him, providing him with the means to carry out his revenge more effectively. Because of Cathy's damning remark that "it would degrade me to marry Heathcliff now," "like Pip in Dickens's *Great Expectations*, he has been made ashamed of his low condition by the girl he loves, and he seeks to transform himself into a gentleman." Heathcliff's transformation, nevertheless, affords him no happy ending; what is more, just like his wealth does not bring him any joy (just the means to seek revenge on his enemies), his revenge does not bring him any happiness either: "he acts like a fiend incarnate, but his actions torture him as much as they torture his victims: they are a part, and the worst part, of the torments of the damned which Heathcliff suffers during his life. When he finds himself capable of a good act, even one so neutral as not persecuting Hareton and Catherine, it is as though his sentence had been at last worked out, and he dies almost joyfully." In *Heathcliff*, because his mentor is Mr. Are, a stand-in for *Jane Eyre*'s Mr. Rochester, who is not a good role model to start with, it is not surprising that Heathcliff only learns the outward signs of gentility. More significantly, in *Heathcliff*, the opportunities provided by the Industrial Revolution are not the way in which he becomes rich, as his money comes from Mr. Are, and is subsequently tainted, since it was taken from Bertha Mason.[13]

Despite Heathcliff's ruthlessness, if we are to understand Brontë's failure to punish Heathcliff in a manner satisfactory to Victorian sensibility, "we must condemn the sin, but pity the sinner." If we do so, "despite everything he does and is, we continue to sympathize with Heathcliff—not, obviously, to admire him or defend him, but to give him our inmost sympathy." That way, Heathcliff is not an essentially evil character, for his evil is the product of the abuses inflicted on him during his childhood and, especially, his unrequited love. Heathcliff's evolution could well have been a from-rags-to-riches story *à la* Dickens but this is not to be for Brontë: "Heathcliff's formation can be said to derive much of its force from Milton's Satan and we can also say that the theological creature that is Satan, is materialized in human form in Heathcliff."[14]

Others are unsure about where to put the blame and, instead, have wondered if Nelly may be the villain or if *Wuthering Heights* might be a villain-free novel. Certainly, Nelly's actions decisively shape the course of the novel, but it is debatable whether she is truly evil—that is, whether she is the mastermind plotting it all. According to Shunami, "Nelly is not the villain of the novel but that her sanctimonious position results from an ignorance of her true role and a misunderstanding of the spirit of others. She is therefore incapable of recognizing the fact that her decisions bring about the tragic crisis of the novel." Whatever her motivations or whether she is driven by ignorance, evil or short-sightedness, the fact remains that Nelly's role is crucial, for with her silences, she is actually changing the course of the action.[15]

In *Heathcliff*, however, her role is more decisive—intercepting Heathcliff's letter to Cathy before her wedding, she dismissed Heathcliff's story of Linton's misbehavior to him at once. Moreover, Nelly's meddlesome ways are not limited to her concealing this letter from Cathy; some pages from it are missing because she destroyed them. Previous letters that Heathcliff sent to Cathy did not reach their addressee either but this Nelly blames on Hindley. In Nelly's portrayal, Cathy comes across as a selfish, materialistic woman who only married Linton out of ambition. She appears as narcissistic and self-centered, since "Miss Catherine was her own true love, along with what she saw of herself in Heathcliff," in Nelly's assessment. At the same time, Cathy is allocated a significant amount of the blame in Heathcliff's outcome, for, in Mr. Are's words, "a woman is as often the source of a man's elevation as she is of his folly."[16]

Whether Heathcliff and Cathy were lovers has generated a great deal of speculation. Apparently, "although the relation between Catherine and Heathcliff is asexual, the great potency for sex is too apparent. Even in death Heathcliff's body is erect, suggesting both the immense libidinous potential in the character." Haire-Sargeant and Condé do see Heathcliff and Cathy's relationship as having been sexually consummated and, in Condé's case, having produced a child. This is further complicated by the question of whether Heathcliff was Mr. Earnshaw's illegitimate child, which would make of him and Cathy the innocent victims of a forbidden love. While "eighteenth-century fiction certainly provided numerous examples of the theme—incest is a plot device in *Moll Flanders, Tom Jones, Humphrey Clinker,* and *Evelinu,*" Brontë stopped short of it. If Heathcliff were Mr. Earnshaw's illegitimate son, this would help explain his desire to own Wuthering Heights (where he suffered endless humiliations) and his decision to stay there instead of moving to his other property, which is much more comfortable. Whereas "the action of the novel discloses an adulterous situation between Heathcliff and Cathy; ... Brontë disappoints simple expectancy and translates the ethical conflict from a physical to a spiritual level. There is no breach of the Ten Commandments, of the statutory code of church and state." Sequels, in this case, take a different stance, as will be seen below. For neither Condé nor Haire-Sargeant were Heathcliff and Cathy brother and sister; Condé, however, takes the incestuous relationship plotline to the next generation in having Razyé as young Cathy's father and then by having her unknowingly have a daughter by Razyé II, the firstborn of Razyé and Irmine, and, consequently, her half-brother.[17]

Haire-Sargeant attempted to give *Wuthering Heights* the aura of reality by including in her novel the Brontë sisters as well as Lockwood, revealing that Heathcliff used to be a friend of Emily's. Lockwood has in his possession Heathcliff's manuscript to Cathy in which he chronicles how he became rich, a manuscript that Nelly intercepted, preventing its reaching Cathy's hands. The day before her wedding, Heathcliff tells Cathy he will claim her on her wedding day if she wants him to. If Brontë's Heathcliff was subject to others' characterization of him, Haire-Sergeant's Heathcliff self-identifies: "Cathy, I am a gentleman." Because the Brontë sisters appear as characters in Haire-Sargeant's sequel, Charlotte's distaste for the violence and cruelty of *Wuthering Heights* is made explicit in *Heathcliff*, where she is outraged by Heathcliff's character—"surely he richly deserved the misfortune that dogged him."[18]

Not only do the Brontës make an appearance in *Heathcliff*, but its plot is closely linked to that of *Jane Eyre*, too. Arriving in the city with nobody to turn to, Mr. Are / Mr. Rochester takes Heathcliff under his wing. This is little more than a passing fancy for him, though. When Heathcliff returns to Thornfield, Mr. Are is no longer interested in advancing his protégé's education, being too busy with the new governess, whom Heathcliff describes as a scheming, ambitious woman—"his new mistress, who, holding back the only trump card one of her station might play, led him a merry game, refusing him what he wanted so he would want it the more."[19]

The connection between Heathcliff and Mr. Rochester had already been noted:

> Heathcliff not only personifies the demonic lower classes. He also stands for everything foreign early nineteenth-century English society feared and abhorred, but which it at the same time often found sexually alluring. Like Rochester in *Jane Eyre*, so too Heathcliff in *Wuthering Heights* has the trappings of a Byronic hero.... Rochester, however, only needs to expiate certain youthful sins and mistakes to remake himself into a mainstay of Victorian society. His purging significantly takes the form of eliminating his first wife, the mad Creole woman.... The role Heathcliff plays in *Wuthering Heights* actually is closer to that of Bertha Mason than that of Rochester.

Haire-Sargeant made this connection more explicit by having Heathcliff as Bertha and Rochester's child, put into a madhouse by Mr. Are due to his mother's insanity. This builds upon the negative view of Creoles in *Jane Eyre*, where

> the book's narrative voice upholds the idea that the law which gives Rochester full possession of his Creole wife's fortune is wholly good, whereas the law that denies him the right to annul his marriage to her, or to consider it void, is wholly bad.... In nineteenth-century England there was a very strong injunction against miscegenation or the "mixing of blood." Racial theories of the time held that such mixing would lead to infertility, and to all sorts of degeneration.

Nevertheless, Rochester's decision is not entirely coherent with *Jane Eyre*—if Mr. Rochester had Bertha Mason hidden in his own house, when he could have easily put her in a faraway asylum, why did he decide to send the child away? As a result of Haire-Sargeant's revelation of Heathcliff's paternity, he then becomes doubly tainted because of his Creole ancestry and the fact that he is the son of a madwoman. It is interesting that *Heathcliff* does not have him as a social outcast but as the disposed legitimate son of a member of the English gentry, deprived of his rightful inheritance and lineage.[20]

Similar to Emma Tennant's *Elinor and Marianne*, Haire-Sargeant sees America as the land where characters constricted by nineteenth-century English rules and social conventions can find freedom and where star-crossed lovers can finally be reunited. Heathcliff begs Cathy in his letter to go with him to America because "there we can be happy and free—free as the aboriginal inhabitants of that vast and beautiful continent, free as the wild wind." These plans have been thwarted by Nelly's intervention, but they will be realized at a later date, as Emily tells Charlotte: Cathy did not die in childbirth, and, because Linton was a magistrate, the records were forged. Actually, Heathcliff came back after the baby was born and gave Cathy a potion to make it look as if she had died because she was resolved to flee with him. Thanks to this scheme, they could get away from Linton, leaving baby Cathy behind, in a rewriting of sorts of *Romeo and Juliet*, but with a happy ending this time. Nelly, to whom "concealment, subterfuge and the like were meat and drink," plotted with Linton to spread the lie that Cathy had died in childbirth, while the couple lived happily together in New Orleans. After Cathy's death, Heathcliff returned to Wuthering Heights.[21]

As in many twentieth-century sequels, homosexuality is introduced in *Heathcliff*, a feature it shares with *Windward Heights*. Thus, at first, Heathcliff is afraid that Mr. Are becomes his protector out of a homosexual interest. Haire-Sargeant's introduction of homosexuality into the text marks her novel as a twentieth-century product. Other flaws in *Heathcliff* involve "modern language slips into the text" and "slips in habits of social convention" as well as mistakes in chronology, as when Mr. Are makes an allusion to George Bernard Shaw's play *Pygmalion,* which did not make it onto the stage until long afterwards, in 1913. Furthermore, Haire-Sergeant's developments were considered inconsistent with Brontë's characterization of her characters since Mr. Are "is much more cheerful than Mr. Rochester," Heathcliff is more cultivated and refined and Blanche Ingram is more sensitive.[22]

Condé's take on *Wuthering Heights* was completely different from Haire-Sargeant's. Born in Guadeloupe in 1937 in a middle class black family, Condé has explained that her parents inculcated in her their pride for being black as well as their Francophilia. Proud of their racial stock and affluent lifestyle, "they discouraged her from associating with poor Black children, considered 'lower-class'; with Mulattoes, whom they considered snobbish; and with white colonists, who scorned persons of colour." In Condé's own words, "in the West Indies, at the beginning of the century, for example, we were obsessed with the color of the skin. My parents were proud and obsessed at the same time by being Black.... You had to prove all the time that you were better than the Mulattoes that you were better than the Whites. As for the Indians, they didn't even count." Given her background, it is not surprising that, in rewriting *Wuthering Heights,* she explored racial issues.[23]

Condé's stated intention was to rewrite *Wuthering Heights* in a respectful manner to the original work, as her dedication testifies: "to Emily Brontë. Who I hope will approve of this interpretation of her masterpiece. Honour and respect!" Heathcliff's name is changed here to Razyé, an "odd name, as if his parents had not bothered to give him a saint's name on the day of his christening," whose origin is due to the fact that "I was found in Guadeloupe as naked as the day I was born, on the barren heath and cliffs—the *razyés.*" "Written during a period of intense social unrest in Britain, while Europe was wracked by revolutions, *Wuthering Heights* thus voices some of the most potent social and political fears of its age," but it does not make any explicit allusion to them. In contrast, the larger political and historical background is made manifest in *Windward Heights. Windward Heights* also alludes to Cuban history, making reference to José Martí's rebellion and the Spanish-American War after the *USS Maine* exploded in port, as Razyé participates in the rebellion. While Brontë denied us knowledge of Heathcliff's whereabouts (to Haire-Sargeant's gain), Condé has Razyé going to Cuba as a mercenary for the Spanish forces before the war, helping to quash Martí's rebellion. Political events play a decisive role in the chronology of the narrative, in sharp contrast to *Wuthering Heights*'s timelessness or historical ignorance, where no political affairs or world events are referenced.[24]

Razyé's wishes that he were white indicate that the class angst of *Wuthering Heights* has been replaced by racial issues in *Windward Heights.* Moreover, while Heathcliff was the only one dissatisfied with his station or social class in *Wuthering Heights,* in *Windward Heights* Cathy shares with her beloved this racial anxiety, even more marked in her case because of her mixed-race status, suspected by both whites and blacks. For Cathy, her color is a burden and "she dreamed of living in a country where neither class nor colour existed." Her mixed-race status is a source of distress for her, provoking an identity crisis: "it's as if there were two Cathys inside me.... One Cathy who's come straight from Africa, vices and all. The other Cathy who is the very image of her white ancestor, pure, dutiful, fond of order and moderation." In the multiracial society of Guadeloupe, characters' racial concerns are central. Moreover, Cathy's racial angst is further compounded by her religious doubts, which lead her to question if Christianity is good for blacks and dream of an afterlife different from Heaven. Her racial anxiety will be exacerbated once she has two sons by her white husband, Aymeric, to whom she feels detached on the grounds of their blonde hair and blue eyes, so different from hers.[25]

Labor issues and the natives' working conditions also occupy space in the narrative and Aymeric is presented as a good, compassionate master improving the free workers' conditions but, despite his efforts, he is not well liked—"but a master is a master. You can't love him." Another topic extensively dealt with by Condé is Heathcliff and Isabella's relationship. In *Wuthering Heights,* it is remarkable that Brontë, raised on books and with little formal schooling and even less socialization with neighbors or people other than her closest family members, punished bookish Isabella by marrying her off to a cruel man who becomes her undoing. Her protected childhood and love for books makes of Isabella an easy prey: "Isabella's bookish upbringing has prepared her to fall in love with (of all people) Heathcliff. Precisely because she has been taught to believe in coercive literary conventions, Isabella is victimized by the genre of romance." Having read a number of romances in which the dark hero sweeps the heroine off her feet, promising a happy ending, Isabella is willing to expect the best from Heathcliff, despite the warning signals that her romance-filled mind refuses to see. Just as Marianne Dashwood in *Sense and Sensibility* almost faces social ruin and death by trying to make reality conform to her romantic readings, it is Isabella's reading that causes her disgrace, as Heathcliff refuses to be the dark hero of her novels to turn out to be a crueler figure. He is a true villain beyond the redemption that literary heroes achieve thanks to the transforming love of a good woman (or maybe he is unwilling to be redeemed). Because *Wuthering Heights* is not a conventional romance, instead Isabella and Heathcliff's "relationship is a caricature of the romantic damsel and the Byronic hero." Despite Isabella's desire to see Heathcliff as somebody who can be saved by her love, she cannot change him and

> Brontë exposes the danger of romanticizing a man like Heathcliff by examining what happens after the romance, that is, during the marriage. For in sentimentalizing him as a brooding and erotic hero, the reader falls victim to the same fraud as Isabella. Even Heathcliff and Catherine's relationship that contributes to the idea of him as a hero proves deceptive by not quite fitting the Byronic model either. Clearly, Brontë makes Heathcliff very Byronic in appearance in order to challenge this literary figure and emphasize the way that fantasy underlies it.

If Austen was warning women about the deceitful nature of courtship and the social dangers of falling for an unsuitable man, Brontë took it much further by actually presenting the utter disaster awaiting those naïve enough to try to get a romantic novel enacted in real life: "the harsh reality that Isabella takes too long in discovering indicates that Brontë wishes to criticize the romantic element of the Byronic hero that emphasizes courtship rather than marriage."[26]

Although "Isabella's only 'crime' against Heathcliff is her youthful and foolish infatuation," she pays dearly for it. She is but the first of Heathcliff's innocent victims whom he harshly punished in spite of her not having contributed to his miseries. Still, it is worth noting that Heathcliff never sets out to deceive Isabella, since he never pretends to be anything other than he is. Isabella is the one who refuses to listen to Nelly and Cathy's warnings and even to take notice of what she actually sees, to cling, instead, to her romantic fantasies. Readers, like Isabella, might want to see Heathcliff under a different light on the grounds of his passion for Cathy. And if Isabella eventually flees from Heathcliff, in *Windward Heights* Irmine never leaves Razyé, staying to bear him a string of children. Irmine's predicament, subjected to abuse, is compared to slaves' circumstances, linking women's submission to slaves' conditions. Thus, she writes that "I hate you, you and your society, who had nothing better to do than invent bondage, the bondage of blacks and the bondage of women." Still, when she marries Razyé and writes home to tell the news, she asks "don't judge me. I loved this man, my executioner." Heathcliff's identification with the devil is also present in *Windward Heights*, as Irmine writes to Lucinda asking if Razyé is a man or a devil.[27]

Homosexuality, as in *Heathcliff*, is also present in *Windward Heights*, where Aymeric's effeminate and delicate features make him an object of male desire and even sexual abuse during his childhood. Razyé's attraction to Justin-Marie, because he reminds him of his aunt Cathy in a way that the young Cathy cannot, also hints at a homosexual subtext. At the same time, Condé is bolder in depicting Razyé and Cathy's relationship as a sexual one. There were insidious insinuations that Cathy might have been no virgin but, later on, they are dispelled with the certainty that Cathy did commit adultery with Razyé, the product of which is her daughter Cathy, whose darker skin points to Razyé's paternity, despite Aymeric's refusal to see it.[28]

Isabella's refusal to see Heathcliff for who he really is until it is too late (and fatal) for her to continue deceiving herself is matched by critics' attempts to see some good (or at least some justification) in Heathcliff. Trying to redeem Heathcliff, it has been argued that "the evil that he does springs not from a love of evil itself, but from the thwarting of the natural processes of love." His evil would not spark from a malevolent, rotten nature but from his harsh upbringing, compounded by the lost love he felt for Cathy and, thus, "modern critics, if they move away from a consideration of the book's mechanism to a consideration of the moral relations of the characters, usually choose to minimize or justify Heathcliff's consistent delight in malice in order to elevate him to the status of hero." In an analogous manner to Isabella's stubbornness in trying to make Heathcliff fit the world of the Byronic hero she wants, readers and critics also try to make Heathcliff conform to their own ideas and see him as a man hurt by his lost love. There has been an evolution in the critical evaluation of Heathcliff—if at first he was regarded as a monster or the very incarnation of the devil, now his image stands closer to that of a tragic hero. In turn, Catherine has undergone the reverse process and she is no longer the defenseless victim of Heathcliff's evil plans but rather a victimizer fully aware of being the cause of Heathcliff's perdition. The result of these parallel processes is that "no one in the novel is entirely guiltless, yet we feel that the nature and degree of guilt among the characters vary considerably."[29]

In having Cathy choose between Linton and Heathcliff, "the choice before her heroine is a straight one between effeminacy and pure virility, black and white." Curiously enough, in the sequels, women are more conventional in that they conform to the expected gender roles to a larger extent than Brontë's characters. Another difference between *Wuthering Heights* and its sequels is that *Wuthering Heights* stood apart from other nineteenth-century novels in that it departed from the urban setting of many nineteenth-century novels to inhabit the Yorkshire moors. Place is also crucial in its sequels—the Creole society of *Windward Heights* defines the action of the novel as much as the Yorkshire moors define Heathcliff and Cathy's relationship while *Heathcliff* takes the action back to the city and the upper circles of society.[30]

The ending of *Wuthering Heights* has been regarded as unsatisfactory and as "the novel's great weakness—a concession by Emily Bronte to the shallow Victorian reader, or a timid, conservative afterthought to the violent portraits of Heathcliff and Catherine." And yet, despite this generalized dissatisfaction, neither Haire-Sargeant nor Condé challenge it. While the aim of Haire-Sargeant's work certainly was not altering the ending of *Wuthering Heights*, or even rewriting it, Condé could have easily changed the ending, but chose to have Razyé die. Condé's ending, maybe to follow up with Brontë's concession to Victorian attitudes, is even bleaker than the original: there is to be no happy ending for the second Cathy, because (although completely ignorant of her lover's true identity) she engaged in an incestuous relationship with her half-brother Razyé II and bore him a daughter, Arthuria. Not only does the second Cathy die but her incestuous origins also make a happy ending for Arthuria unlikely, as her own father fears: "he was absorbed by the thought of Arthuria. Such a lovely child could not be cursed." At the end of *Windward Heights*, Condé, just like Brontë, denies us a happy ending for the protagonist couple and does little to try and improve Heathcliff's character. No happy or proper social order is to be restored by the end of the novel.[31]

Because of the finality of the ending of *Wuthering Heights*, with both Catherine and Heathcliff dead, sequels to it necessarily limit themselves to explain what happened during the years Heathcliff was away or to explore how the novel would read if relocated to the Caribbean. With the main characters dead, a sequel would necessarily have to focus on their descendants, but exploring Heathcliff's years away from Wuthering Heights or setting the story in the Caribbean has seemed more interesting to sequel writers. All in all, the sequels are milder and less daring than *Wuthering Heights*. If the original novel shocked Victorian readers, the sequels are not likely to shock anyone and instead present a more conservative picture of gender roles.

Sequels and all, Heathcliff still haunts the popular imagination and is likely to continue haunting it for years to come. The third book in the mega-best-selling Twilight series by Stephenie Meyer, *Eclipse*, borrows from *Wuthering Heights* in that Bella is, like her namesake Isabella, desperately in love with her particular Heathcliff, Edward, although she is well-aware that with her love she is hurting those who love her. Place, time and circumstances change, but Brontë's characters continue being rewritten.

Chapter 5

"In a Land Where Inequity Is Searched Out, and Punished in the Sight of Rulers and People"[1]

Adultery, Religion and Women's Roles in *The Scarlet Letter* by Nathaniel Hawthorne and John Updike's "*The Scarlet Letter* Trilogy"

One Hester Prynne, who appeared to have been rather a noteworthy personage in the view of our ancestors. She had flourished during the period between the early days of Massachusetts and the close of the seventeenth century. ... She gained from many people the reverence due to an angel, but, I should imagine, was looked upon by others as an intruder and a nuisance. **Nathaniel Hawthorne: *The Scarlet Letter* (1850)**

Met at the glass doors by a large lady, undeformed but unattractive, no doubt chosen for that very quality in this sensitive post. Seemed to be manageress. Named, if my ears, still plugged with jet-hum, deceived me not, Ms. Prynne. Face of a large, white, inexplicably self-congratulating turtle. White neck extended as if to preen or ease a chafing. **John Updike: *A Month of Sundays* (1985)**

Esther, thirty-eight, is fourteen years younger than I—an age difference that has grown, not shrunk, in the fourteen years since we met and coupled and, after my divorce, wed. Though I was a parish minister at the time, she was not among my parishioners; indeed, one of her charms for me was her tranquil indifference, and indifference beyond scorn, to the things of religion. **John Updike: *Roger's Version* (1986)**

I have left you out of love for another. Your own genteel atrocities of coldness and blindness toward me were not by themselves enough. I was too stoical, too Puritan, too much a creature of my society for solitary rebellion; I needed another. Who he is, and where we are together, I will trust you *not* to seek out. **John Updike: *S.* (1988)**

John Updike, probably one of the most famous twentieth-century New Englanders, is especially well-known for being the author of the Rabbit saga or *The Eastwick Witches*. Lesser known is his "*The Scarlet Letter* Trilogy," in which he re-wrote Nathaniel Hawthorne's *The Scarlet Letter* from three different points of view. *The Scarlet Letter* is the story of Hester Prynne, punished in seventeenth-century Puritan Boston for having had a baby born out of wedlock while her husband stayed behind in England, planning to join her at a later date. Hester's refusal to name her baby's father sends her to prison until she is eventually released on the condition that she wears a red A (for adulteress) on her dress at all times. Hester's husband, meanwhile, disappears in a shipwreck on his way to New England and is presumed dead. He was actually rescued by a group of Native Americans among whom he lived for a while. After being freed, he arrives in Boston just in time to see Hester's public humiliation and, since everybody believes him dead, he decides to adopt the name of Roger Chillingworth. This allows him to spy on Hester (whom he swears to secrecy in regards to his true identity) as well as on the Reverend Dimmesdale, baby Pearl's father.

In contrast to Hawthorne's third-person novel, Updike explored the thoughts of Arthur Dimmesdale, Roger Chillingworth and Hester Prynne in loose re-writings in *A Month of Sundays, Roger's Version* and *S.*, respectively. Updike's characters are more complex and multilayered than Hawthorne's, who "remain largely isolated from one another, residing in separate 'spheres' and rarely touching." In the trilogy, Updike examines how individuals face their inner needs in contrast to social constraints which try to suffocate those needs. The idea of how society tries to crush the individual is an important concern in all of Updike's literary production (most notably in the Rabbit saga), so it was not surprising that he decided to explore this idea further in light of America's Puritan heritage. Updike freely borrowed elements from the original novel, playing with the same themes that plagued Hawthorne: "the conflict between matter and spirit; a fascination with community and communal experiments; the anxiety and fear of moral damnation; the relationship between sex and religion; an interest in what Tony Tanner calls the 'unstable triangularity of adultery' and its effect upon a community; and the use of ambivalent symbolism." A sequel's original text is clearly identified as its source, but maybe because "the trilogy is as much a contemporary musing on Hawthorne's themes as an adaptation of Hawthorne's text," some readers and critics have failed to perceive their connection to Hawthorne's work.[2]

In analyzing these two authors, it should be borne in mind that

Hawthorne and Updike, in their respective centuries, were considered the epitome of New Englandness. If in *The Centaur* (1963) and *Couples* (1968) Updike had loosely rewritten and reworked classical and biblical myths, in his trilogy he used a similar approach, reflecting his personal conviction that "*The Scarlet Letter* is not merely a piece of fiction, it is a myth by now, and it was an updating of the myth, the triangle as redefined by D. H. Lawrence, that interested me." Central in Hawthorne's and Updike's novels is the concept and evaluation of sin, which is hardly surprising given America's "fascination and disapprobation with sin and sinners, and our perhaps even greater dislike of those who expose them, [which] still surfaces everywhere in American culture," including American literature, politics, and TV shows.[3]

The Scarlet Letter can be characterized as a story of Puritan punishment which was part of Hawthorne's own legacy; as he stated in the introductory piece "The Custom-House," "I, the present writer, as their representative, hereby take shame upon myself for their sakes, and pray that any curse incurred by them—as I have heard, and as the dreary and unprosperous condition of the race, for many a long year back, would argue to exist—may be now and henceforth removed." Hawthorne's story begins with himself working at the Boston custom-house and his discovery of

> a certain affair of fine red cloth, much worn and faded. There were traces about it of gold embroidery, which, however, was greatly frayed and defaced, so that none, or very little, of the glitter was left.... This rag of scarlet cloth—for time, and wear, and a sacrilegious moth had reduced it to little other than a rag—on careful examination, assumed the shape of a letter. It was the capital letter A. By an accurate measurement, each limb proved to be precisely three inches and a quarter in length. It had been intended, there could be no doubt, as an ornamental article of dress; but how it was to be worn, or what rank, honour, and dignity, in by-past times, were signified by it, was a riddle which (so evanescent are the fashions of the world in these particulars) I saw little hope of solving. And yet it strangely interested me. My eyes fastened themselves upon the old scarlet letter, and would not be turned aside. Certainly there was some deep meaning in it most worthy of interpretation, and which, as it were, streamed forth from the mystic symbol, subtly communicating itself to my sensibilities, but evading the analysis of my mind.[4]

The cloth turns out to have belonged to Hester Prynne, a woman punished for adultery, who, nevertheless, "gained from many people the reverence due to an angel." With this, we are introduced to the idea that there are multiple opinions of her, just as Updike's Sarah in *S.* will be a woman with a personality showing multiple aspects, even contradictory ones. What is more, Hawthorne mentions "the sainted Anne Hutchinson," thus advancing that he is putting forward a favorable opinion of a woman demonized by the Puritans. The same will happen to Hester—a sinner but an angel-like creature at the same time, depending on whose opinion is taken into account.[5]

Hawthorne described *The Scarlet Letter* as "the darkening close of a late human frailty and sorrow" but there is also strength and endurance, rather than fleeing from the consequences of one's actions. Punished as an adulteress, Hester decides to stay and face the consequences of her actions—"giving up her individuality, she would become the general symbol at which the preacher and moralist might point, and in which they might vivify and embody their images of woman's frailty and sinful passion." This is a key issue, for while Updike also deals with the idea of enduring social disapproval, his characters tend to flee from society in the face of adversity: in *A Month of Sundays*, the Reverend Thomas Marshfield is removed from his parish; in *Roger's Version* Roger Lambert willingly leaves his congregation and the ministry to marry Esther and Verna goes back home, leaving her baby daughter behind; and in *S.* Sarah Worth leaves for an ashram in the Arizona desert and eventually to the Caribbean. All of Updike's characters seem to think that a change of place means, up to a certain extent, leaving behind one's previous identity or casting off former responsibilities.[6]

Since her child is the living evidence of her adultery, motherhood is a source of shame, worry, and pain for Hester Prynne:

> when the young woman—the mother of this child—stood fully revealed before the crowd, it seemed to be her first impulse to clasp the infant closely to her bosom; not so much by an impulse of motherly affection, as that she might thereby conceal a certain token, which was wrought or fastened into her dress. In a moment, however, wisely judging that one token of her shame would but poorly serve to hide another, she took the baby on her arm, and with a burning blush, and yet a haughty smile, and a glance that would not be abashed, looked around at her townspeople and neighbours.

Motherhood is certainly problematic in *The Scarlet Letter* and its sequels: Hester often fears that Pearl might be a demon and is afraid of her own child, very much like Verna in *Roger's Version* believes that her baby daughter enjoys torturing her while in *S.* Sarah violently opposes and fights her daughter's life choices, considering them to be mistakes.[7]

Still, whereas Verna's frustration with her daughter leads her to physically abuse her (and almost lose custody) and she eventually abandons her with Roger and Esther to move back home on her own, Hester loves her child as much as she is afraid of her. When local authorities discuss whether it would be wise to separate Pearl from Hester, Hester claims that "she is my happiness—she is my torture, none the less! Pearl keeps me here in life! Pearl punishes me, too!" Although Pearl symbolizes Hester's punishment (her adultery is discovered due to her pregnancy and Pearl herself is a constant reminder of her sin), she is also what prevents Hester from altogether forsaking Puritan society and "from becoming a radical prophetess like Anne Hutchinson. The narrator observes that mothering, like knitting, fortunately 'soothes' Hester's tendency toward conflict." Despite her unconventional ways of thinking and her critical views of society that her isolation allows her, Hester is a mother and for the sake of her daughter she has to conform to conventional womanhood principles, "reinforcing what Nancy Chodorow has called 'the institution of mothering' as the cure for all her ills." But if Hester has to refrain her freethinking so as to continue living as a social being (for all her isolation, she still interacts with her clients) for the sake of her child, Pearl, with her playfulness and her unexpected and unconventional behavior, symbolizes and plays out Hester's repressed feelings, fulfilling a role similar to Hester's sewing.[8]

Puritans scorned art for art's sake, considering that usefulness ranked higher than beauty. Because of this belief, artistic creation was very limited in Puritan New England and only occasionally allowed, provided it was useful and glorified God's work. Hester's art certainly is not destined to glorify God or His doings, for the very object that she embroiders and makes beautiful is the sign of her sin. Because in the patriarchal Puritan society Hester is denied a voice, her artistic concerns become a way to express her true self. Needlework "to Hester Prynne ... might have been a mode of expressing, and therefore soothing, the passion of her life." More importantly, Hester's artistic creations point out her adulterous sexuality and her illegitimate child: "it [Pearl's dress] was the scarlet letter in another form: the scarlet letter endowed with life! The mother herself—as if the red ignominy were so deeply scorched into her brain that all her conceptions assumed its form—had carefully wrought out the similitude, lavishing many hours of morbid ingenuity to create an analogy between the object of her affection and the emblem of her guilt and torture." When Hester finds comfort in sewing an elaborate version of her A or artful dresses for Pearl,

> without benefit of a suitable language, Hester communicates through her feminine artistry of needle-work—an artistry that the narrator recognises as "almost the only within a woman's grasp." The women in the community recognise her non-verbal, feminine form of communication, and thereby recognise—perhaps nothing so definite as their own "outlaw" status as women under patriarchal rule—but possibly a vague sense of the insufficiency of the patriarchal system of language and law to adequately represent and to serve the "unspeakable" needs and desires of women.[9]

Because the A stands for adulteress but neither adultery nor adulteress is ever written out in the novel, the A comes to hold multiple meanings, not all of them negative: "the letter was the symbol of her calling. Such helpfulness was found in her—so much power to do, and power to sympathise—that many people refused to interpret the scarlet A by its original signification. They said that it meant Abel, so strong was Hester Prynne, with a woman's strength." This evolution of the A also transcends society: "they had begun to look upon the scarlet letter as the token, not of that one sin for which she had borne so long and dreary a penance, but of her many good deeds since." Therefore, "the A notoriously hints at all sorts of names while claiming none."[10]

Thanks to Hester's mastery with the needle, "the letter they have 'sentenced' her to wear attempts to define her as a transparent sign—as a transgressor of man's laws, if not as a lawful reflector of man. The attempt, however, backfires—Hester's needle subverts the interpretive code." Because of its changing and evolving meaning,

> the letter will mean whatever people can be persuaded to believe that it means; it has no fixed and permanent reference. This is what Hawthorne shows in the novel: a world wherein different individuals and groups are either trying to persuade others that "their" meaning is the right one, or are simply imposing their meaning by physical force (embroidered by plenty of rhetoric and ceremony), while the letter itself remains susceptible to a variety of meanings. He shows this by introducing the letter to us at a point when its meaning is already being questioned, and never from first to last allowing it to be firmly attached to any single meaning.

With this multiplicity of meanings, Hawthorne shows that laws are also subject to interpretation or even revision and adultery is not necessarily, in other societies, such a hideous crime.[11]

Beginning with the fact that Hester's adultery goes unnamed, naming is a central force in *The Scarlet Letter* and a feature that Updike exploited in his trilogy as well. In Hawthorne's novel, Chillingworth reinvents himself by finding a new name and Hester finds a biblical name of great significance for her daughter. Hester's own name is an anagram of Esther, the biblical queen who "has been brought into 'a false and unnatural relation' with the much older Ahasuerus; she is first brought into his harem and then made his wife." This is not coincidental: "both the book of Esther and *The Scarlet Letter* begin with the public disciplining of a disobedient woman.... The guilt and exemplary banishment of Vashti, Ahasuerus's initial queen and Esther's predecessor, are to be set down in letters and sent throughout the kingdom; Hester is to be made to wear the letter that declares her guilt and her exemplary banishment—her sin is to be published and represented in the form of a text which will continually speak of her disobedience." Like Esther, Hester is a young, beautiful woman trapped into a loveless marriage with a much older man.[12]

Not only does the letter progressively lose its intended, original meaning, but it also provides Hester with a freedom of mind that she would not have obtained had she lived in society: "the scarlet letter was her passport into regions where other women dared not tread. Shame, Despair, Solitude! These had been her teachers—stern and wild ones—and they had made her strong, but taught her much amiss." Hester's punishment can therefore be seen as a mixed blessing in that it allows her to explore unconventional modes of thought and achieve an independence of mind when compared to those who stay within prescribed society. Hester achieves a freedom of mind: "for years past she had looked from this estranged point of view at human institutions, and whatever priests or legislators had established; criticising all." Just as the very scarlet letter itself is subject to multiple interpretations, so is the character of Hester Prynne, whose literary standing has changed from rebellious, punished woman to proto-feminist and martyr of women's rights, or "a feminist heroine of literature, a sacred sister, a model of dignified defiance." Hester, in being an outcast of society and, therefore, able to live on her own, just occasionally engaging in social interaction, can see society from a distance and question it, especially when it comes to women's place in society.[13]

Hester finds in her punishment and isolation from society strength to endure it and, what is more, see society critically. In contrast, her lover, the Reverend Arthur Dimmesdale, is described by Chillingworth as a weakling—"his spirit lacked the strength that could have borne up, as thine has, beneath a burden like thy scarlet letter." Not only is Dimmesdale a hypocrite, a man hiding his true deeds and feelings from society, he is also presented as a hypocrite to Hester herself, who was misled to believe that he was different from what he really is like:

> how deeply had they known each other then! And was this the man? She hardly knew him now! He, moving proudly past, enveloped as it were, in the rich music, with the procession of majestic and venerable fathers; he, so unattainable in his worldly position, and still more so in that far vista of his unsympathizing thoughts, through which she now beheld him! Her spirit sank with the idea that all must have been a delusion, and that, vividly as she had dreamed it, there could be no real bond betwixt the clergyman and herself. And thus much of woman was there in Hester, that she could scarcely forgive him—least of all now, when the heavy footstep of their approaching Fate might be heard, nearer, nearer, nearer!—for being able so completely to withdraw himself from their mutual world—while she groped darkly, and stretched forth her cold hands, and found him not.[14]

Whereas Hester faces society's disapproval and open hostility, Dimmesdale remains silent and conceals his guilt. Instead of facing public opprobrium, "what Dimmesdale sees is the possibility of his redemption according to the Biblical doctrine of inner trial and conversion." Hawthorne expressed it in the following manner:

> there are such men.... But not to suggest more obvious reasons, it may be that they are kept silent by the very constitution of their nature. Or—can we not suppose it?—guilty as they may be, retaining, nevertheless, a zeal for God's glory and man's welfare, they shrink from displaying themselves black and filthy in the view of men; because, thenceforward, no good can be achieved by them; no evil of the past be redeemed by better service. So, to their own unutterable torment, they go about among their fellow-creatures, looking pure as new-fallen snow, while their hearts are all speckled and spotted with iniquity of which they cannot rid themselves.

Dimmesdale is one such man. Inasmuch as his attitude is a sign of his cowardice and his hypocrisy, this makes of him a symbol of Puritanism, in Updike's understanding: "Dimmesdale, in so far as he speaks for Puritanism, is not the hero but the villain, so that we rejoice in his fall."[15]

After the death of Dimmesdale, when Hester lives on and endures "we see the new model for capable womanhood watching the decline of the old model of eighteenth-century fictional values." However, not only was Hawthorne commenting on the situation of women in seventeenth-century New England, but he was also referring to nineteenth-century concepts of womanhood. The nineteenth century ran rife with ideological debates about what the proper role of women was, with the idea of women as the angel in the house being largely prevalent. Moreover, "Smith-Rosenberg notes that nineteenth century Victorian thinking found in female sexuality a metaphor for social order or disorder," very much like Hester is punished for disrupting social mores. Nineteenth-century critics of the novel were quick to appreciate its subversive value and, accordingly, Jane Grey Swisshelm, in her review of *The Scarlet Letter*, "celebrates a novel that ... depicts the bankruptcy of a loveless marriage, raises questions about a woman's legal obligation to remain confined within such a marriage, and supports a woman's desire for sexual fulfillment (even if the result is a child out of wedlock)."[16]

Beginning with Nina Baym's 1982 landmark analysis, many studies have appeared analyzing Hester in feminist terms. For *The Scarlet Letter*, Hawthorne chose both the story of a woman and female writing techniques and styles. Still, the question of whether Hawthorne was sympathetic to Hester's plight has generated an intense critical debate. For Last, the novel is "a narrative of radical sympathy for women suffering under patriarchal oppression." Of a different opinion is Janis Stout, who "observes that the novel's conflicted authorial voice challenges the patriarchal stereotype of the fallen woman and the Puritan treatment of her, but never questions the reality of Hester's sin or guilt." Curiously, Updike's treatment of Sarah in *S.* sparked a similar controversy.[17]

In *A Month of Sundays*, one of his most critically neglected works, Updike used the character of Thomas Marshfield, a minister removed from his parish for sleeping around with several of his female parishioners and who begins a diary during his journey. The minute self-examination of one's inner thoughts, inquiring into the state of one's soul, looking for sins or flaws that might denote eternal condemnation, was a distinctive Puritan feature, which was particularly visible in the detailed diaries they wrote.[18] But in this case Marshfield is forced to write a diary by the people running the shelter he is sent to—"Ms. Prynne tells me to write ... about what interests me most."[19]

If Thomas Marshfield is an alter ego for Dimmesdale, the adulterous minister, the Hester figure does not have a one-to-one correspondence in the novel. Rather, Hester-like elements can be found in a number of female characters in *A Month of Sundays*. The first Hester is Marshfield's wife, Jane Chillingworth, whom he "steals" from her learned father, Dr. Rev. Wesley Augustus Chillingworth. But once married, routine and apathy as well as her innate goodness make her sexually unattractive to her husband. In answer to the question in *The Scarlet Letter* of what would have happened had Hester and Dimmesdale been able to be together, Updike responds that his Dimmesdale would have lost all interest in her and found other parishioners to sleep with.[20]

Marshfield begins several affairs with parishioners, including the deacon's wife, Frankie Harlow, although he cannot fulfill his sexual needs because he is unable to have an erection being with her. He blames it on her being a true believer in contrast to his wife Jane and the church organist, Alice, who does not really believe in God. He is a disbeliever himself and only gets an erection when he forces Frankie to say she does not believe, an instance of the way in which religion and sex are closely interconnected in the novel. Updike has declared that "my central idea there was that clergymen are exposed more than most men to sexual temptations and that, furthermore, there is some deep alliance between the religious impulse and the sexual. Both are a way of perpetuating our lives, of denying our physical limits."[21]

With his portrayal of an unremorseful preacher, "by recasting Dimmesdale as a prankster and a clown, Updike parodies Hawthorne's preacher and demonstrates how sexual attitudes have changed drastically since 1850 (and 1640)." As he acknowledged, "the primary purpose behind *A Month of Sundays* with its fitful Hawthornian echoes was to show how radically American attitudes have changed in regard to adulterous clergy.... As any bishop can tell you, modern clergymen tend to be quite unapologetic about where their bodies take them." If Dimmesdale is a man tortured by remorse, Updike shows that it is possible for a minister to live rather happily being adulterous, without despairing or feeling any kind of remorse, thus rejecting "the notion that literature should inculcate moral principles or precepts."[22]

Although Hester never challenges her punishment for adultery, Hawthorne argues that if adultery is immoral, so is Roger's marriage to Hester in the first place—"I betrayed thy budding youth into a false and unnatural relation with my decay." Whereas the novel does not present Hester regretting her adultery, she does regret her marriage: "she marvelled how she could ever have been wrought upon to marry him! She deemed it her crime most to be repented of, that she had ever endured and reciprocated the lukewarm grasp of his hand, and had suffered the smile of her lips and eyes to mingle and melt into his own. And it seemed a fouler offence committed by Roger Chillingworth than any which had since been done him, that, in the time when her heart knew no better, he had persuaded her to fancy herself happy by his side." Updike has explained the decisive influence *The Scarlet Letter* has had on him in the following terms: "I guess it all goes back to being very impressed by *The Scarlet Letter* when I read it, I don't know when, in my 20's, I guess.... It is our *Anna Karenina* and *Madame Bovary*. It is our contribution to the novel of adultery." In *A Month of Sundays,* Marshfield finds nothing to regret in his sleeping around. He believes that "adultery, my friends, is our inherent condition ... adultery is not a choice to be avoided; it is a circumstance to be embraced." To ease his not very guilty conscience after he begins an affair with Alice, the organist, he tries to bring his wife Jane and his assistant, Ned, together—"my hope was not to convert him, but to alienate him, so he would be eased of guilt, if moved to sleep with my wife." If Chillingworth tortured Dimmesdale for having been Hester's lover, Tom encourages Ned. Curiously enough, Tom encourages his wife to have an affair but is enraged when he finds out his lover does have an affair with Ned.[23]

Remorseless, Marshfield confesses to Alice that "I feel pretty good, actually.... It *is* odd ... that feeling good and being good don't seem to be the same thing." He is so comfortable with adultery that he does not want to change the current situation of sleeping with Alice while not leaving Jane—"how could I leave Jane? How could I make up my betrayal, the lover's perennial betrayal, to Alice?" Marshfield is not willing to leave Jane and the ministry for Alice, this course being the one followed by the minister in *Roger's Version*. For this reason, in a way, *A Month of Sundays* represents the path not taken in *Roger's Version*. "In Updike's novels the dilemma created by this dual morality is often embodied in the women between whom the protagonists must choose" and Marshfield jumps from one woman (one Hester) to another (another version of Hester).[24]

If Marshfield himself is not consumed by the agonizing pangs of remorse that Dimmesdale felt, the same applies to his present-day Hester figures. If Hester accepts her punishment, not defying authorities, Marshfield's lovers are as remorseless as he is: "I was shocked, at first, by how unfussily these seducing women sought out the scrotal concealed in the sacerdotal, how intuitively religious was their view of sex, hasty and improvised though its occasion. Where was their *guilt*? They came to church the next Sunday with clean faces, and listened to the Word intent." What is more, in his view, when it comes to adultery, "women really don't see much wrong with it," which allows him to put all the blame on his lovers:

> the life I have sorrily described is as a departure point at which I am busy hiring various women as porters for the great train of guilt that is my baggage. Jane carried a load for not adoring me as would a mistress or Mary Magdalene; Frankie bore some for adoring me so much I became with her a desexed angel; and now Alice, toward whom I had felt heavy for failing to make her my wife when she was so much my woman ... took on her head the bulky bundle—the struck tent—of my collapsed career. Well, she was thick-waisted and tough and could tote it. Babies and guilt, women are built for lugging.[25]

The protagonist of *Roger's Version*, Roger Lambert, is a professor in an unnamed Northeastern city that well could be Boston while his college could be Harvard Divinity School. To stress the Puritan resonance in the novel, the school his son attends is called Pilgrim School.[26] Touches of Puritanism can be seen in several instances in the novel, most notably in Roger's understanding of the frugality of time. Lambert embraces the Puritan belief that time should not be wasted—"one of the Christian consolations, as I construe them, is that the Lord's unsleeping witness and strict accountancy redeems all moments from pointlessness, just as His Son's sacrifice redeemed Time in the larger sense." However, since sensibilities and social attitudes have changed since Puritan times, often Puritanism is reduced to an issue to make fun of—"Hooker Hall (the often joked-about name of our main building—Thomas Hooker being, of course, a distinguished Puritan divine)."[27]

If Marshfield in *A Month of Sundays* did not dare to leave his wife and the ministry for his lover, Roger Lambert presents himself at the beginning of his first-person account as someone who willingly and rather happily gave up Methodist ministry after leaving his first wife, Lillian, for Esther. This has resulted in his disappointment and distrust of organized religion, which he sees simply as his way to make a living: "to master a few dead languages, to parade sequential moments of the obdurately enigmatic early history of Christianity before classrooms of the hopeful, the deluded, and the docile—there are more fraudulent ways to earn a living. I consider my years spent in the active ministry, before meeting and marrying Esther fourteen years ago, if not exactly wasted, as a kind of pre-existence, the thought of which depresses me." His beliefs stand in stark contrast to those of Dale Kohler, a postgraduate student of his who asks for his endorsement to apply for a research grant. Dale is convinced that, by means of a computer program he plans to design with the funding from the grant, it could be finally proved that "God made Heaven and Earth. It's what science has come to." In his view, far from destroying the veracity of biblical stories in regards to the creation of the world, science should find in nature the clues to ascertain that God is the creator of the world. Like Puritan divines such as Cotton Mather, Dale gives Roger a long list of natural phenomena to support God's existence.[28]

Dale's research is motivated by his frustration at the place God has been given in American society nowadays. In contrast to His prominent role in Puritan society, now God is notably absent from everyday life. According to Dale, "you're afraid. You don't *want* God to break through. People in general don't want that. They just want to grub along being human, and dirty, and sly, and amusing, and having their weekends with Michelob, and God to stay put in the churches if they ever decide to drop by, and maybe to pull them out in the end, down that tunnel of light all these NDEs [near-death-experiences] talk about." Roger is far from offering Dale the support he came looking for, though, since "I must confess I find your whole idea aesthetically and ethically repulsive. Aesthetically because it describes a God Who lets Himself be intellectually trapped, and ethically because it eliminates faith from religion, it takes away our freedom to believe or doubt. A God you could prove makes the whole thing immensely, oh, un*in*teresting." Also, he is convinced of the unfeasibility of the very project: "whenever theology touches science, it gets burned."[29]

When Roger is informed by Dale that his niece Verna, a single teenage mother, is living in town, he decides to pay her a visit. Verna reminds him of Edna, his half-sister, to whom he felt sexually attracted when they were teenagers: "and if my pubescent thoughts had sometimes turned to her ... thoughts are not deeds, not on this mortal plane." Verna, a high school dropout, is violent with her mixed-race daughter Paula, whom she abuses verbally and physically because "Paula *is* Verna's scarlet letter. As the daughter of a black man, Paula marks Verna in the white world as a slut to be shunned and in the black world as a target for passes by black men. Like the letter, Paula represents Verna's shame but also symbolizes Verna's rebellious pride. In a further reversal, Verna does free herself from her scarlet letter."[30]

That Verna's child is a mixed-race is relevant, and comments on little Paula's skin color are numerous throughout the novel. Actually, Verna's social worker attributes her mistreatment of the baby to Verna's desire to be normal (that is, going back to her parents' comfortable home in contrast to her tiny apartment in a disreputable, largely African-American neighborhood). Consequently, at the end of the novel Verna moves back with her parents, leaving Paula behind in the care of Roger and his wife.

If Paula is Pearl, the Hester role is fulfilled by both Esther and Verna: "Esther is Roger's second wife, and like Hester, she is a good deal younger than her husband.... Esther is an angel of mercy, working part-time for little pay at a nearby day-care center (is Updike suggesting that the saintly Hester operates as a mythical predecessor for contemporary females who turn to volunteer work or work for little pay?)" Also, just as Hester expresses her artistry in her embroidery, Esther is an amateur painter. Because his marriage with Esther now lacks all the passion they used to have, Roger begins to feel attracted to Verna: "her fingernails were cut short, like a child's, and this did stir me. Her caresses would not scratch." Roger explains that, with Esther, "boredom wafted from her like the scent of stale sweat" and "long after love goes, there is still habit. Esther was my habit." Updike thus presents the same idea already advanced in *A Month of Sundays*—that routine is the murderer of passion.[31]

Roger invites Verna, Paula and Dale for Thanksgiving even though he suspects that Verna and Dale might be lovers, a possibility that fills him with jealousy. From the very beginning, during their first interview, Roger measures his appreciation of Dale in sexual terms, making assumptions about his sexual life: "I pictured his waxy face, breaking out in a masturbator's pimples. I felt superior to him, being sexually healthy ever since Esther took over from ungainly, barren Lillian. My second wife when unmarried she had been a flexible marvel in bed, her underpants in the sunlight of our illicit afternoons fed to my eyes like tidbits of rosy marzipan."

Nevertheless, despite his own boasted sexual prowess, Roger is jealous of Dale's social abilities.[32]

Roger grows increasingly attracted to Verna, whom he keeps visiting while Dale and Esther begin an affair. Whereas Esther is serious about her relationship with Dale and wants to leave her husband, Dale dissuades her from it because, as a graduate student, he could not financially support her. Meanwhile, Verna gets pregnant after a one-night stand with a stranger, and Roger drives her to an abortion clinic. Soon afterward, Verna beats up Paula viciously and the hospital will not let her take Paula back. Roger convinces the doctors to release the baby to him and not to press charges. When they go back to Verna's apartment, Roger has sex with her.

After this, Verna meets Roger for the last time—she is going back to her parents' home, leaving Paula with Roger and Esther. Verna reveals to Roger that she knows that Dale has been having an affair with a married woman although she ignores the woman's identity. By the end of the novel, Esther and Roger have been appointed the legal guardians of Verna, Dale has lost his faith and left the city while Roger comments that Esther is getting fatter and has taken to going to church, despite her former atheism. The interpretation of the ending varies, with some critics viewing Esther's pregnancy by Dale as his ultimate triumph over Roger, even though Roger succeeded in making him lose his faith. For Wisehart, however, "Roger plots his revenge on them both: on Dale by not only tearing down his arguments but by destroying his faith as well; on Esther by embarking on an incestuous affair with his niece." In a way, Roger causes Dale the same kind of despair that Chillingworth causes Dimmesdale: "it grew to be a widely diffused opinion that the Rev. Arthur Dimmesdale, like many other personages of special sanctity, in all ages of the Christian world, was haunted either by Satan himself or Satan's emissary, in the guise of old Roger Chillingworth. This diabolical agent had the Divine permission, for a season, to burrow into the clergyman's intimacy, and plot against his soul." Yet, it is worth noting that "in Hawthorne's novel, Chillingworth's hatred of Dimmesdale results from his discovery that the minister was Hester's lover. In Updike's novel, Roger's hatred of Dale exists *before* Dale's involvement with Esther. Esther and Dale's adulterous relationship, then, is related only tangentially to Roger's desire to destroy Dale."[33]

Critics have extensively commented on the unreliability of Roger, the first-person narrator of the story. To begin with, the title already hints at the possibility that this is just Roger's version, one of the many possible versions of the same events, in the same way that *Roger's Version* itself is just an instance of retelling *The Scarlet Letter*, the others being *A Month of Sundays* and *S.* Also, Roger narrates in a detailed manner scenes and locations whose knowledge is only available to an omniscient narrator, not to a first-person narrator. How can he describe in such a detailed manner Esther and Dale's lovemaking or the decoration of Dale's campus dorm? Updike, however, has vehemently opposed this categorization of Roger as an unreliable narrator: "what's unreliable about them? They're as reliable as I can make them. Even Roger's visions of his wife and her lover, which might be taken as a pornographic fantasy, are borne out in the end, essentially, by her pregnancy. I know the phrase 'unreliable narrator' is popular critically these days, but I have nothing to do with it. A narrator who's unreliable, why listen to him/her?"[34]

Maybe because some readers of *Roger's Version* have failed to see the novel's connection with *The Scarlet Letter*, the third and final novel in "*The Scarlet Letter* Trilogy," *S.*, opens with two quotations taken from *The Scarlet Letter*. The first quotation refers to Hester's physical description—"she had dark and abundant hair ... how her beauty shone out, and made a halo of the misfortune and ignominy in which she was enveloped." This is a physical description but with a spiritual component to it—she has a halo, almost as if she were a saint. The following quotation ("much of the marble coldness of Hester's impression was to be attributed to the circumstance that her life had turned, in great measure, from passion and feeling, to thought.... The world's law was no law for her mind") illustrates the Puritan dichotomy between passion and thought; in contrast, Hester has a mind of her own. These quotations set the tone for the rest of the novel and make us aware that the protagonist is to be interpreted as a present-day Hester.[35]

In *S.*, Sarah Worth, a New England homemaker and mother, decides to leave her physician husband, tired of his many affairs with his nurses. *S.* is an epistolary novel, using the letters Sarah writes to her husband, daughter, mother, brother, friends, dentist, bank manager, etc. She adopts several identities in the course of the novel, as evidenced in her different names and signatures, depending on who her addressee is—S., Mother, Sarah Worth, Sally Worth, Sarah Worth (Mrs. Charles), Sare, Sarah P. Worth, Sarah (Worth), "your devoted nayika, K.," Sis, Ma Prem Kundalini, Mummy, K., your loving Mother, Sarah née Price. Her names reflect her inner turmoil and her search for a new identity, for she feels Charles's signature branded in her: "I know it so well, that signature, it's been branded into me, I wouldn't be surprised to see it burned into my flank." Naming is a crucial point both in *S.* and in *The Scarlet Letter*. If Hester learns to accept the scarlet letter as part of her identity, Sarah has trouble finding a name for herself. For Sarah, leaving behind her old identity means starting anew: "let me be truly nothing to you, at last. I will change my name. I will change my being. The woman you 'knew' and 'possessed' is no more. I am destroying her."[36]

Hester Prynne embroidered her scarlet letter to express herself; Sarah does not use embroidery, but, rather, the written medium: "I sit inside and embroider my letters and read." Women in the Puritan times were taught to read (so that they could read the Bible) but, believing that reading and writing were two different, unrelated disciplines, girls were not usually taught to write for it was considered that women had nothing worth putting into written words. This modern Hester figure wants to write, not to sew. Women no longer express their inner or artistic concerns by sewing but with writing, just like men.[37]

But if Hester Prynne finds meaning in her life in taking care of her daughter, for Sarah Worth this is not enough once her daughter Pearl is grown-up and moves to study at an English college. In *S.*, motherhood is not self-fulfilling and, what is more, for Sarah it is burdensome and unrewarding: "*I* nursed you, *I* changed your diapers.... You sucked milk out of *my* breasts, took hold of life in *my* belly, not your father's. All he did was clumsily contribute his sperm (I had no climax when you were conceived; I rarely did in those virtually virginal days) ... *raising you was not an equal partnership*, and I *am* hurt, dearest Pearl, by what seems to me not so much your divided loyalty—that perhaps is to be expected and is healthy—but what can only strike me as *dis*loyalty." Instead of finding contentment in the joys of motherhood, a woman has to find meaning within herself, an idea also present at the end of *The Scarlet Letter*, when Hester returns to Boston without Pearl.[38]

Sarah flees from her New England home to an ashram in the Arizona desert, run by the Arhat, an Indian guru whose Buddhist teachings she has gotten acquainted with through her yoga lessons. Sarah sees herself as a "sannyasin," that is, a pilgrim in Sanskrit. The notion of "sannyasin" is very important throughout the whole work. Sarah is a pilgrim to the ashram as much as the Puritans were pilgrims to the New World. Freed after "the previous twenty two years of respectable bondage and socially sanctioned frivolity," Sarah begins to experiment with love and sex at the ashram. She first has an affair with her instructor, Fritz, and then with Alinga, another woman.[39]

For Sarah, "love [is]—a woman's drug." This belief, along with her resentment and bitterness for her broken marriage, makes her totally against marriage. She believes that her husband "took up right where my parents left off, as enforcers of the stale old older," thus continuing with the repression work. Consequently, Sarah violently opposes her daughter's wedding plans with her European boyfriend, whom she considers a pernicious influence (despite having never met him), representing stereotypes of old Europe corrupting fresh, naïve America—"they are everything Americans left Europe to get away from—materialist, class-obsessed, cruel in their smugness, and smug in their dullness.... Pearl needs nice shy American boys, awkwardly full of drive and idealism."[40]

Sarah next embarks on an affair with the Arhat, which abruptly ends when she discovers that he is not Indian-born and his accent is fake—his real name is Arthur Steinmetz and he is an Armenian Jew from Massachusetts. The Arhat turns out to be the man who cannot stand up to Sarah's ideals, very much like Dimmesdale, who is not the good man Hester or the community believed him to be. Sarah's Dimmesdale figure, the false minister, the Arhat, proves to be a weakling who needs women to support him, but contrary to Hester, Sarah rejects him. Through the figure of the Arhat, Updike, very much like Hawthorne, denounces the hypocrisy of so-called holy men. Disappointed, Sarah flees to the Caribbean with the money she withdrew from her joint account with Charles as well as the money she embezzled from the ashram, taking advantage of her capacity as an accountant there.

S. denounces the conservative twist American society took in the 1980s during the Reagan administration. The novel is set in 1986—gone are the hippies but women have not found a place for themselves after the sexual liberation of the sixties and seventies. All in all, *S.* shows that 1980s American society can be as oppressive and restrictive for women as Puritan Boston. The Buddhist-inspired religious beliefs of the ashram turn out to be as soul crushing and oppressive as Puritan values, and twentieth-century society does not give women an independent life of their own either: "what a woman has to realize is that as far as she's concerned she's number 1, too, just like a man.... You know—we're conditioned to think of ourselves as number 2, like Eve and Avis."[41]

Updike's treatment of Sarah was especially controversial. Updike has for long been accused of being "misogynist, elitist, sexually puerile, and too preoccupied with masculine self-pity." Reviewers found the portrayal of Sarah misogynist and the description of Oriental philosophy and practices superficial, reduced to the sexual stuff, without going beyond, giving expression to Roger Chillingworth's misogynist views of what would have happened had Hester Prynne been born again in twentieth-century New England. Critics are divided as to whether Sarah is a disagreeable character, mean, stingy, bitter, manipulative, a control freak, obsessed with money or if she is rather a very complex character, showing her multiple contradictions and the conflicting inner voices that push her. Some critics give Updike a more sympathetic treatment: "though some critics have argued, with cries of sexism and misogyny, that Updike has reduced Hester to 'a wholly hateful woman,' Updike suggests rather that Hester is far more complex, conflicted, defiant, and self-deceptive than is commonly imagined." Sarah herself gives the key to how she should be interpreted when she claims that "we all have a number of skins, especially women I think, because society makes us wriggle more." In this view, she is a complex being, full of contradictions.[42]

For Sarah, all men oppress women. The ashram is just another form of repression and even her male therapist seems to her to be endorsing the patriarchal society she fought against—"looking back at my years of therapy, I confess that it all now seems much more patriarchal and Judeo-Christian than it did at the time. Far from being my ally against Charles as I fantasized, you were *his* ally against my liberation." Sarah is probably Updike's character who feels the pressure of tradition (i.e., the New England past, Puritanism, Protestantism, patriarchy) more acutely than any other in the trilogy because of her being a woman fighting patriarchy.[43]

Updike explicitly defined *S.* as "one attempt to make things right with my, what shall we call them, feminist detractors," similar to *The Witches of Eastwick*, in that it was "a woman's novel by a man." In his own words, *S.*

> was a sincere attempt to write about a woman on the move ... and maybe will somewhat satisfy those women who feel that my women are never on the move, that they're always stuck where the men have put them. I don't know to what extent a writer is responsible for the sociological conditions that he describes. A writer makes his world, but it's very much based on the world he has experienced and seen—and it's been my good fortune to know a lot of independent-minded, bright, shrewd and interesting females, and I suppose that this book is among other things my tribute to the female voice.

For all of Updike's noble intentions, the result did not convince critics. For *The New York Times* critic Michiko Kakutani, Sarah is

> a decidedly unlikable person. Sarah is, by turns, castrating (she refers to her husband's "microscopic ridiculous sperm"), bitter ("Did I not labor for you twenty-two years without wages, serving as concubine, party doll, housekeeper, cook, bedwarmer, masseuse, sympathetic adviser, and walking advertisement") and manipulative ("I feel you, out there, as a dark packet of wounded maleness spitefully taking any tack to 'get at' me, even if it means ruining your daughter's fragile young life"). Apparently she is also stupid or willfully naive: though it's clear from her own descriptions that the

ashram she's joined is thoroughly bogus, she persists in defending its mission, helping to bilk others out of their money and their faith,

nothing to do with Updike's much more sympathetic treatment of Rabbit's flight from his domestic duties.[44]

Money is an important concern of Sarah's. Although a homemaker, she feels entitled to half of her and her husband's assets (and withdraws as much from their joint bank account before leaving) because she took care of their home and daughter while her husband was working. Moreover, she paid his tuition fees in medical school with her own money, even leaving school herself. Sarah complains about American women's dependence on men, inculcated since their very first years—"somehow we American girls are raised for the smell of a man in the house."[45]

At the same time that she is fighting for her own money, she is pressing her mother to give the Arhat her shares—while beginning to embezzle the ashram's accounts so that she can put money aside for herself. For all her claims that "all the material world is a jail," Sarah is stingy, too—she sends friends a tape and demands payment for it. Independence costs money, though, not just a change of mind or place: "the acquisition of money becomes a central concern in *S.* Money enables one to be independent and powerful, and it is through their monopoly on money-making that men for so long have been able to maintain power over women."[46]

Everything in the novel is related to capitalist practices of value and the worth given to products and the price to be paid for those goods. Sarah's maiden name is "Price," a notion she can never forget given that it is minted on her family's heirlooms and Charles's last name is Worth. Sarah claims to have abandoned Puritanism's scorn of money in that she is proud of their money and making use of it—"our comfort did not embarrass me. I know how hard we had worked together to make you a grand grave man."[47] For Schiff, "the title *S.* signifies not only the obvious—Sarah, sannyasin, seductress, sex, self, serpent (Sarah as Eve), Sanskrit—but also $. In a novel primarily about spirituality, religion, and self-renewal, money plays a surprisingly dominant and persistent role. The quest for a new identity, intimately associated with the dream of America, requires money, as does a 'room of one's own.'"[48]

To conclude, Updike's "*The Scarlet Letter* Trilogy" can be considered an updated, satirical, intertextual homage to Hawthorne's Puritan tradition in *The Scarlet Letter*. Updike shows that certain components of American society remain as valid in twentieth-century America as they were in seventeenth-century Puritan Boston such as "the presence and significance of adultery in the community; the struggle on the part of women against patriarchal oppression; the conflicts between matter and spirit, individual and community; and the need to shake off the past and reinvent both the world and the self." Sex, sin, adultery, the dichotomy between bodily urges and religious concerns, remorse (or the lack thereof), false ministers and stray parishioners are all issues rewritten by Updike while Hawthorne's tragedy gets tragicomic overtones in the process and loses its Puritan grimness.[49]

For Updike, the question of how to reconcile religion with adulterous relationships remains unresolved, but it is no longer a source of distress for his characters. Where Dimmesdale despaired, Updike's "characters unify faith and fornication but never wear the A." Different from Hester's stoicism, Updike's Thomas Marshfield, Roger Lambert and Sarah Worth are able to leave their communities and start anew, forging new identities for themselves.[50]

Chapter 6

The Proud Father of Four Little Women

Womanhood, Patriarchy and the Civil War in Louisa May Alcott's *Little Women* and *March* by Geraldine Brooks

> The four young faces on which the firelight shone brightened at the cheerful words, but darkened again as Jo said sadly, "We haven't got Father, and shall not have him for a long time." She didn't say "perhaps never," but each silently added it, thinking of Father far away, where the fighting was. **Louisa May Alcott: *Little Women* (1869)**

> I promised her that I would write something every day, and I find myself turning to this obligation when my mind is most troubled.... I am thankful that she is *not* here, to see what I must see, to know what I am come to know.... I compose a few rote words of spousal longing, and follow these with some professions of fatherly tenderness. **Geraldine Brooks: *March* (2005)**

The interrelationship between the American Civil War (1861–1865) and literature has been very much present since President Abraham Lincoln reportedly referred to Harriet Beecher Stowe, author of the pro-abolitionist novel *Uncle Tom's Cabin* (serialized for forty weeks from June 5, 1851; published as a book in 1852), as the "little woman who wrote the book that made this great war." Stowe's depiction of the cruelties of slavery, "the most damning lie America has ever told itself" in writer James Carroll's words, decisively arouse the public's sympathy towards abolitionism in the years immediately preceding the military conflict. Stowe's depiction of how a noble slave, Uncle Tom, considered almost a family member by his kind master, is sold down South to a terrible life of hardships and corporal punishments, was so moving that many who up to then had remained remiss to adopt a point of view about slavery, now resolved to actively oppose it. Following in Stowe's footsteps, the Civil War has for long occupied a prominent position in the fiction of women writers up to the point that it has become feminized. Actually, the two most famous literary depictions of this war that Stowe inspired were written by women: Louisa May Alcott in *Little Women* when it comes to the Northern side of the war and Margaret Mitchell in *Gone with the Wind* (1936) in regards to the Southern defeat.[1]

A very prolific writer of almost three hundred novels, poems, journalistic pieces, and short stories, Alcott only achieved critical and commercial success after the publication of *Little Women* (1868; second part *Good Wives* published in 1869).[2] Originally an assignment by her editor, she had at first turned it down claiming in her *Journals* that she "never liked girls or knew many except my sisters." She ended up accepting it quite reluctantly and only after much persuading because of pressing financial reasons—by then Alcott was supporting her parents as well as her widowed sister and her two nephews (later on, after the death of her younger sister, another niece joined the Alcott household). Their situation was so strained that at times, much to Alcott's chagrin, they lived on charity. The commercial success of *Little Women* would bring their financial penuries to a close, since "her royalties soared as high as $33,000 in one quadrennium."[3] By 1920, *Little Women* was the best-selling book in the United States, second only to the Bible.[4] With at least thirteen movie adaptations as well as one musical version, it is, with *The Adventures of Huckleberry Finn*, the most well-known nineteenth-century American children's book.[5]

The little women the title alludes to are Meg, Jo, Beth and Amy March, four sisters who live with their mother and a loyal servant, Hannah, while their father is off as a chaplain with the Union Army during the Civil War. Members of a well-reputed but impoverished family, the girls try to make the best out of their poverty, playing games, rehearsing plays that Jo writes, etc. while expecting different things from life. Meg, the eldest and the most serious one, longs for the riches and comforts they used to have before their father went bankrupt; Jo dreams of becoming a well-known author and is persuaded that she will end up a spinster; Beth happily stays at home, too shy to go to school; and Amy wants to marry into money to compensate for the humiliations she suffers from her wealthier classmates.

Little Women was conceived as a girls' story, which meant being "essentially moralistic, ... designed to bridge the gap between the school-room and the drawing room, to recommend docility, marriage, and obedience rather than autonomy or adventure." Yet, despite her initial reluctance, Alcott commented, after reading the proofs, that *Little Women* "read better than I expected. Not a bit sensational, but simple and true, for we really lived most of it, and if it succeeds that will be the reason of it." This markedly autobiographical content obeyed Alcott's own piece of advice, offered in her earlier *Hospital Sketches* (1863), a work inspired by her experiences as a Civil War nurse:

> "I want something to do."
> "Write a book," Quoth the author of my being.
> "Don't know enough, sir. First live, then write."[6]

The autobiographical components in the novel do not end here, for Alcott closely modeled the Marches after her own family. To begin with, Alcott's sisters May, Lizzie and Anna became Meg, Beth and Amy, respectively, while Jo closely resembled herself; their mother, Abba, had Marmee as her alter ego. Critics have had no problem in thoroughly accepting Alcott's one-to-one identification of her life and her novels; thus, in 1889 writer and reformer Ednah Cheney called *Little Women* a "realistic transcript of life, but idealized by the tenderness of real feeling."[7] However, *Little Women* is not the faintly disguised autobiography many have read it as but a fictional rendering of her own life, adding more cheerfulness than the Alcott girls must have felt growing up poor and needy, omitting her own "ongoing private struggles against the constraints of Victorian gender norms, the intellectual world of midcentury Concord, Massachusetts, and the obligations of an eccentric family."[8]

Equally largely ignored in *Little Women* is Alcott's peculiar relationship with her unusual father, as Mr. March is confined to the margins of the narrative for the most part. Alcott had a curious love/hate relationship with her father throughout all her life. She was born on his thirty-third birthday and died on the morning he was buried. Their relationship is mirrored in that of Jo and Mr. March: "she gave him entire confidence, he gave her the help she needed, and both found consolation in the act. For the time had come when they could talk together not only as father and daughter, but as man and woman, able and glad to serve each other with mutual sympathy as well as mutual love." The fact that Mr. March is such a small character was exploited by Geraldine Brooks, who wondered what Mr. March was doing on the front while Alcott was recounting the circumstances of his wife and four young daughters' daily life. *March* follows him to the front to record his war experiences.[9]

Brooks was a correspondent for *The New York Times, The Wall Street Journal, The New Yorker* and *The Guardian* and the author of two nonfiction books before she turned to fiction with *March*. Not surprisingly, her first novel was set in the Civil War, as her husband, Tony Horwitz, is an expert on the period and the author of *Confederates in the Attic* (1998). Brooks explained in an interview that "when we were living in Virginia, I had a crash course in the Civil War by osmosis. One day when we were coming back from an interminable walk through Antietam, we started talking in the car, and it occurred to me that *Little Women* was actually a Civil War novel of a sort, and I just became intrigued by what happened to the absent father, and what, in a war like that, would happen to an idealistic abolitionist New Englander gone to be chaplain for the Union troops."[10]

Brooks is quick to remark that *March* is not a rewriting, revision or an alteration of *Little Women* but an exploration of those topics Alcott omitted. Just as *Little Women* is largely autobiographical, *March* also borrows heavily from Alcott's own life and family. While the March girls are based on the Alcott sisters and Abba Alcott served as inspiration for Marmee, Mr. March's description owed much to Alcott's father, A. Bronson Alcott. Bronson acknowledged this identification with Mr. March, and, moreover, enjoyed his daughter's fame. He capitalized on the popularity of *Little Women* by participating in lecture tours in which he was introduced as "the Father of *Little Women*." Despite his gracious acceptance of this reflection of his daughter's fame on him, Bronson Alcott had a claim of his own to fame, as he was a philosopher, thinker, idealist and an early advocate of pedagogy. He encouraged outdoor exercise as part of the educative curriculum in his short-lived Temple School, where he enrolled a mixed-race student, and advocated a Socratic method of questioning and discussing in the classroom that was too revolutionary at the time. Deeply committed to progress and his ideas, he even moved his family to the utopian community of Fruitlands for a while. Yet, despite his enlightened ideas, "his experiments in education and philosophy inflicted poverty, distress, and, as some critics would say, abuse on his wife and daughters." Abba's brother had warned her by letter that Bronson's "mind and heart are so much occupied with other things that poverty and riches do not seem to concern him," and Ralph Waldo Emerson commented that "he is quite ready at any moment to abandon his wife and children to put any new dream into practice which has bubbled up in the effervescence of discourse." Actually, while in Fruitlands, "the women, especially Bronson Alcott's wife Abba and his four daughters, did most of the work while he traveled to promote his ideas." Alcott herself acknowledged that her father "possesses no gift for money making" and, as a consequence of his disregard and carelessness with money, "from 1844 on the role of the breadwinner was assumed partly by Louisa's mother and sisters, and principally (and finally exclusively) by Louisa herself."[11]

Because, despite his progressive ideas, "none of Louisa May Alcott's twentieth century biographers is kind to Bronson: at best he is portrayed as hapless, at worst abusive," *March* draws on the two-fold need to give March a life of his own and rehabilitate Bronson Alcott's historical figure. Brooks wondered "how did Bronson Alcott become such a belittled man?" whom Emerson called a "tedious archangel." Using Bronson's journals as inspiration, Brooks intertwined the Marches' story with that of American letters, having the Marches befriend Henry David Thoreau and Emerson, both close friends of the Alcotts.[12]

The March girls are, along with Scarlett O'Hara, probably the most famous literary characters experiencing first-hand the difficulties of the Civil War. Yet, the war does not seem to be too disturbing for the four sisters. Certainly, the absence of their father causes them some financial distress and they are forced to economize. But other than this and the fact that their servant, Hannah, limits coffee to once a week, the war does not play a big role and their only knowledge about it comes from Mr. March's letters home. Despite being abolitionists living in Concord, Massachusetts, the Marches do not voice strong abolitionist opinions and Alcott does not dwell on the rights or wrongs of slavery. African-American characters are notably missing from the novel, which does not put forward any view on slavery, maybe because it was published once the war had been won and slavery sufficiently condemned. This silence stands in marked contrast to the Alcotts' involvement with the abolitionist movement. Bronson was one of the founders of Boston's first white abolitionist society and Alcott's mother's family, the Mays, championed abolitionism as well as a number of reform movements. Because of this telling omission, "*Little Women*'s utopia is a fantasy centered on whiteness," which is a characteristic of Civil War–themed writings published after the war that tended to see the conflict as a white-only affair, neglecting African-Americans' participation—as well as women's.[13]

Ironically, although *Little Women* has been cherished as posing sound, traditional role models for girls, Alcott's own displeasure with her work largely derived from these very role models the novel dictated for women. Yet, for all the overt endorsement of traditional female roles, the novel displays some instances of nonconformity or disagreement with them. Very conveniently ignored by most critics is Marmee's anger, which Alcott used to vent her frustrations as a female author as well as her mother's with her role as the family provider due to her husband's inability to support the family. Marmee's anger goes largely undeveloped by Alcott, except for one single reference in passing when Marmee encourages Jo to follow her own example in restraining her temper. As she tells Jo, "you think your temper is the worst in the world, but mine used to be just like it." In a novel about society and traditional family values, women's anger had to be eliminated if social order was to be kept, for it poses a threat to society far more dangerous than women's sexuality.[14]

Although boys' anger was accepted, girls' was repressed from a very early age, as happens with Jo's temper outbursts. In *Little Women,* with the repression of anger at home, the home is portrayed as a laboratory for society, not a shelter from it, a lesson Abba Alcott taught her daughters, despite her advanced ideas about women's education. Through Jo's raging temper, female anger occupies a predominant place in the narrative, as in *Jane Eyre.* If Jane Eyre has Bertha as her double for her anger, illustrating what might befall to women who give free reign to it, Jo has her mother, who instructs her to repress her anger just as she learned to control her own temper, very much like Louisa and Abba. Learning to control her anger and repress her too-quick tongue are just two of the lessons Jo must learn, for "much of the book must be read as a series of lessons designed to teach Jo the value of a more submissive spirit and to reveal to her the wisdom of the doctrines of renunciation and adaptation announced so clearly in the opening pages. Jo is constantly shown the nasty consequence of not following Marmee's model of selflessness and self-control." Jo needs to overcome her temper in order to become a dutiful wife and mother, as Marmee's example illustrates. By the close of the second part, Jo's rebel spirit has been quashed, anticipating the dull matron she becomes in the next two books.[15]

The repression of female anger that Alcott presented as a *fait accompli* is problematized and brought to the forefront in *March,* where Marmee is far from being a traditional or conventional mother: "perhaps one day I will be entrusted with daughters of my own, and if so, I swear I will not see their minds molded into society's simpering ideal of womanhood. Oh, how I would like to raise writers and artists to make the world acknowledge what women can do!" In *March* we see the process by which Marmee learned to control her own anger, prompted by her husband, who complains that "I could see that [John] Brown ignited the very part of my wife's spirit I wished to quench; the lawless, gypsy elements of her nature." He also speaks of her as "my voluble wife" or "this Fury of a wife," treating her as a child. This is another element borrowed from Bronson's biography, as he confided in his writings his frustration with both his wife and Louisa—"two devils, as yet, I am not quite divine enough to vanquish—the mother fiend and her daughter." But far from valuing her husband's "help" in reining off her temper, in *March* her husband teaches a very reluctant Marmee to be calmer.[16]

Although *March* was awarded the 2006 Pulitzer Prize for fiction, some critics resented Brooks's fiery portrait of Marmee, which was very different from Alcott's submissive Marmee, who defers to her husband's greater wisdom: "Brooks turns Mrs. March into a firebrand who excoriates Emerson for his timidity over slavery and whose full-throated admiration for John Brown leaves her husband jealous." This angry Marmee is not entirely a development of Brooks's, though, for in *Little Women* we learn that her current mildness is only the result of a long process to learn to control her fiery temper. In contrast to *Little Women*'s constant portrayal of Marmee's pride and happiness in having conquered her anger, in *March* Marmee resents their poverty because her husband did not ask her before investing their money and, once bankrupt, he withdrew from their creditors, forcing her to deal with them and beg for more credit. It is because of her treatment of Marmee's rage outbursts and her dissatisfaction with her husband's poor financial skills that Brooks's novel has been accused of presenting an unflattering portrayal of the March marriage in contrast to the example of domestic bliss in *Little Women*. A critic commented that "Mr. March comes across as weak-willed, naïve, a bit of a cad, and lacking common sense. And Marmee seems not only to be full of herself, but also ever-ready to pick a fight with anyone that crosses her."[17]

Despite Meg's assertion that "men have to work and women marry for money. It's a dreadfully unjust world," *Little Women* offers a far more complicated picture of gender roles. In contrast to the dominant nineteenth-century ideology that called for women being the angel in the house, secluded and protected from the outside world while reigning in the domestic sphere, Alcott saw how in her own household women were forced into the public world to provide for the family. Reflecting her family's peculiarities, despite *Little Women*'s endorsement of traditional values of domesticity and gender roles, the March marriage does not fully embrace the division of gender roles within the household: "Mrs. March is often sent out into the world while Mr. March remains in the house as counselor and guide for his troubled daughters and friends. He, like a sentimental mother, is immune from the pressures of the working world, whereas Mrs. March, whose struggle against anger is in fact a struggle against her resentment at being continually impoverished by her dreamy spouse, is charged with the work of keeping the family sound, fed, and healthy."[18] What is more, "it is Marmee the one who does all the things putatively ascribed to her husband; it is Marmee who always has the right word of comfort, love, and advice. Indeed, Beth's miraculous recovery is implicitly attributed to the fact that Marmee is merely on her way home." Where Alcott's Marmee does not utter any word of complaint about their financial situation (Amy is the one who bitterly bemoans their impoverishment), in *March* Marmee resents that "where he might retire to his study and be wafted off on some contemplation of the Oversoul, it was I who felt harassed at every hour by our indebtedness and demeaned by begging credit here and there; I who had to go hungry so that he and the girls might eat."[19]

The Marches' father is an ineffectual breadwinner, having driven his family to a delicate position because of his failed business deals. Aware of their father's shortcomings in providing for his wife and daughters, Amy feels confident that "Jo and I are going to make fortunes for you all. Just wait ten years, and see if we don't." Alcott's *Memoir* expressed the same feelings—"I will do something by-and-by. Don't care what, teach, sew, act, write, anything to help the family; and I'll be rich and famous and happy before I die, see if I won't!" Although her family does not take her literary pursuits too seriously (Alcott's literary encouragement from her family was exceptional), it is Jo who provides comforts for the family and pays the bills: "Jo enjoyed a taste of this satisfaction, and ceased to envy richer girls, taking great comfort in the knowledge that she could supply her own wants, and need ask no one for a penny." Jo soon realizes that her writings can provide financial stability to her family:

> the purpose which now took possession of her was a natural one to a poor and ambitious girl, but the means she took to gain her end were not the best. She saw that money conferred power, therefore, she resolved to have, not to be used for herself alone, but for those whom she loved more than life.
>
> The dream of filling home with comforts, giving Beth everything she wanted, from strawberries in winter to an organ in her bedroom, going abroad herself, and always having more than enough, so that she might indulge in the luxury of charity, had been for years Jo's most cherished castle in the air.[20]

Nevertheless, for a woman to go into the outside world, the price to pay involves risking her femininity. Jo's research into the darker aspects of humankind (albeit for the noble goal of writing sensation stories to support her family) leads her to a dangerous course: "she thought she was prospering finely, but unconsciously she was beginning to desecrate some of the womanliest attributes of a woman's character." The narrator's point of view about sensation stories is shared by Professor Bhaer, who declares that "I wish these papers did not come in the house. They are not for children to see, nor young people to read. It is not well, and I haf no patience with those who make this harm.... I do not think that good young girls should see such things. They are made pleasant to some, but I would more rather give my boys gunpowder to play with than this bad trash." Jo defends her stories with an economic argument, which Bhaer doesn't accept and which ultimately causes Jo to cease writing sensation stories. It is paradoxical, then, that a female author financially supporting her family and reaping the benefits of the success of the first part of *Little Women* would have Jo giving up her literary career on the grounds of a man's disapproval.[21]

Another paradox can be found concerning women's voting rights. The Alcotts and Louisa particularly were fierce supporters of a number of reform movements including educational reform, abolition, temperance, female suffrage, vegetarianism, health reform, women's rights, and domestic reform. These reformist ideas, however, are only subtly hinted at in the background of *Little Women*. Although Alcott was very active in the women's suffrage movement, she limited it to a single reference in her most popular work: "on her left were two matrons, with massive foreheads and bonnets to match, discussing Women's Rights and making tatting." Instead of advocating for granting women the right to vote, in *Little Women* the role of women in politics is very much in consonance with the Republican Motherhood ideals:

> this household happiness did not come all at once, but John and Meg had found the key to it, and each year of Married life taught them how to use it, unlocking the treasuries of real home love and mutual helpfulness.... This is the sort of shelf on which young wives and mothers may consent to be laid, safe from the restless fret and fever of the world, finding loyal lovers in the little sons and daughters who cling to them, undaunted by sorrow, poverty, or age, walking side by side, through fair and stormy weather, with a faithful friend, who is, in the true sense of the good old Saxon word, the "house-band," and learning, as Meg learned, that a woman's happiest kingdom is home, her highest honor the art of ruling it not as a queen, but as a wise wife and mother.[22]

According to the Republican Motherhood concept, it was not desirable for women to influence their policy-making husbands; instead, women's role was a didactic one, teaching their sons how to behave properly. Thus, women's influence on politics was more indirect and limited to the possibility of their sons being dutiful citizens and attending to their mothers' teachings. Denied a voice of their own in political affairs, women were assigned a task that was regarded as of crucial importance for the future of the newly-founded republic—being the mothers of future citizens. Accordingly, for Alcott,

> women work a good many miracles, and I have a persuasion that they may perform even that of raising the standard of manhood.... Let the boys be boys, the longer the better, and let the young men sow their wild oats if they must. But mothers, sisters, and friends may help to make the crop a small one, and keep many tares from spoiling the harvest, by believing, and showing that they believe, in the possibility of loyalty to the virtues which make men manliest in good women's eyes. If it is a feminine delusion, leave us to enjoy it while we may, for without it half the beauty and the romance of life is lost, and sorrowful foreboding would embitter all our hopes of the brave, tender-hearted little lads, who still love their mothers better than themselves and are not ashamed to own it.[23]

Moreover, Alcott also partook in contemporary trends that portrayed the American girl "as the visual and literary form to represent the values of the nation and codify the fears and desires of its citizens." And, yet, for all the importance attributed to the American girl, women's influence on society is to be performed only through men: "Amy's lecture did Laurie good, though, of course, he did not own it till long afterward. Men seldom do, for when women are the advisers, the lords of creation don't take the advice till they have persuaded themselves that it is just what they intended to do. Then they act upon it, and, if it succeeds, they give the weaker vessel half the credit of it. If it fails, they generously give her the whole."[24]

If Alcott gave Marmee a conventional veneer, Brooks restored the reformist strain of the Alcotts, and thus, whereas in *Little Women* Marmee concentrates all her energies on her daughters and charity, in *March* her two passions are "the education of our little women and the cause of abolition." Both are closely related and, "if Marmee had been ardent in her abolitionism before the birth of her children, their coming into our lives set her on fire." Her feelings are fueled because she sees women's situation as analogous to slaves'—"you stifle me! You crush me! You preach emancipation, and yet you enslave me." Actually, in the antebellum South "women and slaves were equally uneducated and suffered a situation of 'civil death' since white women were subjected to their husbands (or fathers) as were slaves. Many white women were certainly aware of this, up to the extent that they used the metaphors of bondage and slavery to refer to their own matrimonial circumstances."[25]

If Margaret Mitchell worried that people would find fault with *Gone with the Wind* because, despite its length (over 1,000 pages), only two and a half chapters dealt with the military conflict, in *Little Women* the war does not occupy much space either. While this very omission of the war is one of the reasons for *Little Women*'s enduring popularity and timelessness, it has made Young's claim that it is a war novel questionable. In *Little Women*, despite women's ardent declarations of patriotism, the war remains men's affair, as it is fought far away and has little impact on their daily lives. Even Mr. March's letters home are not too informative: "very few letters were written in those hard times that were not touching, especially those which fathers sent home. In this one little was said of the hardships endured, the dangers faced, or the homesickness conquered. It was a cheerful, hopeful letter, full of lively descriptions of camp life, marches, and military news, and only at the end did the writer's heart over-flow with fatherly love and longing for the little girls at home."[26]

March acknowledges the self-censorship that Mr. March shows in his correspondence: "I did not write of this, for.... I did not think the ears of my little women should be sullied with such things." However, by following him to the battlefield, Brooks restores the Civil War to being men's business and exposes the brutality of slavery in a series of flashbacks to his youth and days as a peddler in the antebellum South so as to vindicate abolitionism and explain the rationale behind Mr. March's involvement in the Civil War. He became an ardent advocate for abolitionism after witnessing how a mixed-race slave (the illegitimate daughter of the plantation owner by a slave woman), Grace, was brutally whipped in retaliation for her having been aware of March teaching another slave girl to read and write (a crime in the antebellum South). *March* also indicts the uselessness of war—"you cannot right injustice by injustice. You must not defame God by preaching that he wills young men to kill one another."[27]

Brooks carried the Marches' political involvement further than Alcott intended and has them as active participants in the abolitionist movement, sheltering fugitives through the Underground Railroad and financially backing up John Brown, whom the Alcotts deeply admired. In *Little Women* we only know that "Mr. March lost his property in trying to help an unfortunate friend" but in *March* we learn that it was as a consequence of his financial support of Brown's schemes.[28]

If in *Little Women* Mr. March's absence was justified because of his war activities, in the three other novels that Alcott wrote recounting the lives of the March sisters, *Good Wives* (1869), *Little Men* (1871), and *Jo's Boys* (1886), she repeatedly denied their father any prominent role. Actually, men in general "are noticeably absent within *Little Women* and the men that are present are feminised, foppish or old and therefore asexual." The March household is a feminine universe in which the few men around are secondary to the females. This was far from being unusual at the time, for although in the nineteenth century the existence of boys was necessary for courtship rituals, their actual presence was not required. Even the apparition of Laurie is an oddity for the March girls: "she liked the 'Laurence boy' better than ever and took several good looks at him, so that she might describe him to the girls, for they had no brothers, very few male cousins, and boys were almost unknown creatures to them." Social mores at the time restricted interaction between single people of different sexes to a limited number of events and always under the supervision of chaperones, resulting in girls living in an almost exclusively feminine universe where they bonded and developed strong ties with other girls, as happens to the four March sisters. As a consequence of this situation and because Laurie is a feminized young man, Jo is unable to consider him a prospective suitor or husband, seeing him as a brother, which helps explain the easy-going relationship he soon forges with the March girls and even with their mother.[29]

While Jo sees the war as a heroic adventure reserved to men (without even considering the possibility of volunteering as a nurse), Brooks, who "simply tried to add some darker adult resonances in the voids of [Alcott's] sparkling children's tale," portrays a much less flattering picture of the war. Despite its noble goal of freeing slaves, *March* shows that not all Union soldiers were in favor of emancipation and deals with "contraband," as freed slaves were called. This unflattering image is due to Brooks's desire not to present an idealized vision of the war. In her own words, "nations inevitably fall into the trap of romanticizing their militaries and are always astonished when the truth of awful atrocities is revealed, as it inevitably is in almost every war. There were plenty of hate-filled racists in Lincoln's army, fighting side by side with the celebrated idealists. March's growing dismay as he learns this in a way reflects my own journey to a more complete understanding." Moreover, despite Marmee's fervent support of the abolitionist cause and her admiration for John Brown, this is far from meaning that she agrees with the war. Upon her husband's departure, she reflects that "I am not alone in this. I only let him do to me what men have ever done to women: march off to empty glory and hollow acclaim and leave us behind to pick up the pieces."[30]

Despite Marmee's hopeful words that "Father's coming will settle everything," once he returns, Mr. March remains for the most part an absent father, even when he is physically at home:

> the war is over, and Mr. March safely at home, busy with his books and the small parish which found in him a minister by nature as by grace, a quiet, studious man, rich in the wisdom that is better than learning, the charity which calls all mankind "brother," the piety that blossoms into character, making it august and lovely. These attributes, in spite of poverty and the strict integrity which shut him out from the more worldly successes, attracted to him many admirable persons.... Earnest young men found the grey-headed scholar as young at heart as they, thoughtful or troubled women instinctively brought their doubts to him, sure of finding the gentlest sympathy, the wisest counsel. Sinners told their sins to the pure-hearted old man and were both rebuked and saved. Gifted men found a companion in him. Ambitious men caught glimpses of nobler ambitions than their own, and even worldlings confessed that his beliefs were beautiful and true, although "they wouldn't pay."

This is a path Laurie will also follow and in *Little Men* and *Jo's Boys* "he becomes like many fathers in nineteenth-century novels: an often absent provider." For Brooks, Mr. March's absence was Alcott's only way to cope with her father's singularity: "to read Bronson Alcott's journals and letters is to understand her difficulty: the truth about her father's character was far too odd and unorthodox to be shoehorned into an idealized, moralistic tale for Victorian children." His radical and unusual ideas about teaching, equality, social organization, and his inability to be a breadwinner all flew in the face of convention.[31]

Nonetheless, even despite his obvious flaws as household head, Alcott is not harsh in passing judgment against Mr. March, and Aunt March is the only one allowed to voice criticisms against his shortcomings as breadwinner—"March never had any stamina." On the contrary, Alcott strove to highlight the important role Mr. March fulfills despite his absence or his discreet presence: "to outsiders the five energetic women seemed to rule the house, and so they did in many things, but the quiet scholar, sitting among his books, was still the head of the family, the household conscience, anchor, and comforter, for to him the busy, anxious women always turned in troublous times, finding him, in the truest sense of those sacred words, husband and father." Although largely absent (be it at war, or secluded in his study), Father knows best, especially better than Marmee, and he is to exercise his correcting moral influence over her rather overindulgent educational methods:

> I seldom give advice unless I've proved its practicability. When you and Jo were little, I went on just as you are, feeling as if I didn't do my duty unless I devoted myself wholly to you. Poor Father took to his books, after I had refused all offers of help, and left me to try my experiment alone. I struggled along as well as I could, but Jo was too much for me. I nearly spoiled her by indulgence. You were poorly, and I worried about you till I fell sick myself. Then Father came to the rescue, quietly managed everything, and made himself so helpful that I saw my mistake, and never have been able to got on without him since. That is the secret of our home happiness.... Each do our part alone in many things, but at home we work together, always.

And yet, sometimes his very erudition and solemn character makes of him a figure of mockery: "Mr. March mildly observed, 'salad was one of the favourite dishes of the ancients, and Evelyn....' Here a general explosion of laughter cut short the 'history of salads,' to the great surprise of the learned gentleman."[32]

While Brooks replicated the failure of Bronson's revolutionary educative methods when Mr. March's teaching a slave girl to read only results in a punishment for Grace for being his accomplice, Alcott paid homage to her father's pedagogy in her writings. Jo and Professor Bhaer's school, Plumfield, and the teaching techniques they employ are heavily indebted to Bronson's Temple School. Additionally, Professor Bhaer's peculiar way of correcting his students, by having them hit his hand with a ruler (instead of the usual practice of hitting students), comes from a corrective employed by Bronson. Mr. March's teaching methods with his grandson Demi are similar to Bronson's, too, while Marmee shares Bronson's abhorrence for corporal punishment.[33]

The Civil War in literature has commonly become a trope for internal conflict and in *Little Women*, with the actual war given a limited role, it is used to signify "the conflict between its overt messages and its covert messages." Because the Civil War caused a "profound sweeping social upheaval and gender role reversals in the North and South [which] deeply affected Alcott's literary life," in *Little Women* the war is used to embody Alcott's life-long gender crisis, echoed in Jo's internal conflict. Despite the war's profound and everlasting effect on Alcott's literary production, life and health, in *Little Women* the war's drama is confined to "translating the pathos of the dying male soldier into that of the dying little sister." Because, very early on, literature began to re-imagine and reinterpret the Civil War as "a whites-only" event, "feminized war literature [had to] insist on the importance of women's contributions to the war effort, but increasingly it argued that women's homefront sufferings were equal to, or even greater than, those of men in battle." During the war and afterwards, there appeared "a wide-ranging popular wartime literature that explored white women's domestic war experiences, imagining them as a source of self-knowledge, an education in patriotism, an initiation into the values of work, the occasion for romance, and, increasingly, the cause of unbearable anguish." In *Little Women*, in spite of the ongoing war, it is telling that Beth's death is the only war casualty.[34]

Despite Jo's professions that "don't I wish I could be a drummer, a vivan—what's its name? Or a nurse, so I could be near him and help [Papa]," her war efforts are quite limited. Jo's words resemble Alcott's in her *Journal:* "I long to be a man; but as I can't fight, I will content myself with working for those who can'" but, despite Jo's claims that "I'm dying to go and fight with Papa. And I can only stay home and knit, like a poky old woman!" her war contribution pales in comparison to men's efforts. Songs, sermons, short stories and novels written during the Civil War all stressed that women's contribution to the war effort was essential if victory was to be achieved. However, in *Little Women,* while girls still have to make small sacrifices for the war effort (Marmee "thinks we ought not to spend money for pleasure, when our men are suffering so in the army"), these are minimal in contrast to the ones undertaken by the author herself, who briefly served as a nurse on the Union lines and volunteered "in Soldiers' Aid Societies, abolitionist organizations, and the Boston auxiliary of the United States Sanitary Commission." Alcott's activities constituted "an assertion of such competence and freedom, the womanly equivalent to taking up arms" but the March sisters did not devote their time to female war-related occupations.[35]

Mr. March, an idealist, sees with distress how men are as bad and racist in any army. Nevertheless, for all the insight Brooks's novel provides into Mr. March's mind, because male ideals and noble ideas do not hold in the face of the brutality of the war, *March* ultimately agrees with *Little Women*'s revolutionary and feminine message of "training the male citizenry of the postwar nation by making a country of little women."[36]

Chapter 7

Last Night I Dreamt I Saw Rebecca Again

Lesbianism, Female Sexuality and Motherhood in *Rebecca* by Daphne du Maurier, *Mrs. de Winter* by Susan Hill and *Rebecca's Tale* by Sally Beauman

> Last night I dreamt I went to Manderley again. It seemed to me I stood by the iron gate leading to the drive, and for a while I could not enter. **Daphne du Maurier: opening lines of *Rebecca* (1938)**

> The undertakers' men were like crows, stiff and black, and the cars were blacklined up beside the path that led to the church; and we, too, were black, as we stood in our pathetic, awkward group waiting for them to lift out the coffin and shoulder it, and for the clergyman to arrange himself; and he was another black crow, in his long cloak. **Susan Hill: opening line of *Mrs. de Winter* (1993)**

> Last night I dreamt I went to Manderley again. **Sally Beauman: opening line of *Rebecca's Tale* (2001)**

"Last night I dreamt I went to Manderley again," begins Daphne du Maurier's most well-known novel, *Rebecca* (1938), and never has a house burned down to ashes been more famously re-visited. The opening is perfect not only from a formal point of view with "its deceptively simple structure (metrically speaking, it is in fact a perfect alexandrine—six successive iambic feet, the stress falling on every second syllable)" but also because of the power of evocation and appeal it has conjured in several generations of readers. For all of the narrator's assurances that "the house was a sepulchre, our fear and suffering lay buried in the ruins. There would be no resurrection," this soon proves to be wishful thinking, since the house comes to life over and over again. Certainly the house is a sepulcher, for it is the abode of the dead Rebecca, who has kept her presence in the house so pervasive and dominant that she cannot be replaced, as her boat's name, "Je Reviens" (I return), advanced. Despite being the house of a dead woman, Manderley is so alive that it is brought back to life not only in *Rebecca* but in its two authorized sequels, *Mrs. de Winter* (1993) by Susan Hill and *Rebecca's Tale* (2001) by Sally Beauman.[1]

"A reader is not a tabula rasa. Even before we pick up a book, we need to know, among other things, certain reading conventions—using the term to refer not to plot formulas but rather to rules that regulate the reader's operations on the text"; accordingly, based on our common-sense knowledge as readers, upon beginning *Rebecca*, we might assume that the Rebecca of the title is the narrator and protagonist of the novel—wrongly, as it soon turns out. The narrator is certainly not Rebecca for Rebecca is already dead by the time the novel begins. What is more, the narrator, despite the pervasive influence of Rebecca, never met Rebecca and never sees a photograph or portrait of Rebecca.[2] Despite the narrator's claims to the contrary, "the more she tries to control her own life, tell her own story, the more she is brought back to Rebecca who has disrupted and defined both. It is Rebecca who is the named subject of the novel, she who dictates its movement, pushes epilogue to prologue, and structures the impossibility of its ending."[3]

Far from being the narrator, Rebecca is the late Mrs. de Winter whereas the narrator is the second Mrs. de Winter, who goes to Manderley as a young bride overawed by the magnificence of the house and the overbearing presence of her predecessor. In contrast to Rebecca's dominant personality, "[Mrs. de Winter] was like a guest, biding [her] time, waiting for the return of the hostess." This Manderley the narrator revisits in her dreams is the house of the Rebecca of the title and, just like the house continues to haunt the narrator, Rebecca's grip on her never ends. For all of the narrator's assurances that "when I thought of Manderley in my waking hours I would not be bitter ... all of us have our particular devil who rides us and torments us.... We have conquered ours," this is evidently not the case. A strong name, Rebecca "includes the suggestion of a revenant: *Re*becca, who comes again, who *beckons* again." Coming from the Hebrew "noose," it poses a threat, all the more powerful because "Rebecca would never grow old. Rebecca would always be the same. And her I could not fight. She was too strong for me." Although Freud identified ghosts as a way for the living to cope with the grief for the death of a loved one, in the case of *Rebecca*, her ghost is rather an impediment for the living to move on with their lives.[4]

At the beginning of *Rebecca*, the narrator and her husband, whose names or identities we ignore, are exiled in continental Europe from Manderley, their former English home. Although the narrator claims that they are never going back to Manderley, the novel is nothing but a testimony of the past, a way to return, in a mental sense, to a place whose destruction has prevented their going back in a physical sense. Manderley, the impossible, the prohibited, is more powerful than their current, placid life. The narrator's need to go back is propelled by the very human need to make sense of the past. But if the biblical Rebecca was turned into a salt statue for looking back, here the ones looking back are the living, not Rebecca. As a result, *Rebecca* "as a whole is about dreams and nightmares, about desire and the repression of desire, about memory and forgetting, about compulsive repetition, about love of place and homesickness."[5]

Homesickness was a central force in both *Rebecca* and in the writing process that led to its very creation. Then living in Alexandria with her husband, Frederick "Boy" Browning (whom she called Tommy), du Maurier missed her homeland, where her two young children had stayed. Her nostalgia led her to write a novel in which the characters longed for a lost house, much as she longed for England. The parallelisms do not end here, for *Rebecca* is at many levels indebted to du Maurier's own life, whose apprehensions and concerns she extrapolated to the second Mrs. de Winter. Two of the main anxieties plaguing du Maurier were jealousy and insecurity, feelings aggravated after finding out that her husband had had affairs with several women before their marriage, including a fiancée, Jan Recardo, whose love letters du Maurier discovered (very much like the young Mrs. de Winter finds Rebecca's handwriting everywhere). Recardo, who committed suicide by throwing herself in front of a train, became the inspiration for Rebecca, a dead woman who continues to disturb the living. Du Maurier also found inspiration in a story she was told about a man who had divorced his wife and remarried a younger woman, which made her wonder "if she had been jealous of the first wife, as I would have been jealous if my Tommy had been married before he married me. He had been engaged once ... perhaps she would have been better at dinners and cocktail parties than I could ever be."[6]

Rebecca, although dead by the beginning of *Rebecca*, is very much alive and present in the lives and minds of those who inhabit Manderley. For Mrs. Danvers, the housekeeper who cherishes Rebecca's memory and keeps her rooms intact, she is still the true owner of the house, and on a daily basis the household is still run according to her organizational skills and preferences. For the young Mrs. de Winter, Rebecca is a menace, a threatening presence, the lover with whom her husband is unfaithful to her. She believes that "he doesn't love me, he loves Rebecca.... He's never forgotten her, he thinks about her still, night and day. He's never loved me.... It's always Rebecca, Rebecca." Rebecca seems to be haunting Maxim de Winter, who, his new wife believes, still remembers and treasures her memory constantly, comparing her to his new wife's inexperience and lack of *savoir faire*, despite his constant assertions to the contrary: "something happened a year ago that altered my whole life, and I want to forget every phase in my existence up to that time. Those days are finished. They are blotted out. I must begin living all over again.... When we climbed the hills and looked down over the precipice. I was there some years ago, with my wife.... You have blotted out the past for me."[7]

The shadow cast by the first wife on the second is hardly a new topic in literature, but du Maurier managed to offer a fresh take on it. Although *Rebecca* might at first resemble the conventional story of the poor girl who marries the rich man, this is not the case since there is no "happily ever after" after their marriage. Accordingly, "unlike traditional romance narratives, the movement from girlhood to womanhood, from sexual naiveté to sentience, does not appear to occur naturally once the heroine marries the hero. *Rebecca* starts where most narratives leave off—the marriage of the central female character. Thus, we must suffer through the difficult transition from adolescent insecurity to a more confident adult identity along with the narrator." *Rebecca* takes inspiration from many sources—*Jane Eyre*, the Gothic romance, fairy tales and romances. Because du Maurier had already tried her hand at Gothic plots with *Jamaica Inn* (1936), we find a series of Gothic features and conventions in the novel—the haunted house, the helpless and innocent heroine, the dark hero, a mysterious landscape, a past murder, passion, a touch of the supernatural, the other woman, a mystery, a ghost-like atmosphere, the weather matching characters' feelings or actions, and a certain violence right beneath the surface about to explode. In *Rebecca*, du Maurier wisely subverts and plays with the conventions of the Gothic genre—contrary to traditional Gothic tales' heroines who are under a severe threat to their life or sanity, *Rebecca*'s narrator is certainly not. The protagonist is a poor orphan, with nobody to take care of her, but neither her life nor her virtue is threatened. Her employer, Mrs. Van Hopper, fastidious as she can be, is a sort of surrogate mother figure (perhaps stepmother) for her, taking care that she behaves properly. Far from being tyrannically enslaved, the protagonist has time to take tennis lessons while in Monte Carlo and Mrs. Van Hopper encourages her to meet young men once they arrive in New York. It is the protagonist's natural, insurmountable shyness that makes her uneasy in social gatherings, not that Mrs. Van Hopper is evil to her.[8]

Even though Mrs. Van Hopper claims that Manderley is like "fairyland," *Rebecca* is not a conventional fairy tale in which the couple lives happily ever after following the wedding, and the "prince in shining armor," far from that, is more of the dark, Gothic hero. Maxim strongly resembles a Gothic hero—he is the handsome man in love with the protagonist but whose happiness is ruined by the secret he conceals from everyone, especially from the heroine, who is often misled to misinterpret the hero's mysterious ways as disinterest or even hatred.[9] In spite of the narrator's attempts to read her courtship and marriage as a love story, she soon realizes that it fails to conform to the standards set up by romance novels, with Mrs. Van Hopper warning her that "you don't flatter yourself he's in love with you, do you? He's lonely, he can't bear that great empty house."[10]

So unromantic is the book that the protagonist herself is misled to believe that Maxim is only proposing out of sheer kindness. Maxim de Winter certainly does not behave like the man who has suddenly fallen in love. His proposal is not very romantic and does not conform to the protagonist's high literary expectations: "I'm asking you to marry me, you little fool," he tells her. Maxim, too, is aware that "I'm being rather a brute to you, aren't I?... This isn't your idea of a proposal. We ought to be in a conservatory, you in a white frock with a rose in your hand, and a violin playing a waltz in the distance." For his soon-to-be bride, "it was as though the King asked one. It did not ring true. And he went on eating his marmalade as though everything were natural. In books men knelt to women, and it would be moonlight." Yet, in her infatuation with Maxim, she accepts a simple wedding, finding comfort in the thought that "that was what people would say. It was all very sudden and romantic. They suddenly decided to get married and there it was. Such an adventure" although she is still capable of realizing that "he had not said anything yet about being in love." This stands in marked contrast to her passionate later profession of love—"you know I love you more than anything in the world. There has never been anyone but you. You are my father and my brother and my son."[11]

Rebecca is rich in literary echoes. In playing with the conventions of the happily ever after ending in fairy tales, du Maurier recreated the fairy tale of "Bluebeard," whose young bride discovers that her husband has killed his other wives. In *Rebecca*, Maxim is the murderer of his first wife but this revelation, far from filling the narrator with horror, comes as a relief. For the narrator, it confirms that he never loved Rebecca but hated her so much he killed her. Some critics have also noted connections with

> Le Fanu's "Carmilla" ... published in 1872, ... a picture which appears to "come to life." An old family portrait of one "Marcia Karnstein," once restored by a local picture-cleaner, reveals a portrait of Mircalla, Countess Karnstein, painted in 1698. She is "the effigy of Carmilla," to the astonishment of Laura, who also recognises her own family likeness to the portrait.... What Laura "sees" in the portrait of Countess Karnstein, of course, is arguably the "unspoken" of patriarchal culture: she glimpses evidence of the maternal line's ghostly resurrection in the face of what Irigaray has diagnosed as Western society's cultural dynamic of matricide, made manifest in the obliteration of maternal genealogy. What she also sees is a woman she desires, in so far as the portrait bears an uncanny resemblance to the young house guest, Carmilla.[12]

Rebecca has for long been regarded as a twentieth-century rewriting of the *Jane Eyre* romantic subplot—young, innocent maiden meets her prince charming but he turns out to be not so charming because of the pervasive presence of his first wife (alive in the case of Rochester's, dead but definitely not at rest in the case of Maxim de Winter's). If Rochester's Thornfield Hall is burned down by his mad wife, Manderley is destroyed by the wife's mad companion. Crippled and with his house and social standing gone, Rochester became Jane Eyre's social equal, inasmuch as a marriage between them as equals was possible. The burning and the death of his first wife thus removed all the impediments for their marriage. But is the burning of Manderley a positive outcome? Critics have debated whether it is positive (Rebecca is such an overbearing presence in the house that it is hard to believe they could live happily ever after there) or not (since it forces them into exile). Probably the key is in du Maurier's intended ending, where she had the couple maimed. The original ending of *Rebecca* was closer to that of *Jane Eyre*—Henry de Winter and his second wife ended up in exile, crippled as a result of a car accident on their way back to Manderley from London after meeting Rebecca's doctor.[13] Yet, for Jackson, despite these similarities, "the poor little anonymous narrator of *Rebecca* lacks the strength and conviction of *Jane Eyre*'s titular heroine. Du Maurier's is a darker novel than Bronte's and her protagonist's final victory is dubious at best. While both novels have gothic elements, *Jane Eyre* strives for realism; *Rebecca* is a sinister fairy tale, with its melodrama and stilted, exaggerated characters."[14]

Maxim's relationship with both of his wives is largely determined by sexuality. At first, "he pursues the narrator precisely because of her difference from Rebecca and because her boyish lack of sexuality poses little threat to his fragile identity." But Rebecca stands between them: "in the traditional female Gothic plot, it is other women who must die or otherwise be removed in order to facilitate the heroine's happiness. These figures, as Bertha Mason in *Jane Eyre*, often embody a dangerous, threatening aspect of the female condition that the heroine must learn to shun before being rewarded with marriage. That is, she must learn to separate herself from threatening, unregulated female passions (not only sexuality but rage as well)." That Rebecca is dead, far from making things any easier, only complicates matters further—how to fight an absent and seemingly perfect adversary? Once in Manderley, Maxim's aloofness and strangeness bedazzle his new wife but rather than trying to get to know her husband better, she wants to know what Rebecca was like in order to become a better wife. It is manifest that Rebecca and the narrator pose two diametrically different conceptions of womanhood and sexuality.[15]

In *Rebecca*, the protagonist will only have a true marriage once she learns that Maxim never loved Rebecca and killed her after she told him she was pregnant with another man's child. The catalyst of Maxim's confession is the imminent discovery of Rebecca's corpse—ironically, it brings about the truth about his first marriage and the possibility of sending him to prison as well. Previous hints that Rebecca was not so well liked by everybody had been lost on the narrator, who is totally absorbed in the fiction of Rebecca as the perfect wife and hostess. She misinterprets her in-laws' reluctance to visit Manderley during Rebecca's life (in contrast to their quick befriending of her) or Frank Crawley's assertion that "I don't know very much about women ... but I should say kindliness, and sincerity, and ... modesty—are worth far more to a man, to a husband, than all the wit and beauty in the world." The power that Rebecca had on the narrator on the grounds of Maxim's devoted love to Rebecca (as the narrator wrongly believes) vanishes with his confession that "Rebecca was not drowned at all. I killed her. I shot Rebecca in the cottage in the cove." It is only after this that he can say express his love for his second wife. The revelation of the truth makes the narrator grow up and give up childhood and, far from being horrified by the fact that her husband is an uxoricide (or that his only remorse is his second wife's loss of innocence, not the loss of Rebecca's life), she identifies with him completely. For the narrator, Rebecca now truly dies—"I did not hate her any more. Now that I knew her to have been evil and vicious and rotten I did not hate her any more.... Her body had come back, but I was free of her forever."[16]

Maxim's hatred for Rebecca and his love for his second wife testify to both his revulsion at unregulated female sexuality and his endorsement of conventional female sexuality, as personified by his two wives. Because of Rebecca, Maxim

> has lost faith in the authenticity of the constructed identity that the narrator and perhaps the reader alike expect him to find alluring. As we later learn and perhaps suspect all along, the ideal of Rebecca as perfect wife has been a carefully crafted fantasy. Through her private rejection of marriage tenets and her participation in extramarital sexual relations with, some assume, both men and women, Rebecca openly mocks the belief in a primary or stable gender identity that is presented by her very public performance of a proper woman.

Until the discovery of Rebecca's true self, Maxim and his second wife's expressions of love had been formal—"he had kissed me too, a natural business, comforting and quiet. Not dramatic as in books," almost like those to a pet: "he stroked my hand absently, not thinking, talking to Beatrice. 'That's what I do to Jasper [the dog].... He likes me in the way I like Jasper.'" Theirs had so far been an asexual marriage in which "representations of passion and erotic charge are confined to Rebecca who, problematically for the narrative in terms of gender, activates and inspires sexual interest. The failure to construct a heterosexuality that is passionate leaves open the interpretations of the paradigm of sexuality/gender." They will only be passionate once he has been acquitted—"we began to kiss one another, feverishly, desperately, like guilty lovers who have not kissed before."[17]

Because of the narrator's attempts at emulating Rebecca, "what makes the narrator's transformation possible is Maxim's certification of the hitherto envied Rebecca's deviancy from proper womanhood." In this outcome, Rebecca "is the character through whom the fiction of romance is undermined and whose murder will rescue and re-establish its norms." Because she is "associated with adultery, deceit, degeneracy, lesbianism at the plot level and with Jewishness, vampirism and a polymorphous sexuality at the level of metaphor, Rebecca clearly functions as a figure of abjection in the novel." And yet, she is not an utterly deplorable character:

> she also had an amazing gift of being attractive to everyone; to men, to women, to children, relatives, dogs and casual acquaintances. Or that, although Scarlett O'Hara "was not beautiful," men "seldom realized it, when caught by her charm as the Tarleton twins were." Regardless of their manifest lack of certain ideally feminine virtues, by making Rebecca and Scarlett seem both naturally and artificially and *always* exceptionally attractive to men, Daphne du Maurier and Margaret Mitchell make them interesting and enviable to most women.[18]

Sequels are born out of a perceived absence in the original work—a character left unexplored, an unsatisfactory or too open ending, plotlines not conveniently explained, and characters' past lives being unexplored. For Watson, *Rebecca* paves the way for a sequel for three reasons:

> First *Rebecca* disappointingly refuses to provide the expected romance ending. In common with the other blockbuster of its decade, Margaret Mitchell's *Gone with the Wind* (1936), however, *Rebecca* signally fails to deliver happy heterosexual romance with its conventional promise of domesticity and procreation. Second, *Rebecca* is based, ... on substitution and repetition. There is no real reason that the narrator should not give way again to her obsession about Rebecca, since it is clear that her marriage remains fundamentally unsatisfactory. Such repetition could carry on in Rebecca's obsessive fashion. Third, the novel as a whole is organized as an investigation into the mystery of Rebecca herself; structurally, the reader—along with the narrator—is dripped revelations about the dead woman.[19]

Because of the long shadow Rebecca casts, *Rebecca* and its two sequels go back to the past. *Rebecca* is a long flashback, seen from the "safe" present that Mr. and Mrs. de Winter enjoy abroad; *Mrs. de Winter* has the second wife, alone, remembering the events that took them back to England, and finally *Rebecca's Tale*, although covering past events missing in *Rebecca* and which date back to 1931, opens in 1951, that is, the twentieth anniversary of Rebecca's death, to do an exercise of memory. Even though the second Mrs. de Winter thought that returning was no longer possible, over and over again, in all three novels, we always go back to Manderley.

Mrs. de Winter and *Rebecca's Tale*, like *Scarlett* or *Rhett Butler's People* to *Gone with the Wind*, constitute a special case of literary rewritings in that all were commissioned by the heirs of a late writer. Du Maurier died in 1987, leaving many questions about her masterpiece unanswered. Although *The Rebecca Notebook*, a compilation of the notes she took during the writing process, was supposed to answer these questions, it did not really solve all the enigmas and much still remained shrouded in mystery. In 1990 Susan Hill, who had already tried her hand at the Gothic genre with *The Woman in Black*, was unexpectedly commissioned by the du Maurier estate, in the hands of her three children, to write a sequel.[20]

In having the de Winters eventually return to England, Hill was altering du Maurier's intended meaning. Not only had du Maurier put the de Winters in exile abroad at the end of *Rebecca*, what is more, in her original *Rebecca* epilogue, the de Winters had resolved never to return to England: "we shall never live in England again, that much is certain. The past would be too close to us. Those things we are trying to forget and put behind us would stir again, and that sense of fear, of furtive unrest struggling at length to master unreasoning panic—now mercifully stilled, thank God—might in some manner unforeseen become a living companion, as did before." Even worse, preventing any plan to return home, as was already dreaded in *Rebecca*, "this summer Manderley opens as a country club."[21]

Hill's story began immediately after the end of the Second World War, with Maxim and his second wife living in their self-imposed exile to explore "two features of the original—the narrator's unacknowledged fear of and anger at the husband, and Maxim's guilt as a murderer." After twelve years abroad, they are still afraid of being recognized. Their exile is not only physical, but also psychological for Maxim often retreats to his own private world, leaving his wife out. He constantly strives to leave the past behind and not remember anything, with his wife helping him to achieve it, living quietly and anonymously. However, she longs to return to England even if she no longer dares to speak to Maxim about her secret longing—to have children.[22]

For the second wife, being alive is her vengeance on Rebecca—they are alive while Rebecca is long dead and buried in Manderley's crypt. Yet, she knows she is obsessed with Manderley even if she was unhappy there. Problems arise when the idea that her husband is a murderer begins to jump into her mind from time to time. At night, fears prey on her mind and she blames herself for not letting the ghosts rest and bringing them back. Eventually, they return to England, where they live quite happily until the second wife accidentally runs into Jack Favell, who then begins to blackmail her. The return of the past, in the form of a visit from Mrs. Danvers, puts another nail in the coffin and ends with Maxim driving at night to Manderley and dying in a car accident.[23]

For Watson, "*Mrs de Winter* perhaps registers the increasing ability of women to express scepticism about the condition of modern marriage," a topic that would be more thoroughly explored by Beauman. For Hill, "*Rebecca* is a novel of power and atmosphere. It is about obsession. It is about evil and its power and about the influence and hold of the past over us in the present. It is about vulnerability and loss, about fear, about death. It is a ghost story and a detective story." Consequently, what she tried to do in *Mrs. de Winter* was not to recover the past but to show how the past can still contaminate the present. Although Beauman's is also a commissioned sequel, Hill's and Beauman's respective approaches to *Rebecca* are altogether different. Hill did purposefully not want to include elements or themes that would have complicated and altered our reading of *Rebecca*: "I believe very firmly that no reader should of course have to read a sequel and that I would not do anything in my novel that retrospectively affected anything Daphne du Maurier already had done. So that the reader reading *Mrs de Winter* would not then go back to Rebecca and find that, after what I had done the characters in the future, the past was altered."[24]

In contrast, Beauman made a point of filling in missing information she found implicit in *Rebecca*. "Last night I dreamt I went to Manderley again," opens Beauman's *Rebecca's Tale*. However, although her novel begins with the very same sentence as *Rebecca*, all similarities end there. In this case, Rebecca is a character in a nightmare and this dreamer is not the second wife but Colonel Julyan, thus challenging our expectations. This will be only the first time our expectations are shattered in that Beauman's approach to sequel writing was entirely different from Hill's.[25]

One of the weaknesses of *Rebecca* was that, although Rebecca was very much present in the minds of those who loved and hated her and her presence in the house is almost another dweller, the real Rebecca is missing. Because in *Rebecca* we sympathize with the murderer of an evil woman with no redeeming features, *Rebecca's Tale* tries to introduce some grey shadows into the black-and-white picture presented in *Rebecca*. Because "recalled through others' memories, never in flashback as perceptual evidence, Rebecca is intimately tied to the fictionality of desire, always in the process of construction for the reader, recalled 'through the eyes' of a number of characters," Beauman wrote Rebecca's side of the story to recover her as a living woman. Beauman's point was that "there was never a trial, so no advocate ever spoke for Rebecca. She's been condemned to silence for twenty years. She can't defend herself or correct the lies. Could I perform that service for Rebecca?" Beauman envisaged her novel as performing a task similar to Jean Rhys's *Wide Sargasso Sea* in that she was also recovering the early life of the first wife.[26]

The obvious heroine of *Rebecca* is the narrator, as Rebecca is dead and a thoroughly despicable character. Nevertheless, according to Beauman's reading of *Rebecca*, du Maurier's true heroine was Rebecca, not the unnamed second Mrs. de Winter, but du Maurier, writing in the thirties, could not show her preference for Rebecca too obviously because of social conventions and moral concerns about the sexual propriety of women. For Beauman,

> in Mrs. de Winter, the famously "anonymous" second wife who tells the story, she created the first unreliable narrator in popular fiction. De Winter is a narrator so convincing and so persuasive that most readers never look beyond the gaucheries of her prose, and never notice the devices du Maurier uses to undermine it. Certainly, reviewers leapt to the assumption that the narrator's views and the author's were one and the same. Examine *Rebecca* closely, and you begin to see how wrong they were. The novel may seem to celebrate the sweet "feminine" virtues embodied in the second Mrs. de Winter—obedience, modesty, sexual inexperience, naivety, a willingness to conform to male ideas as to suitable female or wifely behaviour—but does it actually do that? No. The woman who rises triumphant from the novel is Rebecca, the disobedient and profoundly transgressive first wife.

The unreliability of the second wife is a key point for Beauman, who claims that

> there's a clear assumption that the first readers of *Rebecca* must have made which is a very dangerous and strange one. I've never read a single thing that was written about the book at the time of publication which pointed out that the second wife is prepared completely to accept what her husband tells her about her predecessor, and to assume that because he says his first wife was promiscuous, the murder was justified and it is all right for her to give him her support. Nobody questioned it. The book was marketed by Gollancz as "an exquisite love story," and in a way it is. But du Maurier is a dark author. There are elements of Bluebeard here, and if you reread the novel, you can see that du Maurier is pointing it up.

Add to this Beauman's interest in exploring feminism in popular literary works and we have *Rebecca's Tale*.[27]

Beauman's developments were regarded as consistent with *Rebecca*—"*Rebecca's Tale* is the story that du Maurier hinted at but never explicitly told." Beauman also kept up with the developments introduced by Hill, which is not always the case when we have several sequels to the same work. A particular strength of *Rebecca's Tale* is that "cannily assuming that buyers of *Rebecca's Tale* would not only be familiar with du Maurier's text and perhaps with *The Rebecca Notebook* but also with Hitchcock's film, and more especially with Hill's *Mrs. de Winter*, she scrupulously incorporated these intertexts into her story as part of the parent text." In Beauman's work, following Maxim's death on his way to Manderley, the second Mrs. de Winter has moved to Canada, and all attempts to contact her are prevented by her lawyers.[28]

If Beauman believed that *Rebecca* was a study on an unreliable first-person narrator, in *Rebecca's Tale* she follows the same pattern and has three different characters, Colonel Julyan, Terence Grey, and Ellie Julyan. The three of them produce first-hand, written accounts which are unreliable up to a certain point. Each of these stories provide a new perspective on who Rebecca was. Characters' differing opinions of what Rebecca was really like contribute to defy the second wife's version, as stated in *Rebecca* and continued in *Mrs. de Winter*.

Colonel Julyan's version is the first one in the book and it passes as the "official" account since he was the local magistrate at the time of Rebecca's death. Also, he was a life-long friend of Maxim, whom he had tutored as a child, and was infatuated with Rebecca, whom he claims to have known better than most people. These are his qualifications to support his conviction that he is the most appropriate one to find out what had happened at Manderley. Acknowledging "the power she would come to exert in my life and my imagination," it is his resolve to tell the truth at last. The second account is penned by Terence Grey, who first shows up in Kerrith, the closest town to Manderley, as a young historian who has accepted a part-time job as archivist and cataloguer at the local library, a job that consists of cataloguing the de Winter papers donated by the second Mrs. de Winter.[29]

Rebecca's story, Rebecca's tale, is the third section of the book, the notebook that Rebecca writes for the child she believes is growing inside her (although actually she suffers from cancer). Rebecca presents herself as a person with suicidal tendencies who attempted to kill herself after her father's death but now wants to get Maxim to kill her. Not only will Rebecca become a ghost—she also sees ghosts, and she even sees the ghost of the second wife, whom she kisses, thus advancing the lesbian undertones of the relationship of Mrs. Danvers (as a surrogate for Rebecca and keeper of Rebecca's memory) and the second wife in *Rebecca*. If *Rebecca* at times echoes *Jane Eyre*, *Rebecca's Tale* at times echoes *Wide Sargasso Sea*. Just like, at the end of *Wide Sargasso Sea*, Bertha Mason sees the ghost of Jane Eyre, Rebecca sees the ghost of the second Mrs. de Winter.[30]

Ellie Julyan, the spinster daughter of the colonel, who gave up a college scholarship to stay at home to take care of her elderly parents, has been influenced by her father's fascination with Rebecca all her life. As a child (she was eleven at the time of Rebecca's death), Ellie saw many instances of her father making a fool of himself because of his admiration for Rebecca, which were even more painful for his wife. The sudden return of the second wife provides yet another insight into Rebecca. The second wife puts forward her own opinion of Rebecca:

> it was me Maxim loved, not Rebecca. She claims she made herself so memorable—but once Maxim and I left this place, he rarely thought of her.... Rebecca was childish, that's what I've decided ... she never really grew up, not emotionally. She even writes in a childish way.... I think it's *very* childish. It's just like some silly fairy tale, with curses and ogres. I was surprised by that. I'd expected her to be sophisticated.... She can't have been at all normal, can she, to behave as she did, or write as she did? I can see why she made Maxim so miserable; he was a man of such high principles—and she had no principles at all.... She was *childish*. Infantile. I was quite disappointed in her. She wasn't *nearly* as interesting as I'd imagined her to be.... I decided she was really rather pathetic, writing to some fantasy child, when all the time she was barren.... She was barren in many ways, I think—barren of normal affections. Not warm-hearted. Not womanly. Once I realised that, I felt so much better, so much stronger.... Maxim could never have loved her.[31]

Rebecca is thus seen by an admirer, by a historian searching for a truth that comes too close to home for historical rigor sometimes (he suspects he might be Rebecca's illegitimate child but he turns out to be Rebecca's mother's love child, put up for adoption because their mother died in childbirth), by herself, by Ellie, whose father's obsession with Rebecca has had a permanent effect on her life, and by a rival woman such as the second Mrs. de Winter.

Rebecca is, in a way, a warning for the second wife—"they function in the same way that Rochester's first wife functions as a vision of Jane Eyre's future, since Jane sees the madwoman in the attic on the eve of her wedding," but one which she chose not to listen to. However, for Ellie, at the end of the novel, Rebecca certainly is a role model, teaching her a valuable lesson: that being a wife might not be the best option and that marriage comes with a high price for women—their freedom. Ellie's fear of becoming a dull wife like the second wife prompts her to turn down the local doctor's marriage proposal in order to be free; contrary to the second wife, the lesson she has learned from Rebecca is how to handle men. With these role models, Ellie decides to break free from social conventions or her father's wishes and go to Cambridge, as she has always wanted to do, to pursue an education for herself. This is not such a shocking departure from *Rebecca* as it might seem at first, given that the limitations that marriage imposes upon women is not a topic foreign to du Maurier's literary production. In *Rebecca, Frenchman's Creek* and *Jamaica Inn,* "like her male protagonists, the women of these novels are trapped and passive; but unlike men, they do not have the counterbalancing social power to make their stories either interesting or resonant."[32]

Reviewers found Beauman's novel a good match to du Maurier's mastery, with critic Linda Grant giving Beauman the upper hand—"while both du Maurier and Beauman are great storytellers, Beauman really is the better prose writer." If *Rebecca* is a modern rewriting of *Jane Eyre,* some have seen in *Rebecca's Tale* echoes of such different voices as Shakespeare, Emily Brontë and the Grimm Brothers. Beauman also made use of du Maurier's biography: Rebecca and her mother worked for a while in a dramatic troupe, a hint to du Maurier's own life, as her parents were both actors. Acting and the theatrical world, which come to the foreground in *Rebecca's Tale,* formed the background of du Maurier's life and it is fitting that Rebecca's might have been in the theater as well. For Zlosnik and Horner, du Maurier's "career as a writer negotiates a triangulated relationship between her own family history, her sense of identification with Cornwall and her own struggle for self-definition and identity as a writer" and Beauman makes use of du Maurier's biography in order to illuminate Rebecca's early life.[33]

Sexuality and gender roles play a key role in the three novels. For the characters, the issue of sexuality or sexual identity proves to be a major concern around which some of the most important anxieties in the novels are built. In *Rebecca*, the young wife finds comfort in that Rebecca had her own bedroom, separate from Maxim's (not to mention her London apartment or that she often slept in the cottage), whereas they always sleep in the same bed. The very names of Rebecca and Maxim signal their different approach to sexuality: "'R' might encompass the idea of ... the sexual innuendo of a female body (sloping in Rebecca's monogram), with spread legs suggesting availability. 'Maxim de Winter' is a name with connotations of an ancient and foreign lineage, both Latin and French, and aristocratic in an ersatz way. It also means the maximum or worst of winter, a cryptonym of coldness, desolation, and ultimately death." According to Mrs. Danvers, for Rebecca "love-making was a game with her, only a game. She told me so. She did it because it made her laugh. It made her laugh." Rebecca's open attitude toward sex is a male one, or, at least, one more socially acceptable for men than for women. In *Rebecca*, Rebecca's non-normative sexual life has to be punished—either at the hands of her husband or by nature (cancer) because in literature, there is "a social norm which requires, after the fact of an illicit sexual act, a failure of the health of the woman." In contrast, in *Rebecca's Tale* sex between Maxim and Rebecca is presented as violent at times, passionate, and full of ardor: "Maxim is certainly not the suave, irresistible, strong and silent type we all thought he was. Nothing at all like Sir Laurence Olivier portrayed him in the famous movie. Frankly I always thought Maxim was a bounder, and could never understand any woman falling for a patronising toff who addresses her as 'young little fool.'"[34]

Sexuality is closely connected to class differences in *Rebecca*—Light points out that with this it is made clear that "obviously their [Maxim and the second wife's] marriage is not one of social equals. Maxim makes this explicit in a comparison which demonstrates how class interprets and regulates sexual behaviour and expectations."[35] The issue of female sexuality also resonates with gothic overtones: "the Female Gothic gives form to female desire; heroines in transitional status, usually in love or coming-of-age, find themselves suddenly in the midst of a Gothic plot, suggesting that female desire itself is the symbolic threat to the protagonist. In modern Gothic tales, men are not as important as women's own psychological concerns, which are expressed through struggles between female characters for houses."[36]

For Dorothy Allison, "always I read as a lesbian.... But looking for self-defined lesbian books was never how I approached the subject. I always reinterpreted books to give me what I needed. All books were lesbian books—if they were believable about women at all, and particularly if they were true to my own experience." Without going so far as to turn every book into a lesbian book, it is obvious that there is a lesbian subtext in *Rebecca*. The "invisibility" of lesbians, whose relationship can often be read as close female friendship, has been a central issue in Gay/Lesbian/Bisexual/Transsexual Studies. Berenstein notes the Hollywood movie convention of having lesbians characterized as ghosts, which "is, then, directly linked to cultural attitudes and anxieties about homosexuality. The lesbian is a paradoxical figure; she is an invisible—yet representable—threat." That "when it comes to lesbians ... many people have trouble seeing what's in front of them," may explain why lesbianism in *Rebecca* has often been conveniently overlooked by a majority of readers and viewers, consciously or not.[37]

Du Maurier's own biography hints at some instances of lesbianism. Margaret Forster's *Daphne du Maurier* in 1993 disclosed the author's relationships with women and that "throughout her adolescence and early adulthood, Daphne seems to have been drawn to strong-minded women—even after her marriage to Tommy in 1932." Du Maurier is suspected of having had a crush (if nothing else) on Fernande Yvon, principal of the Parisian school she attended, although du Maurier spoke of this relationship as a maternal one because of her estrangement with her own mother during most of her life. Later on, she was extremely close to the wife of her American editor, whom she gave the original of *The Rebecca Notebook* as a gift (it was returned to du Maurier after her death). According to Moore, "like so many mid-century, rather misogynist women novelists, du Maurier managed the tension between public propriety and a private life that included erotic adventures with women."[38]

The fascination that Rebecca exerts on her "successor" reads like lesbianism at times, as does the morbid adoration of Mrs. Danvers for her employer. Mrs. Danvers's frightening the new mistress has lesbian overtones, as most of this peculiar "courtship" takes place in Rebecca's bedroom by showing her Rebecca's personal belongings, including her lingerie. Rebecca herself is a peculiar character for whom, we are told through Mrs. Danvers, men were nothing but a pastime. Rebecca and Mrs. Danvers "are depicted as a fixed (although sexually challenged) class apart, and this is replicated in the relationship between Mrs Danvers and the second Mrs de Winter (and between the dead Rebecca and the second wife for whom she is a fantasy figure laced with same-sex flavour). While the encounters between these women are unsettling, this is a temporary matter—and one which the heterosexual pre-eminence of the plot counters." Mrs. Danvers's relationship with Rebecca is a complex one that goes well beyond that of a faithful servant towards her mistress. Their relationship is sexually charged and loaded with overtones of sexual impropriety, threats to the heterosexual marriage, and class division and blurring: "lesbian fantasy across class divisions has its own history. From the early modern period, at least, homosexuality was frequently associated with a double transgression, a socially inverted sexual corruption of higher class innocents by members of a lower order. Female servants are often presented as corrupters of a middle-class youth, introducing their mistresses to the pleasure/sin of same-sex eroticism." Because "Rebecca and the second Mrs de Winter are, by definition, married, while Mrs Danvers' title hints at a married past. The lesbian protagonists are thus (potentially at least) transgressors of matrimony, of sexuality, and of class." However, in *Rebecca* there is no reference to what might have happened to Mrs. Danvers's husband and in *Rebecca's Tale* it is confirmed that she never married, Mrs. being the formal title for housekeepers at the time.[39]

The second wife and Mrs. Danvers are natural antagonists—the former young, inexperienced, naïve; the latter much older, more knowledgeable, and with an agenda of her own. They immediately develop a complex relationship: "in the Gothic form, in which characters always encounter their doubles such that individual identity is undermined, the mistress and servant become natural doubles, engaged in perverse, erotic, and competitive relationships. They share a privacy and intimacy normally reserved only for lovers. Yet they struggle for power until one or the other dies or leaves the house." One of the main topics in romance is "the doubts and delights of heterosexuality." Although *Rebecca* has more than its share of doubts about heterosexuality (advanced by Rebecca and Mrs. Danvers's equivocal relationship), it is not so clear that the delights of heterosexual life/marriage are present: "romance is inherently a soothing and tender genre that aims to reconcile women to traditional lives whose common denominator is home.... Home in *Rebecca* is an *unheimlich* [uncanny] monstrosity whose only alternative is exile. If Daphne du Maurier writes romances at all, their achievement is to infuse with menace the lives women are supposed to want.... For [Mrs. de Winter] wifehood is an excruciating ordeal.... *Rebecca* ... is indelible ... as a study of menacing domesticity."[40]

For the second wife, domestic life is fraught with unrest and distress, not only because of Rebecca's domineering presence but also because of her own inadequacy—"as a daughter of the professional middle classes, she has not been trained up to the semi-aristocratic set-up that is Manderley." Maxim, however, does not accept his wife's excuse that she was not raised to run an estate. He claims that "it's not a question of bringing up, as you put it. It's a matter of application," thus blaming her for her lack of enthusiasm or her unwillingness to fulfill her role as Manderley's mistress. He also turns down her excuses that she is not good enough for the task.[41]

Beginning with du Maurier's editor, *Rebecca* has conventionally been mislabeled as a romance, or as a love story.[42] Characterized in the flap cover as "an atmosphere that alternates between the doom of impending disaster and the ecstasy of an exquisite love story," many a reader has been swept away by the love story between the unnamed second Mrs. de Winter and the widower Maxim de Winter, who saves her from a destiny worse than death (or so she thinks)—going to New York as Mrs. Van Hopper's companion. Harbord advances that "both psychoanalysis and conventional romance narratives are discourses that depend on, and reproduce, a dialectic of past and present.... Yet in neither psychoanalysis nor romance fiction is the past successfully contained, closed off, hermetically sealed. The past returns to haunt, to ghost the present and disturb the familiarity of 'home.'" This might explain why *Rebecca* has been misidentified as a romance.[43]

The lesbian subplot, present in both the novel and the movie, is absent in *Mrs. de Winter*. In *Rebecca's Tale*, although there is no lesbianism and Rebecca is presented as definitely heterosexual, we have homosexuality. Maxim is rumored to be a closeted homosexual, carrying on a several decades-long discreet affair with Frank. More visible is the case of Terence Grey, who turns down Ellie's romantic advances claiming to be in love with another person. Because Grey is being haunted by the memories of the recently deceased Julia, the wife of his best friend, Nicky, Ellie jumps to the conclusion that he must have been in love with her. However, it turns out to be Nicky whom Terence is in love with.[44]

Rebecca is a sexually ambiguous character. Although she does not claim to have female lovers in *Rebecca's Tale*, she used to play adolescent boys in Shakespeare's plays. Curiously enough, for all of the "sins" that Beauman attributes to Rebecca, she stops short of incest and lesbianism. Her cousin Jack Favell's claims of having been Rebecca's lover are dispelled given Rebecca's hatred for him. At the same time, Mrs. Danvers's obsessive love for Rebecca, with occasional hints of lesbianism, is a burden Rebecca lives with because of the advantages that having Mrs. Danvers as her ally involve, even though she can hardly put up with her obvious and excessive worshipping.

After the publication of *Rebecca*, du Maurier was repeatedly asked why she had not given her protagonist a Christian name. The narrator tells us that she has an unusual name, chosen by her father, which is never revealed. We know, though, that "my name was on the envelope, and spelt correctly, an unusual thing" for "you have a very lovely and unusual name," as Maxim tells her. Readers wondered why the second wife had no name, among them Agatha Christie, who publicly asked it, in turn earning du Maurier's enmity. Du Maurier claimed that the reason for this namelessness was that "I began the novel in the first person and I avoided giving the heroine a name because it became an interesting exercise in writing and technique."[45]

Even more telling, the narrator lacks both a Christian name and a last name of her own. Her lack of a name is indicative of her lack of a well-defined identity. She does not feel comfortable in her own skin and after being introduced to Maxim for the first time, "I wished I was older, different." Without ever having given her name, she declares her intention that "I am going to be Mrs. de Winter. I am going to live at Manderley. Manderley will belong to me." Her namelessness denotes a lack of an identity of her own and her subsequent struggle to acquire one. Lacking a name, "the crucial fact about this woman is that she has no identity: her achievement of identity depends upon her discovering the secret on which her existence as Max de Winter's wife, as Mrs. de Winter, is conditioned, the woman whose attainment of status and identity entails the destruction of the coveted Manderley and the crippling (actual in the first draft, metaphorical in the published novel) of its patriarch."[46]

Literary critics have found it a daunting task to find a way to refer to her. The most popular options are "the second wife" or "the girl." While I personally like the former, because it emphasizes that she will always be the second wife and this is how she feels throughout the novel, as an inferior and inadequate successor to Rebecca, "the girl" also stresses that she is inadequate. She is not a woman, as Rebecca was, but a girl who cannot run Manderley nor replace Rebecca effectively. Not that Maxim seems to mind it at all—"it's a pity you have to grow up," he complains. He treats her "as a child, rather spoilt, rather irresponsible, someone to be petted from time to time when the mood came upon him but more often forgotten.... I wished something would happen to make me look wiser, more mature," contrary to Maxim's wishes. In contrast to Rebecca, who keeps her first name, the second wife's first name is lost to her new name as Mrs. de Winter, although she sometimes fails to identify herself as "Mrs. de Winter."[47]

The new identity she adopts, that of Mrs. de Winter, soon turns out to be problematic, for she cannot live up to Rebecca's example. When on her first morning in the lady of the house's office she answers Mrs. Danvers's address on the phone for Mrs. de Winter replying that Mrs. de Winter died, she is acknowledging that she has yet to feel her new name as her own. Living in Rebecca's house, "I had to teach myself that all this was mine now." Her namelessness is an effective device that contributes greatly to our identifying more closely with her as well as to mark her insignificance, versus the notoriety of Rebecca's name, which, years after her death, is still a word seen everywhere—a name that, if spoken, is rich with meaning.[48]

In contrast to the multiplicity of instances where Rebecca's name is written, "we hardly ever see the narrator writing anything, and especially never signing or 'naming' anything, whereas Rebecca's pre-empting pre-eminence is expressed in the physical prevalence of her writing, especially her monogram and signature." Not only does she keep her own name, Rebecca has the power to name her husband—"she called him Max.... Max was her choice, the word was her possession.... And I had to call him Maxim." Meanwhile, the only instance in which the second wife's name is written is when it has been written by others—by Maxim in the note he sends to her room in Monte Carlo when he first meets her in *Rebecca*, and by Jack Favell when he blackmails her in *Mrs. de Winter*.[49]

It is hard for the narrator to assert her identity as different from Rebecca's since she had no strong identity to start with. Rebecca casts too large a shadow for her to surpass and stands between Maxim and his new wife: "there, I had said it at last, the word that had hovered on my tongue for days. Your wife. It came out with ease, without reluctance, as though the mere mention of her must be the most casual thing in all the world. Your wife. The word lingered in the air once I had uttered it, dancing before me, and because he received it silently, making no comment, the word magnified itself into something heinous and appalling, a forbidden word, unnatural to the tongue. And I could not call it back, it could never be unsaid." Her trying to become a good wife and hostess is a struggle for her, one that almost ends up as failure when she dresses up as Caroline de Winter for the annual costume ball at Manderley, thus adopting the identity of another woman, or rather, of two, since that was the costume Rebecca wore at her last costume ball. For all of her wishing to be like Rebecca, with this dress, "she has her wish; she becomes Rebecca so successfully, not least in Rebecca's delight in deceit, masquerade and multiplicity, that in a cruel reversal of the Cinderella myth, Maxim does finally see her as Rebecca, and to her astonishment violently repudiates her."[50]

So much does the second wife lack an identity of her own that "the girl herself is only a remembered and invented persona—relayed back to us by the older-woman narrator with whom we started the novel. The narrator is already projecting back into the feelings and thoughts of an imaginary younger self." No longer a girl, "the narrator establishes girlhood as an ex-identity not to be remembered fondly but with contempt." This process of repudiating her old self begins to take place very early in the novel, since, after her first meeting with Maxim, she believes that "I was a person of importance, I was grown up at last. That girl who, tortured by shyness, would stand outside the sitting-room door twisting a handkerchief in her hands, while from within came that babble of confused chatter so unnerving to the intruder—she had gone with the wind that afternoon. She was a poor creature, and I thought of her with scorn if I considered her at all."[51]

Many have identified the protagonist of *Rebecca* with du Maurier herself because the story is written in the first person and there are several parallelisms between du Maurier's life and the second wife's. Actually, during the filming of *Rebecca,* cast and crew referred to the protagonist, played by Joan Fontaine, as Daphne. Shallcross, a close friend of du Maurier's during her last years and her biographer, recalls a conversation in the course of which du Maurier "told me this was something like the truth, and that she was the girl in the story." Still, du Maurier also wrote that "the cottage on the beach could be my hut. Rebecca's lovers could be my books."[52]

Electra echoes are easily identifiable in *Rebecca,* too. In a way, Rebecca is a mother figure for the second Mrs. de Winter since she knows best and is older than the inexpert second wife.[53] Moreover, the narrator herself acknowledges that "I did not want to be a child. I wanted to be his wife, his mother." In turn, Maxim for her is "my father, my brother and my son" but not her husband or lover. She keeps fond and tender memories of her father, who died during her childhood, and worships Maxim as an almost divine creature, superior to her, which can again be traced back to du Maurier's admiration for both her father and her husband. Light interprets the novel in terms of an oedipalization process: "*Rebecca* might also be seen—like all romances—as being about adolescence and as such a reenactment of the choices and traumas of Oedipalization: Maxim replaces the girl's lost father ... but is only able to become her lover once the girl has moved from identification with Rebecca's clitoral (phallic) sexuality. Mrs Danvers is important here as Rebecca's lover in an almost lesbian relationship. The girl moves to a passive 'vaginal' femininity, organized and defined by Maxim." Because of the age gap between Maxim and his second wife and the pervasive shadow of Rebecca, some critics have proposed a psychoanalytic reading:

> du Maurier's story of the young bride who comes across a skeleton in her Bluebeard's castle, Manderley, invites a conventional psychoanalytic reading in which the new wife fears encountering the primal scene between her "parents": her husband, Max de Winter, who is much older than she ... and his first wife, Rebecca (whose surrogate, Mrs. Danvers, stands prohibitively between the ingénue and the scene of sexuality, figured particularly through Rebecca's bedroom). Release from this neurotic fixation is accomplished by knowledge of the truth ... and by elimination of the surrogate mother, Mrs. Danvers, who dies in the holocaust that consumes the family home.[54] The young wife is now able to engage in a fully sexual relationship with her father/husband, but the incest taboo is not lightly broken; the couple must endure a childless exile, consumed by nostalgia for England, cricket, and so on.[55]

If there are problems with the father/daughter relationship, motherhood is problematic in *Rebecca*, too. Rebecca believes herself pregnant with the child of one of her sporadic lovers only to discover that she is dying of uterine cancer; the second wife, despite her desire to produce an heir for Manderley, is unable to (both in *Rebecca* and in *Mrs. de Winter*) and Mrs. Danvers is a single woman whose mothering instincts seem to have been fulfilled by taking care of Rebecca. Motherhood is further problematized in *Rebecca's Tale* because Rebecca's mother dies of septicemia, a childbirth-related disease, a circumstance of which Rebecca is not informed until well into her adulthood.[56]

Mothers in *Rebecca's Tale* are, at best, incompetent, unable to provide for their children. Maxim's mother dies when he is three, leaving him alone, in the care of his domineering grandmother (his father being too busy, first with his love affairs and later with syphilis, to pay him any attention). Little Rebecca is at first presented very much as a mama's girl, for they live in Brittany completely isolated from the outside world, including males, with the sole company of her *Maman*. Hers is a feminine universe, where only her fastidious cousin brings some (but scarce) male presence. Her mother proves to be an ineffectual parent—they are always short of money and when the checks they regularly receive stop being regular, it is Rebecca who has to ask the owner of a theatrical company to employ both of them. Although Rebecca proves to be great playing Puck first and then doomed boys in Shakespeare's plays, her mother is a bad actress whose low voice cannot be heard. Her mother cannot protect Rebecca, either financially or especially from men: Rebecca is raped at age seven on the beach by an older boy.

For Rebecca, motherhood is the key to personal salvation. Although she is unsure about which of her lovers fathered the child she believes is growing in her womb (certainly not Maxim, with whom she had not slept with in a year), she sees her baby as a possibility to redeem her past sins and, even better, reinvent herself. Despite its not being Maxim's biological child, she is also confident that once Maxim sees the child he will grow fond of it and this might open up the way for reconciliation. Rebecca's pregnancy, however, turns out to be a growing cancer that is rapidly killing her, without a possibility for treatment.[57]

Rebecca's Tale is also fraught with issues of property laws—should women be dispossessed or should they be the transmitters of property? Rebecca wants to give Manderley to her child, even if it is not Maxim's. For Shapiro, "according to Beauman, the real Rebecca was actually a strong-minded feminist born decades ahead of her time.... Owing to a complicated parentage and a firm belief that inheritance should pass through the female side of the family, she was convinced she had a rightful claim to Manderley. She spent her life obsessed with the place, but the only way to get hold of it was to marry Maxim. Then—rotten luck—he suddenly changed into an Othello crazed with fantasies about Rebecca's sexual adventuring." Maxim, forced to produce an heir to bequest Manderley to, is unable to father a child, first with Rebecca and then with his second wife.[58]

All in all, "*Rebecca* says something about the situation of women," especially married women at the time it was first published. For her disregard and violation of social norms regarding moral and sexual propriety, Rebecca is punished by death, but the alternative, as posed by the second wife, is not too appealing and makes Ellie reject that option of womanhood. It is fitting that Beauman has Rebecca become a role model for women, acknowledging that the quandaries of the second wife are not to be shared by her twenty-first century readers: "in 1901, over one and a quarter million women were employed as domestic servants. By 1950 the figure had dwindled to a fraction of that, and many a suburban villa was a miniature Manderley, with an intimidated, socially insecure wife struggling to achieve a sense of possession of her own home.... Half a century later, when women head households and pay mortgages, the poignancy of Mrs de Winter's situation is lost." What Beauman does, in opposition to the two possible understandings of femininity posed by Rebecca and the second wife, is introduce a third competing alternative—Ellie, who is single and unwilling to get into a conventional marriage even though she is capable of passionate love. She is not a spinster but a woman who embraces single life as a proper alternative for women. Rebecca eventually leaves behind her role as a temptress or a corrupt woman to become, instead, a valid alternative to conventional sexuality and marriage and a role model for younger women.[59]

Conclusion: The End?

In their attempt to explain what happened after "the end" of a novel, in sequels, happy marriages are problematized, minor or secondary characters are brought to the forefront, stories are set in a different time and location, the formerly mysterious past of a character is revealed, and an unappealing character is redeemed. Or, readers may become the protagonists themselves and change the course of the story depending on their choices. Whereas the original authors refused to let us know certain things, sequel writers make their trade by telling us what would have otherwise remained silenced or ignored. For example, thanks to sequels we know Mr. Darcy's private thoughts when he was introduced to Elizabeth Bennet. We learn first-hand how he despaired upon realizing her admiration for the worthless rascal Wickham while she only had contempt for Mr. Darcy. We also learn that their marital life is fraught with misunderstandings and family tensions. Other Austen happy marriages are also found to be less than perfect and even though Austen promised Elinor and Marianne marital felicity, Elinor only finds loneliness and a weak husband who won't support her against his insane mother. Marianne's fate is even worse, as she faces incomprehension from both a husband whose age deeply concerns her and an elder sister who, far from offering her any solace, just criticizes her.

If happy marriages turn sour, evil characters are rediscovered so as to understand them better. Bertha Mason, before she was given a name that was not her own and taken away from her native country to England, was not the deranged, adulterous woman her husband claimed, but a woman forced into an unwanted marriage to a stranger she did not understand at all. Not evil but much suspected of wicked inclinations, Adèle, her mother's daughter, aspired to be an actress too, despite the curbing influence of Jane Eyre. Heathcliff's whereabouts when he left Wuthering Heights are finally revealed, as is his parentage—he turns out to be Mr. Rochester and Bertha Mason's child. Nevertheless, sequels and all, his and Cathy's relationship seems to be impossible, for even if it had taken place in the West Indies, it would have been doomed to disaster.

Women characters particularly have been the focus of new interpretations by sequel writers. Hester Prynne was a victim of the strict Boston Puritan society that punished her for her adulterous relationship. Since the nineteenth century, attitudes towards sex have greatly changed in America and, rewriting Hawthorne's trio of protagonists, Updike shows us a dissatisfied housewife joining a yoga-inspired commune, a womanizer minister and an adulterous professor whose wife cheats on him too. Another female character undergoing a major revision is Marmee March, who was not just a loyal wife supporting her husband's decisions. She becomes a brave woman with a temper who does not mind giving a piece of her mind to anyone, especially if it is in order to defend her two most cherished ideals—women's rights and abolitionism. But the major rewriting of a female character is that of Rebecca. We learn that Maxim de Winter and his second wife returned from exile in Europe to live (not happily ever after, but just the contrary, as it turned out) in England and that Rebecca was not the seducer and temptress her husband/murderer claimed she was, but a troubled, unhappy woman likely to be a positive role model for younger women.

Endings are far from random. For them to be meaningful, they have to provide a conclusion to the novel. It is the very effectiveness and role of endings that makes "every reader, however naïve, ... recognise that it is not reality but an imitation of it, not a slice of life but a statement about it." Previous events coming to such a conclusion are to present a coherent, logical narrative whereas open endings deny that life (and, by extension, literature, inasmuch as literature is a portrayal of life itself) might have any meaning, as nothing is resolved and no conclusion is reached. Therefore, "with the acceptance of the open ending in modern fiction, the ending which is satisfying but not final, the recognition of ambiguity or uncertainty in experience is institutionalised as form." Sequels, in turn, deny the finality of any ending to continue the action after the original writer put a stop to it.[1]

The feminist (or anti-feminist, as in the case of *S.*) subtext is at the core of many sequels, which examine the original novels from a new perspective, giving to previously silenced female characters a voice of their own, as is the case with Marmee in *March*. Not only are women the ones who lacked a voice and are given one by these modern writers, but also minority groups such as Western Indians in *Windward Heights* or *Wide Sargasso Sea*. Sometimes, new writers introduce a diametrically different approach. Jean Rhys and Maryse Condé brought a postcolonial discourse into the colonial and politically incorrect *Jane Eyre* and *Wuthering Heights*, respectively. In their bringing alive these old stories, sequel writers have brought to them their own twentieth- and twenty-first-century sensibility, envisioning changes, plots, and storylines that writers of the period could not have envisioned, such as postcolonialism. Others, like Geraldine Brooks, deliberately decided that "I would only go where Louisa May Alcott had chosen not to go."[2]

Some sequels change the ending of famous novels or expand it. Others, however, reject this possibility and leave the ending as it was, such as *March, Heathcliff: The Return to Wuthering Heights* or the sequels to *Jane Eyre*. *Wide Sargasso Sea*, being a prequel, cannot change the ending much. Other sequels limit their scope to expand a well-known story, without challenging the ending or the content of the original novel but simply adding extra information or filling up the gaps with more details. Other sequels, however, re-write the original novel in a more extensive and far-reaching manner. For instance, *Pemberley* provides a further reason why Mr. Darcy did not want Bingley to marry Jane Bennet so suddenly. Whatever the path that a sequel takes and its approach to the original work, endings provide a vital point for our understanding of sequels and the very process of sequel writing.

Still, in some cases the original novel remains much more revealing and more profound than its successor. This may be due to the literary skills of the next writer, which do not match their predecessor's or because sequel writers do not dare to go into the possibilities hinted at in the original work. The latter is the case of *Rebecca*, whose lesbian subplot, a matter of much debate and discussion and to which the new biographies of Daphne du Maurier (revealing the author's own lesbian impulses) have brought new life, is conspicuously absent from the two authorized sequels to the book.

While many sequels are born to offer a far more benevolent take on a previously neglected or vilified character (such as Heathcliff in Haire-Sargeant's homonymous novel), at times, the fuller exploration of a female character that the sequels pursue does not shed a positive light on that character. Thus, Updike's take on Hester Prynne in *S.* is a frankly negative one, presenting her alternatively as a thief, an easily deluded woman, an embittered wife, a fraudster, and a bad mother. His several Hester figures in *Roger's Version* are rather negative too while their counterpart in *A Month of Sundays* is such a sketchy, minor character that not much can be said about her. However, sometimes, in their providing their female characters with a range of choices not offered by the original authors, sequel writers defy social conventions of propriety beyond what would have been acceptable back then. All texts are bound by considerations surrounding their author such as historical period, setting, current situation, social conventions and manners. Sequel writers, living in a different time period with a completely different set of circumstances, despite their attempts at accuracy, sometimes bring their own conditions to the novel they are writing, resulting in anachronisms—would Elizabeth Darcy and Marianne Brandon dare to leave their husbands, at a time when even women abandoned by their husbands were social pariahs with nobody to turn to for help or even employment? Maybe in an attempt to successfully break with social conventions, it is remarkable that sequel writers seem to find America as a solution to their characters' problems. In *Elinor and Marianne,* Willoughby plans to embark on a journey to found a community in America and in *Heathcliff,* Heathcliff takes Cathy with him to live in America.

If barely sketched female characters are given a more profound treatment, the reverse process is also true and male characters whose previous lives were a mystery in women novelists' works are given a distinctive past in the sequels, making up for the omissions and half-hinted events in the original novels. Through sequels we learn about Mr. March's Civil War experiences as well as his youthful years, about Mr. Darcy's involvement in the war in France, and about Heathcliff's first years as an orphan in Liverpool and his years away from Wuthering Heights. In some instances sequels do not offer a continuation of the plot but explain previous events, such as *Heathcliff, The French Dancer's Bastard, Wide Sargasso Sea* or *March.* We learn how Heathcliff or Rebecca became the people they were, in an attempt to explain the darker aspects of their personalities. They become better known and some of their worst characteristics (Heathcliff's cruelty, Rebecca's promiscuity) are accounted for on the grounds of their difficult childhoods. Mr. Darcy's somber moods are also the focus of sequels and he is very conveniently given a heroic role in the French-English War. Even seemingly anodyne characters, such as Mr. March, are given a more interesting past. Secondary characters who were on the sidelines because it was not their story are now pushed front and center in sequels to have *their* story told, such as Adèle, the second Mrs. de Winter or Marmee.

It seems that while loose rewritings such as Updike's or Condé's could be read separately from the original works, this is not the case with those novels that continue a story and whose meaning largely draws on events, characterizations and circumstances taken from the original novels. Heathcliff's pursuit of a formal education and wealth are not so urgent if one does not know about the humiliations he suffered at Wuthering Heights. We better understand Elizabeth Darcy's tendency to jump to erroneous conclusions when we recall her prejudiced disposition in *Pride and Prejudice*—and the misunderstandings it led to. We would not know the reason for Mrs. Ferrars's animosity towards Elinor without having read *Sense and Sensibility*. Why are the de Winters so afraid of returning to England if not for what had happened in *Rebecca*? Why do we need yet another Civil War novel about a Northern chaplain if it were not for its significance to *Little Women*? Why would Adèle's brief life be of any interest without her governess? Meanwhile, "*The Scarlet Letter* Trilogy" could be read as a take on adultery, religion and its role and ministers in twentieth-century America and *Windward Heights* and *Wide Sargasso Sea* could be interpreted as explorations of the evils and after-effects of European colonialism in the West Indies. In some cases, one gets the impression that it would have been better if the characters had been left alone, though. This is especially true when the sequels reveal that figures of mystery and romance are no longer that mysterious and, accordingly, not so romantic anymore. Was the ending of *Pride and Prejudice* not more surprising than that of Grange's sequel, *Mr. Darcy's Diary*? Could it be that we had imagined Heathcliff's whereabouts and activities during his time away from Wuthering Heights as more exotic and dashing than Haire-Sargeant had them?

Some authors seem to have found a liking to writing sequels, such as Emma Tennant. In turn, some authors' works seem to be more likely than others to be continued. Austen's novels, because of their enduring popularity since the nineteenth century and their being free of copyright and the constraints imposed by reluctant heirs, are a favorite among writers of literary sequels. Works still under copyright are, for the time being, denied being continued in published sequels. That new sequels continue to be written, that old stories keep being told, but with a new outlook, does not testify to the obsoleteness of the original stories. Just the opposite, for the very fact that they are revisited (and often modernized in the process) means that they continue to have validity in the twenty-first century.

That, in most cases, sequels are written to works that have long been in the public domain is not only a testament to the modern-day currency of classical works; it is also an act of necessity. Daring to write a sequel to a novel still under copyright protection is an automatic way for a sequel writer to get a lawsuit. The year 2009 saw the controversy surrounding the publication of *Sixty Years Later: Coming through the Rye* in which Swedish writer Fredrik Colting (under the pseudonym of J. D. California) imagined the life of an aged Holden Caulfield (identified as Mr. C.) living in a retirement home. Federal judge Deborah Batts's ruling on June 17, 2009, that Colting's use of the characters of *Catcher in the Rye* violated Salinger's copyright set a precedent in U.S. jurisdiction, for it was the first time that a single character appearing in one single literary work was regarded as copyrightable. The case was especially salient because of Salinger's tight control over his works as well as his own life. After Colting's appeal was successful in September 2009 at the Second Circuit of Appeals, an out-of-court settlement put an end to the dispute and, according to *Publisher's Weekly*, "Colting has agreed not to publish or otherwise distribute the book, e-book, or any other editions ... in the U.S. or Canada until *The Catcher in the Rye* enters the public domain." Also, "Colting cannot include 'Coming Through the Rye' as part of the book title. In addition, the author cannot refer to Salinger, *The Catcher in the Rye*, or his legal battles in the book."[3]

A few years earlier, news of the publication of *The Wind Done Gone*, a work whose author, African-American Alice Randall defined as a parody of *Gone with the Wind*, had made it to the headlines and into legal annals. The subsequent legal battle between Randall and her publisher and the estate of Margaret Mitchell did not merely deal with legal matters and copyright protection, but also with questions such as history writing, historical revisionism, prejudices and racism in literature and race issues. Finally, after an appeal turned down a previous verdict and gave Randall the right to have her work published, the Mitchells, instead of appealing again, reached an agreement according to which *The Wind Done Gone* was to be sold as "an unauthorized parody." Lauretta Hugo, the wife of the great-grandson of Victor Hugo, complained publicly about the publication of a sequel to *Les Misérables*, arguing that "the distortion of works of heritage for commercial ends must be stopped. It's time to defend culture and creativity against the savagery of free enterprise, which seems to want to tarnish everything and reduce every cultural product to the level of the market place." *Cosette, ou, Le temps des illusions* by François Ceresa came out in 2001 and sold 65,000 copies in the first week.[4]

It is problematic to decide who is entitled to write a sequel, as the *Gone with the Wind* legal battle or the J. D. Salinger case illustrate. Can somebody else, with or without the authors' heirs' or relatives' permission, write new developments that obviously the author did not intend to be told or known? Even sequel writers have ambivalent feelings about ownership and copyright. Updike, with three sequels to Hawthorne's *The Scarlet Letter* and another one to Hamlet (*Gertrude and Claudius*) under his belt, asked about his own trilogy in regards to the publication of *Lo's Diary*, an unauthorized sequel to Vladimir Nabokov's *Lolita* from the female protagonist's point of view, argued that "Hawthorne is not under copyright." Yet, he admitted that, were a sequel to one of his works published, "I would be upset.... I think of my characters as mine. I wouldn't want someone handling them with dirty fingers."[5]

Updike's opinion on sequel writing, establishing a distinction between copyrighted works and works in the public domain, puts a finger on the sequels that we might expect to be written—or at least published. Because of the lawsuits against those attempting to continue contemporary works, "it is of course possible that the risk of being held an infringer is deterring rewritings of texts that are still copyrighted and is steering authors to set their revisionary sights instead on public domain works. With the recent copyright term extension, one wonders how many more canonical works will be shielded by long copyright terms, and how many rewritings will not be produced because authors cannot get permission to create them." Books still protected by copyright will have to wait to have sequels published. In the meantime, however, these sequels frequently appear on the Internet in the form of fan fiction stories. So far, the Internet has been free from copyright infringement lawsuits and fan fiction authors have generally been left alone, with original authors looking the other way. Exceptions have been J. K. Rowling or Anne Rice, who have had letters from their lawyers sent to fan fiction writers, although these have been not followed up by any legal procedure.[6]

The popularization of the Internet and the spread of fan fiction make us realize that the need to write a continuation to a well-beloved literary work is far from extinct. Fan fiction is a peculiar case of sequel writing—more democratic, open to anyone and, what is more, with fewer constrictions. Although it has a negative reputation, being often perceived "as a semi-literate, usually pornographic genre providing nothing but in-jokes for geeks," fan fiction pieces "are derivative works taking not just the characters but frequently the whole fictional world of the original work. The Fan Fiction works operate within shared worlds which develop and complement the world in the original work.[7] Fan Fiction writers have a devout admiration for the original text and there is no intention to produce a competitive work which would exploit the commercial success of the original." Only time will tell if fan fiction pieces of works still under copyright protection will give way to the legal publication of sequels once the original novels go into the public domain.[8]

Chapter Notes

Introduction

1. Henry James, "Eugene Pickering," 1874, Project Gutenberg, 8 May 2005, www.gutenberg.org/files/2534/2534-h/2534-h.htm (accessed 2 September 2012).

2. David Lodge, *Working with Structuralism: Essays and Reviews on Nineteenth- and Twentieth-Century Literature* (London: Routledge & Kegan Paul, 1981), 143–155. Quoted in Lodge, *Working with Structuralism*, 147.

3. Lodge, *Working with Structuralism*, 148. Grace Moore, "Great Expectations," *The Literary Encyclopedia*, 9 December 2004, www.litencyc.com/php/sworks.php?rec=true&UID=4892 (accessed 16 May 2012).

4. Quoted in Sheryl A. Englund, "Reading the Author in *Little Women*: A Biography of the Book," *American Transcendental Quarterly* 12.3 (1998): 204.

5. Kurt Vonnegut, Jr., *Slaughterhouse-Five, or the Children's Crusade* (1969; New York: Delacorte Press/Seymour Lawrence, 1994), 20. Terry Castle quoted in Tamara S. Wagner, "Rewriting Sentimental Plots: Sequels to Novels of Sensibility by Jane Austen and Another Lady," in *Second Thought: Updating the Eighteenth-Century Text*, ed. Elizabeth Kraft and Debra Taylor Bourdeau (Newark: University of Delaware Press, 2007), 210. Marjorie Garber, "'I'll Be Back': Review of *Part Two: Reflections on the Sequel*," *London Review of Books* 21.16 (1999), www.lrb.co.uk/v21/n16/marjorie-garber/ill-be-back/print (accessed 19 January 2010).

6. M. Carmen Gomez-Galisteo, *The Wind Is Never Gone: Sequels, Parodies and Rewritings of* Gone with the Wind (Jefferson, NC: McFarland, 2011), 64.

7. Although the law grants copyright for seventy-five years after the author's death, in some cases authors' relatives have sought and obtained an extension of their copyright.

8. Quoted in Henry Jenkins, *Textual Poachers: Television Fans and Participatory Culture* (New York: Routledge, 1992), 24. Roland Barthes, "The Death of the Author," trans. Richard Howard Aspen, www.ubu.com/aspen/aspen5and6/threeEssays.html (accessed 9 February 2009). Wagner, "Rewriting Sentimental Plots," 239.

9. Marianne Brace, "'Last Night I Dreamt I Went to Manderley Again...' and Again and Again," *The Independent*, 29 September 2001, www.independent.co.uk/arts-entertainment/books/reviews/rebeccas-tale-by-sally-beauman-752125.html (accessed 9 January 2009). Philip Hensher, "What Rebecca Did Next, If You Care," *The Observer*, 23 September 2001, www.guardian.co.uk/books/2001/sep/23/fiction.features (accessed 9 January 2009). Susan Hill, "Mrs. De Winter," Susanhill.com, www.susan-hill.com/pages/books/the_

books/mrs_de_winter.asp (accessed 12 January 2009).

10. Asunción López-Varela Azcárate, "Recepción e intertextualidad," E-Excellence, Biblioteca de recursos electrónicos de Humanidades, Liceus, n.d., 3. Quoted in Louise Tucker, "A Colonized Imagination: Louise Tucker Talks to Geraldine Brooks," in Geralding Brooks, *March* (2005; London: Perennial, 2006), 4.

11. Jeffrey D. Grossett, "*The Wind Done Gone*: Transforming Tara Into a Plantation Parody," *Case Western Reserve Law Review* 52.4 (2002): 1113. Hill, "Mrs. De Winter," Sally Beauman, "Living with Rebecca," *The Guardian*, 12 September 2001. Alan Howard website, www.alanhoward.org.uk/living.htm (accessed 9 January 2009).

12. Quoted in Michael Thorpe, "The Other Side: *Wide Sargasso Sea* and *Jane Eyre*," *Ariel* 3 (1977): 99.

13. Celia Brayfield, "Now discontent is our de Winter: *Mrs. De Winter*—Susan Hill," *The Independent*, 10 October 1993, www.independent.co.uk/arts-entertainment/book-review—now-discontent-is-our-de-winter-mrs-de-winter—susan-hill-sinclairstevenson-1299-pounds-1509933.html (accessed 25 May 2009). Garber, "I'll Be Back." Quoted in Karen Newman, "Can This Marriage Be Saved: Jane Austen Makes Sense of an Ending," *ELH* 50.4 (1983): 693. Quoted in Charles Soukup, "Television Viewing as Vicarious Resistance: *The X-Files* and Conspiracy Discourse," *The Southern Communication Journal* 68.1 (2002): 17.

14. Jeannie Suk, "Originality," *Harvard Law Review* 115 (2002), http://papers.ssrn.com/sol3/papers.cfm?abstract_id=1136322 (accessed 1 March 2010). Brayfield, "Now discontent is our de Winter," Eleanor Robinson, "Once Upon a Time ... a Happy Ending for the Unauthorised Sequel?" *The New Zealand Law e-Journal* 4 (2006): 2. Martin Arnold, "After that Night in the Airport," *The New York Times*, 22 October 1998, www.nytimes.com/1998/10/22/movies/making-books-after-that-night-at-the-airport.html (accessed 25 May 2009). Garber, "I'll Be Back." Laura Shapiro, "Manderley Confidential," *The New York Times*, 14 October 2001, www.nytimes.com/2001/10/14/books/manderley-confidential.html?pagewanted=print (accessed 25 May 2009).

15. Lisa Schwarzbaum, "Rebecca Redux," *Entertainment Weekly*, 22 October 1993, www.ew.com/ew/article/0,,308500,00.html (accessed 9 June 2009).

16. Adrienne Rich, *On Lies, Secrets, and Silence: Selected Prose, 1966–1978* (1979; London: Virago Press, 1986), 37–38, 35. Sandra M. Gilbert and Susan Gubar, *The Madwoman in the Attic: The Woman Writer and the Nineteenth-Century Literary Imagination* (1979; New Haven: Yale University Press, 1984), 6.

17. Louisa May Alcott, *Little Women*, 1868, Oxford Text Archive, University of Virginia Library, Electronic Text Center, 2003, http://etext.lib.virginia.edu/modeng A.browse.html (accessed 4 June 2009), 270.

Chapter 1

1. An alternative name is "Janeites," coined around 1894. Allison Thompson, "Trinkets and Treasures: Consuming Jane Austen," *Persuasions On-Line* 28.2 (2008), www.jasna.org/persuasions/on-line/vol28no2/thompson.htm (accessed 16 June 2009).

2. Garber quoted in Brandy Foster, "Pimp My Austen: The Commodification and Customization of Jane Austen," *Persuasions On-Line* 29.1 (2008), www.jasna.org/persuasions/on-line/vol29no1/foster.html (accessed 10 June 2009). Quoted in Brooke Allen, "Jane Austen for the Nineties," *New Criterion* 14.1 (1995), retrieved from Academic Search Premier (accessed 30 June 2009).

3. During the 1990s Austen became "the most powerful woman in Hollywood, never mind that she died in 1817," As of 2007, there had been "seven [cinematographic] adaptations in the past 12 years (not including *Clueless*)." Elisabeth Chretien, "Gentility and the Canon Under Siege: *Pride and Prejudice and Zombies*, Violence, and Contemporary Adaptations of Jane Austen" (M.A. Thesis, University of Nebraska–Lincoln, 2011), 16. Elsa Solender, "Recreating Jane Austen's World on Film," *Persuasions On-Line* 24 (2002): 103. Sally Williams, "Not So Plain Jane," *Telegraph*, 17 February 2007, www.telegraph.co.uk/

culture/3663235/Not-so-plain-Jane.html (accessed 3 December 2009).

4. Williams, "Not So Plain Jane." Salber quoted in Foster, "Pimp My Austen." Marjorie Garber, "'I'll Be Back': Review of Part Two: Reflections on the Sequel," *London Review of Books* 21.16 (1999), www.lrb.co.uk/v21/n16/marjorie-garber/ill-be-back/print (accessed 19 January 2010). Matthew Reisz, "Review of *What Matters in Jane Austen*? Twenty Crucial Puzzles Solved," *Times Higher Education*, 7 June 2012. www.timeshighereducation.co.uk/story.asp?sectioncode=26&storycode=420217&c=2 (accessed 11 June 2012). Julia Braun Kessler, "Murdering Miss Austen," *California Literary Review*, 6 December 2007, http://calitreview.com/292 (accessed 30 October 2008). Gerhard Joseph, "Prejudice in Jane Austen, Emma Tennant, Charles Dickens—and Us," *Studies in English Literature, 1500–1900* 40.4 (2000): 679. Carmen Lara Rallo, "*Sense and Sensibility* Revisited: Emma Tennant's *Elinor and Marianne*," *Odisea: Revista de Estudios Ingleses* 4 (2003): 86.

5. The next sequels, *Mad About the Boy* and *Bridget Jones' Baby*, are not connected to Austen's works.

6. Foster, "Pimp My Austen."

7. James Bowman, "The Inexhaustible Adaptability of Jane Austen," *The New York Sun*, 11 February 2005, www.jamesbowman.net/articleDetail.asp?pubID=1595 (accessed 15 May 2007). Foster, "Pimp My Austen," Kaplan quoted in Thompson, "Trinkets and Treasures," Tamara S. Wagner, "Rewriting Sentimental Plots: Sequels to Novels of Sensibility by Jane Austen and Another Lady," in *Second Thought: Updating the Eighteenth-Century Text*, ed. Elizabeth Kraft and Debra Taylor Bourdeau (Newark: University of Delaware Press, 2007), 211. Claire Radcliffe, "Updating Austen: Jane Austen's Stories in a Modern World," Earl Gregg Swem Library, College of William and Mary, http://dspace.swem.wm.edu/jspui/bitstream/10288/622/1/Radcliffe.pdf (accessed 16 June 2009). Jennifer Frey, "The Patron Saint of Chick Lit," *Los Angeles Times*, 1 September 2004, http://articles.latimes.com/2004/sep/01/entertainment/et-frey1?pg=1 (accessed 30 June 2009).

8. Foster, "Pimp My Austen." Quoted in Sue Parrill, *Jane Austen on Film and TV: A Critical Study of the Adaptations* (Jefferson, NC: McFarland, 2002), 3. Emma Campbell Webster, *Being Elizabeth Bennet: Create Your Own Jane Austen Adventure* (London: Atlantic Books, 2007), 360.

9. Kessler, "Murdering Miss Austen," Martin Amis, "Jane's World," *The New Yorker*, 8 January 1996: 31–35, www.newyorker.com/archive/1996/01/08/1996_01_08_031_TNY_CARDS_000374562?currentPage=all (accessed 22 June 2009). Deborah Kaplan, "Mass Marketing Jane Austen: Men, Women, and Courtship in Two of the Recent Films," *Persuasions On-Line* 18 (1996), www.jasna.org/persuasions/printed/number18/kaplan.htm (accessed 9 June 2009).

10. In real life, though, scholars' vast knowledge of Austen does not seem to be so exhaustive or detailed: "'when the Jane Austen Society has quizzes,' says John Mullan, professor of English at University College London, 'academics always do rather badly. One scholar implied it was rather to their credit, as if there are more important things to know about than how old Mr. Collins is or how far Kellynch Hall is from Uppercross.'" Quoted in Reisz, "Review of *What Matters in Jane Austen?*"

11. Lynch quoted in Foster, "Pimp My Austen." Lara Rallo, "*Sense and Sensibility* Revisited," 86. Wagner, "Rewriting Sentimental Plots," 210. Judy Simons, "Classics and Trash: Reading Austen in the 1990s," *Women's Writing* 5.1 (1998): 33–34. Gwyn Cready, *Seducing Mr. Darcy* (New York: Pocket Books, 2008), 208.

12. Wagner, "Rewriting Sentimental Plots," 233, 222. Charles H. Hinnant, "Jane Austen's 'Wild Imagination': Romance and the Courtship Plot in the Six Canonical Novels," *Narrative* 14.3 (2006): 294. M. Carmen Gomez-Galisteo, "A Damsel in Distress: Jane Austen's *Emma* Goes *Clueless*," in *Current Trends in Anglophone Studies: Cultural, Linguistic and Literary Research*, ed. Javier Ruano García et al. (Salamanca, Spain: Ediciones Universidad de Salamanca, 2011), 235.

13. John Tierney, "The Big City; Fab Dads and Wanton Wives," *The New York Times Magazine*, 11 February 1996, www.

nytimes.com/1996/02/11/magazine/the-big-city-fab-dads-and-wanton-wives.html?pagewanted=all&src=pm (accessed 17 July 2012). Hinnant, "Wild Imagination," 297–298.

14. Julia Prewitt Brown, "The Feminist Depreciation of Austen: A Polemical Reading," *Novel* 23.3 (1990): 306.

15. Wagner, "Rewriting Sentimental Plots," 212–213.

16. Robert Clark, "Jane Austen," *The Literary Encyclopedia*, 8 January 2001, www.litencyc.com/php/speople.php?rec=true&UID=5167 (accessed 12 May 2008). F. B. Pinion, *A Jane Austen Companion. A Critical Survey and Reference Book* (London: Macmillan, 1973), 84, 19. Barbara M. Benedict, "Jane Austen's *Sense and Sensibility*: The Politics of Point of View," *Philological Quarterly* 69.4 (1990): 454–455. Elisabeth Lenckos, "'…[I]nventing Elegant Letters,' Or, Why Don't Austen's Lovers Write More Often?" *Persuasions On-Line* 26.1 (2005), www.jasna.org/persuasions/on-line/vol26no1/lenckos.htm (accessed 4 December 2009).

17. F. P. Lock, "The Geology of *Sense and Sensibility*," *Yearbook of English Studies* 9 (1979): 255.

18. This dissatisfaction with the ending is largely responsible for the novel's critical neglect or snubbing, notwithstanding that, as Austen's first published novel, it reveals the topics and concerns she would explore in the rest of her literary production. However, despite its merits, "*Sense and Sensibility* is Jane Austen's least loved and least respected novel" along with *Northanger Abbey*. Ana-Karina Schneider, "Sense and Sensibility," *The Literary Encyclopedia*, 9 January 2008, www.litencyc.com/php/sworks.php?rec=true&UID=2122 (accessed 31 July 2012). David Kaufmann, "Law and Propriety, *Sense and Sensibility:* Austen on the Cusp of Modernity," *ELH* 59 (1992): 385. Edward Joseph Shoben, Jr., "Impulse and Virtue in Jane Austen: *Sense and Sensibility* in Two Centuries," *Hudson Review* 35.4 (1982–1983): 529. Claudia L. Johnson, "The 'Twilight of Probability': Uncertainty and Hope in *Sense and Sensibility*," *Philological Quarterly* 62.2 (1983): 171.

19. Marilyn Butler, "Sensibility and Jacobinism," in Sense and Sensibility *and* Pride and Prejudice*: New Casebooks*, ed. Robert Clark (Basingstoke: Macmillan, 1994), 44. Karl Kroeber, "Jane Austen as an Historical Novelist; *Sense and Sensibility*," *Persuasions On-Line* 12 (1990): 10–18, www.jasna.org/persuasions/printed/number12/kroeber.htm (accessed 2 September 2012).

20. Margaret, in contrast, is used in the film *Sense and Sensibility* (1995) to present a romanticized image of childhood and to voice the questions modern audiences might have about nineteenth-century English social practices. Nora Foster Stovel, "From Page to Screen: Emma Thompson's Film Adaptation of *Sense and Sensibility*," *Persuasions On-Line* 32.1 (2011), www.jasna.org/persuasions/on-line/vol32no1/stovel.html (accessed 19 July 2012). Patrice Hannon, "Austen Novels and Austen Films: Incompatible Worlds?" *Persuasions On-Line* 18 (1996): 24–32, www.jasna.org/persuasions/printed/number18/hannon.htm (accessed 4 August 2012). Devoney Looser, "Jane Austen 'Responds' to the Men's Movement," *Persuasions On-Line* 18 (2006), www.jasna.org/persuasions/printed/number18/looser.htm (accessed 2 September 2012).

21. Emma Tennant, *Elinor and Marianne* (London: Simon & Schuster, 1996), 85. Carmen Lara Rallo, "*Sense and Sensibility* Revisited: Emma Tennant's *Elinor and Marianne*," *Odisea: Revista de Estudios Ingleses* 4 (2003): 91–92.

22. Charles H. Hinnant, "Jane Austen's 'Wild Imagination': Romance and the Courtship Plot in the Six Canonical Novels," *Narrative* 14 3 (2006): 296. Butler, "Sensibility and Jacobinism," 38. Pinion, *Austen Companion*, 86. Schneider, "Sense and Sensibility." Johnson, "Twilight of Probability," 172.

23. Susan Morgan, "Polite Lies: The Veiled Heroine of *Sense and Sensibility*," *Nineteenth-Century Fiction* 31.2 (1976): 188. Susan Morgan, *In the Meantime: Character and Perception in Jane Austen's Fiction* (Chicago: University of Chicago Press, 1980), 7. Alastair Duckworth, "Improving on Sensibility," in Sense and Sensibility *and* Pride and Prejudice*: New Casebooks*, ed. Robert Clark (Basingstoke:

Macmillan, 1994), 27. Kaufmann, "Law and Propriety, *Sense and Sensibility*," 399. Yasmine Gooneratne, *Jane Austen* (Cambridge: Cambridge University Press, 1970), 79. Kroeber, "Austen Historical Novelist."

24. Not that young age is a valid excuse—"for Austen, youth is never an excuse. Everybody past childhood, say about age 13, is regarded by Austen as a responsible moral agent, capable of acting with ethical correctness. Of course, almost nobody in her novels does act correctly. That—alas—makes her a realist." Kroeber, "Austen Historical Novelist,"

25. Gila Reinstein, "Moral Priorities in *Sense and Sensibility*," *Renascence* 35.4 (1983): 269, 276–277, 279. Kaufmann, "Law and Propriety, *Sense and Sensibility*," 399.

26. Julie A. Shaffer, "The Ideological Intervention of Ambiguities in the Marriage Plot: Who Fails Marianne in Austen's *Sense and Sensibility?*" in *A Dialogue of Voices: Feminist Literary Theory and Bakhtin*, ed. Karen Hohne and Helen Wussow (Minneapolis: University of Minnesota Press, 1994), 128–129. Morgan, "Polite Lies," 191–192, 194.

27. Shaffer, "Ambiguities in Marriage Plot," 139. Shoben, Jr., "Impulse and Virtue," 531. Duckworth, "Improving on Sensibility," 29. M. Carmen Gomez-Galisteo, *The Wind Is Never Gone: Sequels, Parodies and Rewritings of* Gone with the Wind (Jefferson, NC: McFarland, 2011), 107. Jane Austen, *Sense and Sensibility*, 1811, Project Gutenberg, 25 May 2008, www.gutenberg.org/ebooks/161 (accessed 11 July 2012).

28. Johnson, "Twilight of Probability," 173. Austen, *Sense and Sensibility*.

29. Johnson, "Twilight of Probability," 177. Hinnant, "Wild Imagination," 306. Shaffer, "Ambiguities in Marriage Plot," 148. Kathleen Lundeen, "A Modest Proposal? Paradise Found in Jane Austen's Betrothal Scenes," *Review of English Studies* 41.161 (1990): 67. Carlos J. Gómez Blanco, "Story and History: Jane Austen and the Politics of Fiction," *BABEL AFIAL* 2 (1993): 19–20.

30. Hinnant, "Wild Imagination," 304. Austen, *Sense and Sensibility*.

31. Kaufmann, "Law and Propriety, *Sense and Sensibility*," 397. Austen, *Sense and Sensibility*.

32. Shaffer, "Ambiguities in Marriage Plot," 141. Austen, *Sense and Sensibility*.

33. For Stovel, Emma Thompson, author of the screenplay for the 1995 cinematographic adaptation, enhances Edward's appeal by omitting several instances of his deviousness towards Elinor in Lucy's conversation with Elinor. Similarly, Alan Rickman's Colonel Brandon is "far sexier than Austen intended him to be," perhaps to atone for the fact that, in Alistair Duckworth's words, "Marianne's marriage to the rheumatic Colonel Brandon is a gross over-compensation for her misguided sensibility." Stovel, "From Page to Screen." William H. Magee, "Instrument of Growth: The Courtship and Marriage Plot in Jane Austen's Novels," *Journal of Narrative Technique* 17.2 (1987): 200. Deborah Kaplan, "Mass Marketing Jane Austen: Men, Women, and Courtship in Two of the Recent Films," *Persuasions On-Line* 18 (1996): 171–181. Nachumi quoted in Stovel, "From Page to Screen." Quoted in Michael Kramp, *Disciplining Love: Austen and the Modern Man* (Columbus: Ohio State University Press, 2007), 172.

34. Shaffer, "Ambiguities in Marriage Plot," 140. Austen, *Sense and Sensibility*. Morgan, "Polite Lies," 190. Butler, "Sensibility and Jacobinism," 40. Mary Watson, "A Defense of Edward Ferrars: Austen's Hero as a Nexus of *Sense and Sensibility*," *Persuasions On-Line* 32.1 (2011), www.jasna.org/persuasions/on-line/vol32no1/watson.html (accessed 19 July 2012). Stovel, "From Page to Screen."

35. Lundeen, "A Modest Proposal?" 67–68.

36. Shaffer, "Ambiguities in Marriage Plot," 140–141. Duckworth, "Improving on Sensibility," 31.

37. Morgan, "Polite Lies," 199. Austen, *Sense and Sensibility*. Pinion, *Austen Companion*, 11. Butler, "Sensibility and Jacobinism," 42–43.

38. Reinstein, "Moral Priorities," 275. Kimiyo Ogawa, "Marianne's Addiction: Amorous Pleasures in *Sense and Sensibility*," *Persuasions On-Line* 32.2 (2012), www.jasna.org/persuasions/on-line/vol32no2/ogawa.html (accessed 18 July

2012). Mudrick quoted in Johnson, "Twilight of Probability," 171. Johnson, "Twilight of Probability," 175–176.

39. Johnson, "Twilight of Probability," 174. Morgan, "Polite Lies," 196, 199–200. Duckworth, "Improving on Sensibility," 29.

40. Karen Newman, "Can This Marriage Be Saved: Jane Austen Makes Sense of an Ending," *ELH* 50.4 (1983): 695. Judith Lowder Newton, "*Pride and Prejudice*: Power, Fantasy, and Subversion in Jane Austen," *Feminist Studies* 4.1 (1978): 27. Shaffer, "Ambiguities in Marriage Plot," 135, 142.

41. Schneider, "Sense and Sensibility." Fuller quoted in Stovel, "From Page to Screen." Austen, *Sense and Sensibility.*

42. Austen, *Sense and Sensibility.* Johnson, "Twilight of Probability," 182–183. Kaufmann, "Law and Propriety, *Sense and Sensibility*," 394.

43. Shaffer, "Ambiguities in Marriage Plot," 135. Serena Hansen, "Rhetorical Dynamics in Jane Austen's Treatment of Marriage Proposals," *Persuasions On-Line* 21.2 (2000), www.jasna.org/persuasions/on-line/vol21no2/hansen.html (accessed 4 December 2009).

44. Newman, "Can This Marriage Be Saved," 693–694. Shaffer, "Ambiguities in Marriage Plot," 145.

45. Tennant, *Elinor and Marianne*, 28. Lara Rallo, "*Sense and Sensibility* Revisited," 86, 89.

46. "Both Scott and Austen are concerned more with the sheer facts of social transformations than with telling us how things *ought* to change—or *ought* to *have* changed. But both are biased toward the underdog, the losers, the people formal and official history ignores.... For Jane Austen the underdogs were women—the majority underclass of Regency England." Kroeber, "Austen Historical Novelist."

47. Kaufmann, "Law and Propriety, *Sense and Sensibility*," 401. Karl quoted in Virginia Lyn Neylon, "Reading and Writing the Romance Novel: An Analysis of Romance Fiction and Its Place in the Community College Classroom," n.d., www.cuyamaca.net/lyn.neylon/Romance/Reading%20and%20writing%20romance.doc (accessed 4 September 2007), 10.

48. Shaffer, "Ambiguities in Marriage Plot," 145–146. Pinion, *Austen Companion*, 88.

49. Tennant, *Elinor and Marianne*, 26–28, 106.

50. Jane Austen, *Mansfield Park*, 1814, Project Gutenberg, 22 January 2010, www.gutenberg.org/ebooks/141 (accessed 14 July 2012).

51. Glenda A. Hudson, "'Precious Remains of the Earliest Attachment': Sibling Love in Jane Austen's *Pride and Prejudice*," *Persuasions On-Line* 11 (1989): 125–131, www.jasna.org/persuasions/printed/number11/hudson.htm (accessed 6 November 2009). Lara Rallo, "*Sense and Sensibility* Revisited," 91–92.

52. Lara Rallo, "*Sense and Sensibility* Revisited," 91.

53. Schneider, "Sense and Sensibility," Tennant, *Elinor and Marianne*, 128.

54. Quoted in Lara Rallo, "*Sense and Sensibility* Revisited," 86. Tamara S. Wagner, "Rewriting Sentimental Plots: Sequels to Novels of Sensibility by Jane Austen and Another Lady," in *Second Thought: Updating the Eighteenth-Century Text*, ed. Elizabeth Kraft and Debra Taylor Bourdeau (Newark: University of Delaware Press, 2007), 233. Tennant, *Elinor and Marianne*, 4–5.

55. Reinstein, "Moral Priorities," 275. Duckworth, "Improving on Sensibility," 29. Shoben, Jr., "Impulse and Virtue," 532–533. Tennant, *Elinor and Marianne*, 28.

56. Tennant, *Elinor and Marianne*, 108, 123, 83. Morgan, "Polite Lies," 188.

57. Quoted in Shaffer, "Ambiguities in Marriage Plot," 129. Gómez Blanco, "Story and History," 23.

58. Tennant, *Elinor and Marianne*, 149.

59. Morgan, "Polite Lies," 190. Tennant, *Elinor and Marianne*, 125–126, 122, 12. Watson, "Defense of Ferrars."

60. Lara Rallo, "*Sense and Sensibility* Revisited," 87.

Chapter 2

1. Quoted in F. B. Pinion, *A Jane Austen Companion. A Critical Survey and Reference Book* (London: Macmillan, 1973), 325.

2. Elisabeth Lenckos, "'...[I]nventing

Elegant Letters,' Or, Why Don't Austen's Lovers Write More Often?" *Persuasions On-Line* 26.1 (2005), www.jasna.org/persuasions/on-line/vol26no1/lenckos.htm (accessed 4 December 2009). Robert Clark, "Jane Austen," *The Literary Encyclopedia*, 8 January 2001, www.litencyc.com/php/speople.php?rec=true&UID=5167 (accessed 12 May 2008).

3. James Edward Austen-Leigh, *A Memoir of Jane Austen*, 1870, 2d ed. (London: Richard Bentley and Son, 1871), Project Gutenberg, 2006, www.gutenberg.org/files/17797/17797-h/17797-h.htm (accessed 4 December 2009), 1–2. Quoted in Laura Carroll, "Jane Austen's Abandoned Romances," *Meanjin* 67.2 (June 2008), http://meanjin.com.au/editions/volume-67-number-2-2008/article/jane-austen-s-abandoned-romances/ (accessed 1 August 2012). Linda Troost and Sayre Greenfield, "Appropriating Austen: Localism on the Global Scene," *Persuasions On-Line* 28.2 (2008), www.jasna.org/persuasions/on-line/vol28no2/troost-greenfield.htm (accessed 1 August 2012).

4. Deidre Lynch, "See Jane Elope: What *Becoming Jane* Gets Wrong About Jane Austen's Love Life," *Slate Magazine*, 3 August 2007, www.slate.com/id/2171615/ (accessed 4 December 2009). Dyalan Govender, "*Becoming Jane:* Adapting Female Authority," *Sydney Studies* 34 (2008): 86–108, http://escholarship.usyd.edu.au/journals/index.php/SSE/article/viewFile/641/683 (accessed 29 October 2009), 89.

5. *Pride and Prejudice*'s indebtedness to Austen's life, according to *Becoming Jane*, is analogous to the idea of Shakespeare's life inspiring *Romeo and Juliet* that *Shakespeare in Love* put forward. Marina Cano López and Rosa María García-Periego, "Becoming Shakespeare and Jane Austen in Love: An Intertextual Dialogue between Two Biopics," *Persuasions On-Line* 29.1 (2008), http://jasna.org/persuasions/on-line/vol29no1/cano-garcia.html (accessed 30 July 2012).

6. Carroll, "Austen's Abandoned Romances." Quoted in Sally Williams, "Not So Plain Jane," *Telegraph*, 17 February 2007, www.telegraph.co.uk/culture/3663235/Not-so-plain-Jane.html (accessed 3 December 2009). Penny Gay, "Book Review of *Becoming Jane Austen* by Jon Spence," 14 February 2004, The Jane Austen Society of Australia, www.jasa.net.au/books/spence2.htm (accessed 4 December 2009).

7. In its hardback edition, the original title was *Darcy's Diary*.

8. In the United States, the book was published under the title *Lost in Austen*.

9. Ana-Karina Schneider, "*Pride and Prejudice*," *The Literary Encyclopedia*, 19 January 2008, www.litencyc.com/php/sworks.php?rec=true&UID=2575 (accessed 12 May 2008).

10. Clark, "Jane Austen." Janis P. Stout, "Jane Austen's Proposal Scenes and the Limitations of Language," *Studies in the Novel* 14.4 (1982): 316–317.

11. Barbara Sherrod, "*Pride and Prejudice*: A Classic Love Story," *Persuasions On-Line* 11 (1989): 66–69, www.jasna.org/persuasions/printed/number11/sherrod.htm (accessed 6 November 2009). Deborah Kaplan, "Mass Marketing Jane Austen: Men, Women, and Courtship in Two of the Recent Films," *Persuasions On-Line* 18 (1996): 171–181, www.jasna.org/persuasions/printed/number18/kaplan.htm (accessed 9 June 2009). Quoted in Cecilia Salber, "Bridget Jones and Mark Darcy: Art Imitating Art ... Imitating Art," *Persuasions On-Line* 22.1 (2001), www.jasna.org/persuasions/on-line/vol22no1/salber.html (accessed 31 July 2012).

12. Carol McDaid, "There's No Escaping Mr. Dacy," *The Independent*, 9 June 2000, www.spring.net/karenr/articles/independent060900.html (accessed 2 August 2012). James Rampton, "Forever Darcy," *The International Express*, 26 December 2000, http://hem.passagen.se/lmw/articles.html (accessed 2 August 2012). Quoted in Patrice Hannon, "Austen Novels and Austen Films: Incompatible Worlds?" *Persuasions On-Line* 18 (1996): 24–32, www.jasna.org/persuasions/printed/number18/hannon.htm (accessed 4 August 2012). Sheenagh Pugh, "The Democratic Genre: Fan Fiction in a Literary Context," *Refractory* 5 (2004), http://blogs.arts.unimelb.edu.au/refractory/2004/02/03/the-democratic-genre-fan-fiction-in-a-literary-context-sheenagh-pugh/ (accessed 19 January 2010).

13. Charles H. Hinnant, "Jane Austen's

'Wild Imagination': Romance and the Courtship Plot in the Six Canonical Novels," *Narrative* 14.3 (2006): 306, 303. Susan Morgan, *In the Meantime: Character and Perception in Jane Austen's Fiction* (Chicago: University of Chicago Press, 1980), 82.

14. Serena Hansen, "Rhetorical Dynamics in Jane Austen's Treatment of Marriage Proposals," *Persuasions On-Line* 21.2 (2000), www.jasna.org/persuasions/on-line/vol21no2/hansen.html (accessed 4 December 2009).

15. Stout, "Austen's Proposal Scenes," 316–317. Hansen, "Rhetorical Dynamics." Brooke Allen, "Jane Austen for the Nineties," *New Criterion* 14.1 (1995), retrieved from Academic Search Premier (accessed 30 June 2009). Quoted in Kathleen Lundeen, "A Modest Proposal? Paradise Found in Jane Austen's Betrothal Scenes," *Review of English Studies* 41.161 (1990): 65. Quoted in Joan D. Peters, "Finding a Voice: Towards a Woman's Discourse of Dialogue in the Narration of Jane Eyre," *Studies in the Novel* 23.2 (1991): 224–225.

16. Lundeen, "A Modest Proposal?" 72. Stout, "Austen's Proposal Scenes," 317, 320–322. Jane Austen, *Pride and Prejudice*, 1813, Project Gutenberg, 26 August 2008, www.gutenberg.org/ebooks/1342 (accessed 11 July 2012). Allen, "Austen for the Nineties."

17. Stout, "Austen's Proposal Scenes," 323, 317. Hansen, "Rhetorical Dynamics." Allen, "Austen for the Nineties." Lundeen, "A Modest Proposal?" 73. Sherrod, "A Classic Love Story,"

18. Joseph Wiesenfarth, "Jane Austen's Family of Fiction: From Henry and Eliza to Darcy and Eliza," *Persuasions On-Line* 22.1 (2001), www.jasna.org/persuasions/on-line/vol22no1/wiesenfarth.html (accessed 4 December 2009). Karen Newman, "Can This Marriage Be Saved? Jane Austen Makes Sense of an Ending," *ELH* 50.4 (1983): 703, 695. Hansen, "Rhetorical Dynamics." Quoted in Ruth Perry, "Sleeping with Mr. Collins," *Persuasions On-Line* 22 (2000): 119–135, www.jasna.org/persuasions/printed/number22/perry.htm (accessed 14 September 2012). John McAleer, "The Comedy of Social Distinctions in *Pride and Prejudice*," *Persuasions On-Line* 11 (1989): 70–76, www.jasna.org/persuasions/printed/number11/mcaleer.htm (accessed 14 September 2012).

19. Austen, *Pride and Prejudice*. Judith Lowder Newton, "*Pride and Prejudice*: Power, Fantasy, and Subversion in Jane Austen," *Feminist Studies* 4.1 (1978): 30. Philippa Levine, "'*So* Few Prizes and So Many Blanks': Marriage and Feminism in Later 19th-Century England," *The Journal of British Studies* 28.2 (1989): 150.

20. Judith Lowder Newton, "Women, Power and Subversion," in Sense and Sensibility *and* Pride and Prejudice*: New Casebooks*, ed. Robert Clark (Basingstoke: Macmillan, 1994), 122, 32. Hansen, "Rhetorical Dynamics." Pinion, *Austen Companion*, 95. Morgan, *In the Meantime*, 15.

21. Gina Wisker, "Pemberley," *The Literary Encyclopedia*, 1 November 2002, www.litencyc.com/php/sworks.php?rec=true&UID=2861 (accessed 10 October 2008). Austen, *Pride and Prejudice*. Gerhard Joseph, "Prejudice in Jane Austen, Emma Tennant, Charles Dickens—and Us," *Studies in English Literature, 1500–1900* 40.4 (2000): 682.

22. Austen, *Pride and Prejudice*. Newman, "Can This Marriage Be Saved," 706. William H. Magee, "Instrument of Growth: The Courtship and Marriage Plot in Jane Austen's Novels," *Journal of Narrative Technique* 17.2 (1987): 205.

23. Pinion, *Austen Companion*, 95–96. Barbara Laughlin Adler, "'A disagreement between us': Gendered Argument in Austen's Novels," *Persuasions On-Line* 24 (2002), retrieved from FindArticles.com, http://findarticles.com/p/articles/mi_6747/is_24/ai_n28132583/ (accessed 18 December 2009).

24. Emma Tennant, *Pemberley* (London: Hodder & Stoughton, 1993), 6.

25. Julieta Ojeda Alba, "Elizabeth Bennet and Her Weaknesses," *BABEL AFIAL* 3-4-5 (1996): 70.

26. For a novel just taking place a year after *Pride and Prejudice*, there is just no material time for Lydia's many children and Jane's second pregnancy.

27. Tennant, *Pemberley*, 7, 11, 15, 51.

28. Tennant's second sequel deals more extensively with Elizabeth and Mr. Darcy's marriage and their grown children.

29. Tennant, *Pemberley*, 138, 47.

30. Tennant, *Pemberley*, 26, 18. Jennifer Preston Wilson, "'One has got all the goodness, and the other all the appearance of it': The Development of Darcy in *Pride and Prejudice*," *Persuasions On-Line* 25.1 (2004), www.jasna.org/persuasions/on-line/vol25no1/wilson.html (accessed 3 November 2009).

31. Tennant, *Pemberley*, 37–38. Clark, "Jane Austen." Irvine quoted in Barbara K. Seeber, "A Bennet Utopia: Adapting the Father in *Pride and Prejudice*," *Persuasions On-Line* 27.2 (2007), www.jasna.org/persuasions/on-line/vol27no2/seeber.htm (accessed 1 August 2012). Newton, "Power, Fantasy, and Subversion," 29–30. McAleer, "Comedy of Social Distinctions."

32. Tennant, *Pemberley*, 136, 69, 182, 184. Danny Yee, "Review of *Pemberley: A Sequel to Pride and Prejudice* by Emma Tennant and *Presumption: An Entertainment* by Julia Barrett," March 1997, http://dannyreviews.com/h/Pemberley_Presumption.html (accessed 19 May 2008).

33. Tennant, *Pemberley*, 143. Hobson quoted in Michael Kramp, *Disciplining Love: Austen and the Modern Man* (Columbus: Ohio State University Press, 2007), 151. Quoted in Wisker, "Pemberley." Wisker, "Pemberley." Tamara S. Wagner, "Rewriting Sentimental Plots: Sequels to Novels of Sensibility by Jane Austen and Another Lady," in *Second Thought: Updating the Eighteenth-Century Text*, ed. Elizabeth Kraft and Debra Taylor Bourdeau (Newark: University of Delaware Press, 2007), 233. Martin Arnold, "After that Night in the Airport," *The New York Times*, 22 October 1998, www.nytimes.com/1998/10/22/movies/making-books-after-that-night-at-the-airport.html (accessed 25 May 2009).

34. Amanda Grange, *Mr. Darcy's Diary* (2005; Naperville, IL: Sourcebooks, 2007), 2–3, 6, 26. Glenda A. Hudson, "'Precious Remains of the Earliest Attachment': Sibling Love in Jane Austen's *Pride and Prejudice*," *Persuasions On-Line* 11 (1989): 125–131, www.jasna.org/persuasions/printed/number11/hudson.htm (accessed 6 November 2009). Kramp, *Disciplining Love*, 12.

35. Grange, *Mr. Darcy's Diary*, 34–36, 38, 41, 167, 79, 239, 245, 283.

36. Grange, *Mr. Darcy's Diary*, 192, 136, 301, 86.

37. Grange, *Mr. Darcy's Diary*, 220, 329, 307, 283, 298.

38. Bruce Stovel, "Secrets, Silence, and Surprise in *Pride and Prejudice*," *Persuasions On-Line* 11 (1989): 85–91, www.jasna.org/persuasions/printed/number11/stovel.htm (accessed 6 November 2009).

39. Gwyn Cready, *Seducing Mr. Darcy* (New York: Pocket Books, 2008), 37, 47, 49.

40. "Time-Travel Tango," Review of *Seducing Mr. Darcy* by Gwyn Cready, *Book Page*, August 2008, www.cready.com/pics/bookpage_Aug_2008.jpg (accessed 15 December 2009). Cready, *Seducing Mr. Darcy*, 290, 305. Stephanie Rosenbloom, "Living Your Dreams, in a Manner of Speaking," *The New York Times*, 16 September 2007, www.nytimes.com/2007/09/16/fashion/16lucid.html?_r=1&pagewanted=print (accessed 15 December 2009).

41. Cready, *Seducing Mr. Darcy*, 37.

42. Cready, *Seducing Mr. Darcy*, 7, 90, 15, 92.

43. Cready, *Seducing Mr. Darcy*, 61, 142, 177, 141.

44. Cready, *Seducing Mr. Darcy*, 36, 146. Wagner, "Rewriting Sentimental Plots," 233.

45. Emma Campbell Webster, *Being Elizabeth Bennet: Create Your Own Jane Austen Adventure* (London: Atlantic Books, 2007).

46. Jane Austen and Seth Grahame-Smith, *Pride and Prejudice and Zombies* (Philadelphia: Quirk Books, 2009), 5, 2, 42, 77, 13, 104.

47. Austen and Grahame-Smith, *Pride and Prejudice and Zombies*, 13, 34.

48. Austen and Grahame-Smith, *Pride and Prejudice and Zombies*, 26, 87, 82. Macy Halford, "Jane Austen Does the Monster Mash," *The New Yorker*, 8 April 2009, www.newyorker.com/online/blogs/books/2009/04/jane-austen-doe.html (accessed 28 July 2012).

49. Austen and Grahame-Smith, *Pride and Prejudice and Zombies*, 6, 80.

50. Seeber, "A Bennet Utopia." Troost and Greenfield, "Appropriating Austen."

Carol M. Dole, "Jane Austen and Mud: *Pride & Prejudice* (2005), British Realism, and the Heritage Film," *Persuasions On-Line* 27.2 (2007), www.jasna.org/persuasions/on-line/vol27no2/dole.htm (accessed 30 July 2012). Halford, "Austen Does the Monster Mash." Elisabeth Chretien, "Gentility and the Canon Under Siege: *Pride and Prejudice and Zombies*, Violence, and Contemporary Adaptations of Jane Austen" (M.A. Thesis, University of Nebraska–Lincoln, 2011), 36.

51. Chretien, "Gentility and the Canon Under Siege," abstract, 7, 12.

52. Chretien, "Gentility and the Canon Under Siege," 27, 40, 30. Kramp, *Disciplining Love*, xi.

53. Wilson, "Development of Darcy."

54. Marilyn Francus, "Austen Therapy: *Pride and Prejudice* and Popular Culture," *Persuasions On-Line* 30.2 (2010), www.jasna.org/persuasions/on-line/vol30no2/francus.html (accessed 1 August 2012).

55. Francus, "Austen Therapy." Penny Gay, "Pictures of Perfection? Filming Jane Austen," *Sydney Studies in English*. 23 (1997): 41–57, http://ojs-prod.library.usyd.edu.au/index.php/SSE/article/download/520/492 (accessed 28 July 2012), 41. Quoted in Karen Joy Fowler, "What Would Jane Cut?" *Persuasions On-Line* 29 (2007): 169–173, www.jasna.org/persuasions/printed/number29/fowler.pdf (accessed 31 July 2012).

56. Leah Orcutt, "How to Find Mr. Darcy," *Take Root and Write*, 17 August 2009, www.takerootandwrite.com/2009/08/how-to-find-mr-darcy.html (accessed 2 August 2012). "How to Find a Modern Day Mr. Darcy," Wikihow, www.wikihow.com/Find-a-Modern-Day-Mr.-Darcy (accessed 24 July 2012). Kramp, *Disciplining Love*, 14.

57. Cherry Potter, "Why Do We Still Fall for Mr. Darcy?" *The Guardian*, 29 September 2004, www.guardian.co.uk/film/2004/sep/29/books.gender (accessed 1 August 2012). Marina Cano López, "Looking Back in Desire: or, How Jane Austen Rewrites Chick Lit in Alexandra Potter's *Me and Mr. Darcy*," *Persuasions On-Line* 31.1 (2010), www.jasna.org/persuasions/on-line/vol31no1/cano-lopez.html (accessed 28 July 2012). Marina Cano López, "*Persuasion* Moves to Chicago: Rewriting Austen's Classic in *The Lake House*," *Persuasions On-Line* 29.1 (2008), www.jasna.org/persuasions/on-line/vol29no1/cano-lopez.html (accessed 31 July 2012). Kramp, *Disciplining Love*, 12.

58. Hudelet quoted in Cano López and García-Periego, "Becoming Shakespeare and Austen." Penny Gay, "Pictures of Perfection?" 53. Martin Amis, "Jane's World," *The New Yorker*, 8 January 1996: 31–35, www.newyorker.com/archive/1996/01/08/1996_01_08_031_TNY_CARDS_000374562?currentPage=all (accessed 22 June 2009). Potter, "Why Do We Still Fall for Mr. Darcy?"

59. Potter, "Why Do We Still Fall for Mr. Darcy?"

60. Kramp, *Disciplining Love*, 1–2.

61. Potter, "Why Do We Still Fall for Mr. Darcy?" Quoted in Potter, "Why Do We Still Fall for Mr. Darcy?" Quoted in Cano López, "Looking Back in Desire." Francus, "Austen Therapy." María Elena Rodríguez Martín, "La influencia de la ficción breve de Jane Austen en su obra posterior y en la adaptación al cine de su novela *Mansfield Park*," *El Cuento En Red* (2004), http://148.206.107.15/biblioteca_digital/estadistica.php?id_host=6&tipo=ARTICULO&id=3281&archivo=10-242-3281pfp.pdf&titulo=La influencia de la ficción breve de Jane Austen en su obra posterior y en la adaptación al cine de su novela Mansfield Park (accessed 4 August 2012).

62. Amis, "Jane's World." Carroll, "Austen's Abandoned Romances." Dole, "Austen and Mud."

63. Frey, "Patron Saint of Chick Lit." Gina Wisker, "Pemberley," *The Literary Encyclopedia*, 1 November 2002, www.litencyc.com/php/sworks.php?rec=true&UID=2861 (accessed 10 October 2008). Wagner, "Rewriting Sentimental Plots," 239.

Chapter 3

1. Quoted in Kathy Mezei, "And It Kept Its Secret: Narration, Memory, and Madness in Jean Rhys' *Wide Sargasso Sea*," *Critique* 28.4 (1987): 195.

2. *The French Dancer's Bastard* is Ten-

nant's rewriting of her previous *Adèle: Jane Eyre's Hidden Story* and her later *Thornfield Hall* (2007) is another reissue of *The French Dancer's Bastard.*

3. Mona Fayad, "Unquiet Ghosts: The Struggle for Representation in Jean Rhys's *Wide Sargasso Sea*," *Modern Fiction Studies* 34.3 (1988): 442. Emma Tennant, *The French Dancer's Bastard* (London: Maia Press, 2006), 8.

4. Jean Rhys, *Wide Sargasso Sea*, ed. Hilary Jenkins (1966; London: Penguin, 2001), 150. Peter Hulme, "Jean Rhys," *The Literary Encyclopedia*, 21 January 2001, www.litencyc.com/php/speople.php?rec=true&UID=3758 (accessed 15 October 2009).

5. Quoted in Rose Kamel, "'Before I Was Set Free': The Creole Wife in *Jane Eyre* and *Wide Sargasso Sea*," *Journal of Narrative Technique* 25.1 (1995): 3. Jenkins, *Wide Sargasso Sea*, 149.

6. This stands in marked contrast with Jane's claims that "I feel now that I was right when adhered to principle and law, and scorned and crushed the insane prompting of a frenzied moment. God directed me to a correct choice: I thank His Providence for the guidance!" Charlotte Brontë, *Jane Eyre* (1847; London: Penguin, 1994), 356.

7. Brontë, *Jane Eyre*, 5. *Notes on Charlotte Brontë's* Jane Eyre (London: Methuen Educational, 1967), 37. Tom Winnifrith, "Charlotte Brontë and Mr. Rochester," in *Brontë Facts and Brontë Problems*, ed. Edward Chitham and Tom Winnifrith (London: Macmillan, 1983), 13.

8. Glyn Hughes, *Brontë* (New York: St. Martin's Press, 1996), 285. Arthur Pollard, *Charlotte Brontë* (London: Routledge & Kegan Paul, 1968), 2. Tom Winnifrith and Edward Chitham, *Charlotte and Emily Brontë: Literary Lives* (Basingstoke: Palgrave Macmillan, 1989), 111.

9. Judy Giles, "Jane Eyre," *The Literary Encyclopedia*, 2001, www.litencyc.com/php/sworks.php?rec=true&UID=4360 (accessed 10 July 2009). Rosa María García Rayego, "Apuntes sobre la evolución del punto de vista en la ficción de Jean Rhys: *Wide Sargasso Sea*," *Revista Alicantina de Estudios Ingleses* 3 (1990): 50. Carine Melkom Mardorossian, "Double (de)colonization and the Feminist Criticism of *Wide Sargasso Sea*," *College Literature* (1999), http://findarticles.com/p/articles/mi_qa3709/is_199904/ai_n8836640/ (accessed 13 July 2009).

10. Brontë, *Jane Eyre*, 90, 103, 146, 103–104. Richard Benvenuto, "The Child of Nature, the Child of Grace, and the Unresolved Conflict of *Jane Eyre*," *ELH* 39.4 (1972): 623.

11. Brontë, *Jane Eyre*, 123, 140–141, 299, 146. Tennant, *French Dancer's Bastard*, 67–69.

12. Tennant, *French Dancer's Bastard*, 20, 34, 47, 49, 94.

13. Tennant, *French Dancer's Bastard*, 115, 156, 159–160.

14. Tennant, *French Dancer's Bastard*, 160, 216–217, 219.

15. Tennant, *French Dancer's Bastard*, 14, 124, 219.

16. Tennant, *French Dancer's Bastard*, 88, 94, 107, 135, 141, 219.

17. Tennant, *French Dancer's Bastard*, 37, 40, 67, 42, 143.

18. Quoted in Mardorossian, "Double (de)colonization." Sandra M. Gilbert, "Plain Jane's Progress," *Signs* 2.4 (1977): 796, 780–781. Fayad, "Unquiet Ghosts," 438. Liz Lewis, "The Representation of the Doubleness of Selfhood in Charlotte Bronte's *Jane Eyre* and Jean Rhys's *Wide Sargasso Sea*," London School of Journalism, 2001, www.english-literature.org/essays/bronte_rhys.html (accessed 29 June 2009). Peter Grudin, "Jane and the Other Mrs. Rochester: Excess and Restraint in *Jane Eyre*," *Novel* 10.2 (1977): 157. Kamel, "The Creole Wife," 17. Robert Kendrick, "Edward Rochester and the Margins of Masculinity in *Jane Eyre* and *Wide Sargasso Sea*," *Papers on Language & Literature* 30.3 (1994): 242. Parama Roy, "Unaccommodated Woman and the Poetics of Property in *Jane Eyre*," *Studies in English Literature, 1500–1900* 29.4 (1989): 720.

19. Sandra M. Gilbert, "*Jane Eyre* and the Secrets of Furious Lovemaking," *Novel* 31.3 (1998): 360. Grudin, "Jane and the Other Mrs. Rochester," 147. Roy, "Unaccommodated Woman," 720. Catherine Parayre, "'Madness' and Desire: *Jane Eyre* and *Wittgenstein's Nephew*," *The Brock Review* 10.2 (2009): 2, 5. Valerie Beattie, "The Mystery at Thornfield: Representa-

tions of Madness in *Jane Eyre*," *Studies in the Novel* 28.4 (1996): 496, 501. Joyce Carol Oates, "Romance and Anti-Romance: From Brontë's *Jane Eyre* to Rhys's *Wide Sargasso Sea*," *Virginia Quarterly Review* 61.1 (1985): 51. Fayad, "Unquiet Ghosts," 437. Valerie P. Roper, "Woman as Storyteller in *Wide Sargasso Sea*," *Caribbean Quarterly* 34.1-2 (1988): 31. Gilbert, "Plain Jane's Progress," 782–783. Margaret Howard Blom, *Charlotte Brontë* (London: George Prior/ Boston: Twayne, 1977), 93. Benvenuto, "The Child of Nature," 623.

20. Roy, "Unaccommodated Woman," 720–721. Kamel, "The Creole Wife," 3. Quoted in Michael Thorpe, "The Other Side: *Wide Sargasso Sea* and *Jane Eyre*," *Ariel* 3 (1977): 101.

21. John Buchan, "'Jane's All White': An Examination of Victorian Chromatic Anxiety in Brontë's *Jane Eyre*," 8 May 2001, Queen's University of Belfast, www.qub.ac.uk/schools/SchoolofEnglish/imperial/carib/chromatic-anxiety.htm (accessed 29 June 2009). Parayre, "'Madness' and Desire," 5. Brontë, *Jane Eyre*, 302. Kamel, "The Creole Wife," 8–9. Tennant, *The French Dancer's Bastard*, 45.

22. Brontë, *Jane Eyre*, 309. Tennant, *The French Dancer's Bastard*, 39, 37.

23. Jean Rhys, *Wide Sargasso Sea* (1966; London: Penguin, 2001), 70, 86, 95, 46, 39.

24. Parayre, "'Madness' and Desire," 2. Brontë, *Jane Eyre*, 302, 304. Fayad, "Unquiet Ghosts," 444–445. Rhys, *Wide Sargasso Sea*, 44.

25. Brontë, *Jane Eyre*, 259. John Kucich, "Passionate Reserve and Reserved Passion in the Works of Charlotte Brontë," *ELH* 52.4 (1985): 931–932. Roy, "Unaccommodated Woman," 720–721, 723.

26. Roy, "Unaccommodated Woman," 714, 718. Kendrick, "Rochester and the Margins of Masculinity," 246.

27. Dianne F. Sadoff, "The Father, Castration, and Female Fantasy in *Jane Eyre*," *Psychoanalytic Criticism*, www.ux1.eiu.edu/~rlbeebe/d%20sadoff%20—%20Jane%20Eyre.pdf (accessed 29 June 2009), 527–528. F. A. C. Wilson, "The Primrose Wreath: The Heroes of the Brontë Novels," *Nineteenth-Century Literature* 29.1 (1974): 45. Oates, "Romance and Anti-Romance," 52. Brontë, *Jane Eyre*, 440, 431. Kendrick, "Rochester and the Margins of Masculinity," 254. Roy, "Unaccommodated Woman," 724. Giles, "Jane Eyre." Adrienne Rich, *On Lies, Secrets, and Silence: Selected Prose, 1966–1978* (1979; London: Virago Press, 1986), 106. Ruth Yeazell, "Fictional Heroines and Feminist Critics," *Novel* 8.1 (1974): 34.

28. Micael M. Clarke, "Brontë's *Jane Eyre* and the Grimms' *Cinderella*," *Studies in English Literature, 1500–1900* 40.4 (2000): 695. Brontë, *Jane Eyre*, 430, 202. Roy, "*Unaccommodated Woman*," *725*. Gilbert, "*Plain Jane's Progress*," 803. Tennant, *French Dancer's Bastard*, 147.

29. See chapter 4 for Lin Haire-Sargeant's reinterpretation of the plot of *Jane Eyre* in connection to the plot of *Wuthering Heights* in *Heathcliff: The Return to Wuthering Heights*.

Chapter 4

1. Quoted in Arnold Krupat, "The Strangeness of *Wuthering Heights*," *Nineteenth-Century Literature* 25.3 (1970): 269.

2. Charlotte Brontë, *Jane Eyre* (1847; London: Penguin, 1994), 252. F. A. C. Wilson, "The Primrose Wreath: The Heroes of the Brontë Novels," *Nineteenth-Century Literature* 29.1 (1974): 44. Quoted in Sandra M. Gilbert, "*Jane Eyre* and the Secrets of Furious Lovemaking," *NOVEL: A Forum on Fiction* 31.3, Thirtieth Anniversary Issue III (1998): 354. Adrienne Rich, *On Lies, Secrets, and Silence: Selected Prose, 1966–1978. 1979* (London: Virago Press, 1986), 106. Tom Winnifrith and Edward Chitham, *Charlotte and Emily Brontë: Literary Lives* (Basingstoke: Macmillan, 1989), 116.

3. Winnifrith and Chitham, *Charlotte and Emily Brontë*, 117–118. Quoted in Steven Vine, "Wuthering Heights," *The Literary Encyclopedia*, 30 June 2002, http://litencyc.com/php/sworks.php?rec=true&UID=8891 (accessed 12 November 2009). Quoted in Miriam Allott, ed., *Emily Brontë:* Wuthering Heights*: A Casebook*, rev. ed. (1970; Basingstoke: Macmillan, 1992), 48.

4. Winnifrith and Chitham, *Charlotte and Emily Brontë*, 112. Vine, "Wuthering Heights."

5. Ertugrul Koç, "*Wuthering Heights:* A Hybrid That Rejects Classification," *Journal of Arts and Sciences* 7 (2007): 121. Quoted in Vine, "Wuthering Heights." Quoted in Harriett Hawkins, *Classics and Trash: Traditions and Taboos in High Literature and Popular Modern Genres* (Toronto: University of Toronto Press, 1990), 170.

6. Charlotte Brontë, "Editor's Preface to the New Edition of *Wuthering Heights*," in Emily Brontë, *Wuthering Heights* (1847; London: Penguin, 1994), 13, 15–16. Charlotte Brontë, "Biographical Notice of Ellis and Acton Bell," in Emily Brontë, *Wuthering Heights* (1847; London: Penguin, 1994), 10.

7. John E. Jordan, "The Ironic Vision of Emily Brontë," *Nineteenth-Century Fiction* 29.1 (1965): 2. Emily Brontë, *Wuthering Heights* (1847; London: Penguin, 1994), 92. Craik quoted in Koç, "Hybrid that Rejects Classification," 119. C. M. Yang, "A Deleuzian Reading of *Wuthering Heights:* The Micropolitics of Minorization," *Arts and Social Sciences Journal* 44 (2012), http://astonjournals.com/manuscripts/Vol2012/ASSJ-44_Vol2012.pdf (accessed 2 August 2012), 4.

8. Melvin Watson, "Tempest in the Soul: The Theme and Structure of *Wuthering Heights*," *Nineteenth-Century Fiction* 4, no 2 (1949): 89. John Allen Stevenson, "'Heathcliff is Me!': *Wuthering Heights* and the Question of Likeness," *Nineteenth-Century Literature* 43.1 (1988): 72. Anne Leslie Harris, "Psychological Time in *Wuthering Heights*," *The International Fiction Review* 7.2 (1980): 115. Philip Drew, "Charlotte Brontë as a Critic of *Wuthering Heights*," *Nineteenth-Century Fiction* 18.4 (1964): 379.

9. Stevenson, "*Wuthering Heights* and the Question of Likeness," 68. Quoted in Carolyne Van der Meer, "Interrogating Brontë Sequels: Lin Haire-Sargeant's *The Story of Heathcliff's Journey Back to Wuthering Heights*," *Brontë Studies* 29.1 (2004): 77.

10. Quoted in "Study Guide for *Wuthering Heights* by Emily Brontë," in *The Glencoe Literature Library* (New York: Glencoe McGraw-Hill, n.d.), 10. Winifred Gérin, *Emily Brontë: A Biography*. (Oxford: Clarendon Press, 1971), 225.

11. Vine, "Wuthering Heights."

12. Stevenson, "*Wuthering Heights* and the Question of Likeness," 75. Theo D'haen, "Space as Live Experience in Postcolonial Literature: Retellings of the Caribbean," *Esercizi Filosofici* 7 (2012): 16. Vine, "Wuthering Heights."

13. Katrín Júlia Pálmadóttir, "Heaven and Hell—a Human Creation: Emily Brontë's Vision of an Earthly Heaven an Hell in *Wuthering Heights* with a Miltonic Comparison" (B.A. Thesis, Sigilum Universitatis Islandiae, 2012), http://skemman.is/stream/get/1946/10652/26493/1/B.A_essay...pdf (accessed 2 August 2012), 17. Michael Kramp, *Disciplining Love: Austen and the Modern Man* (Columbus: Ohio State University Press, 2007), 12. Stevenson, "*Wuthering Heights* and the Question of Likeness," 70. Brontë, *Wuthering Heights*, 80. John Hagan, "Control of Sympathy in *Wuthering Heights*," *Nineteenth-Century Fiction* 21.4 (1967): 310. Drew, "Charlotte Brontë as a Critic of *Wuthering Heights*," 380.

14. Hagan, "Control of Sympathy," 305, 312, 317–318. Arnold Kettle quoted in Hagan, "Control of Sympathy," 305–306. Edgar F. Shannon, Jr., "Lockwood's Dreams and the Exegesis of *Wuthering Heights*," *Nineteenth-Century Literature* 14 (1959): 104–108. Pálmadóttir, "Heaven and Hell," 2.

15. Gideon Shunami, "The Unreliable Narrator in *Wuthering Heights*," *Nineteenth-Century Fiction* 27.4 (1973): 452, 457.

16. Lin Haire-Sargeant, *Heathcliff: The Return to Wuthering Heights* (London: Century, 1992), 207, 205, 208, 266, 56.

17. Koç, "Hybrid that Rejects Classification," 123. Eric Solomon, "The Incest Theme in *Wuthering Heights*," *Nineteenth-Century Literature* 14.1 (1959): 81, 83. Shannon, Jr., "Lockwood's Dreams," 100.

18. Haire-Sargeant, *Heathcliff*, 1–6, 123, 9, 12, 15–16, 192.

19. Haire-Sargeant, *Heathcliff*, 210–211.

20. D'haen, "Space as Live Experience," 15, 12. Haire-Sargeant, *Heathcliff*, 248. Wilson, "The Primrose Wreath," 50.

21. Haire-Sargeant, *Heathcliff*, 256, 270–271, 273–280.

22. Haire-Sargeant, *Heathcliff*, 50. Van

der Meer, "*The Story of Heathcliff's Journey*," 78–79.

23. Laurence M. Porter, "Maryse Condé," *The Literary Encyclopedia*, 23 March 2011, www.litencyc.com/php/speople.php?rec=true&UID=5580 (accessed 7 December 2012). Quoted in Mohamed B. Taleb-Khyar, "An Interview with Maryse Condé and Rita Dove," *Callallo* 14.2 (1991): 354.

24. Maryse Condé, *Windward Heights* [*La migration des coeurs*], trans. Richard Philcox (1995; London: Faber and Faber, 1998), 117, 8–9, 116. D'haen, "Space as Live Experience," 15.

25. Condé, *Windward Heights*, 30, 140, 142, 40, 81, 60.

26. Condé, *Windward Heights*, 52, 196. Sandra M. Gilbert and Susan Gubar, *The Madwoman in the Attic: The Woman Writer and the Nineteenth-Century Literary Imagination* (1979; New Haven: Yale University Press, 1984), 288. Jordan, "The Ironic Vision of Emily Brontë," 14. Alison Masters, "Heathcliff: Byronic Challenge," *Occasions* www.colorado.edu/pwr/occasions/articles/Masters_Heathcliff.pdf (accessed 2 August 2012), 2–3.

27. Hagan, "Control of Sympathy," 307. Condé, *Windward Heights*, 76, 106, 78.

28. Condé, *Windward Heights*, 53, 107, 68, 95.

29. Watson, "Tempest in the Soul," 92. Philip Drew, "Charlotte Brontë's Insight into *Wuthering Heights*," in Miriam Allott, ed., *Emily Brontë:* Wuthering Heights*: A Casebook*, rev. ed. (Basingstoke: Macmillan, 1992), 199. William A. Madden, "*Wuthering Heights:* The Binding of Passion," *Nineteenth-Century Fiction* 27.2 (1972): 128.

30. Wilson, "The Primrose Wreath," 51–52.

31. Francis Fike, "Bitter Herbs and Wholesome Medicines: Love as Theological Affirmation in *Wuthering Heights*," *Nineteenth-Century Fiction* 23.2 (1968): 145. Condé, *Windward Heights*, 348.

Chapter 5

1. Nathaniel Hawthorne, *The Scarlet Letter*, in *Novels* (New York: The Library of America, 1983), 170.

2. Ceri Gorton, "The Unitary Self and Conflicting Voices in John Updike's *S*," *Working with English: Medieval and Modern Language, Literature and Drama* 2.1 (2006): 30. James A. Schiff, "Updike's *Scarlet Letter* Trilogy: Recasting an American Myth," *Studies in American Fiction* 20.1 (1992): 20, 18. Donald J. Greiner, "Body and Soul: John Updike and *The Scarlet Letter*," *Journal of Modern Literature* XV.4 (1989): 475.

3. Quoted in Schiff, "Updike's *Scarlet Letter* Trilogy," 19. Jill Jones, "Hags and Whores: American Sin and Shaming from Salem to *Springer*," *The Journal of American Culture* 32.2 (2009): 148,146.

4. Hawthorne, *The Scarlet Letter*, 127, 145–146.

5. Hawthorne, *The Scarlet Letter*, 146, 159.

6. Hawthorne, *The Scarlet Letter*, 159, 185.

7. Hawthorne, *The Scarlet Letter*, 163, 200.

8. Hawthorne, *The Scarlet Letter*, 203–214. David Leverenz, "Mrs. Hawthorne's Headache: Reading *The Scarlet Letter*," *Nineteenth-Century Fiction* 37.4 (1983): 559–560. Suzan Last, "Hawthorne's Feminine Voices: Reading *The Scarlet Letter* as a Woman," *Journal of Narrative Technique* 27.3 (1997): 363–364.

9. Hawthorne, *The Scarlet Letter*, 190, 204–205. Robert K. Martin, "Hester Prynne, *C'est Moi*: Nathaniel Hawthorne and the Anxieties of Gender," in *The Scarlet Letter and Other Writings*, ed. Leland S. Person (New York: W. W. Norton, 2005), 519. Last, "Hawthorne's Feminine Voices," 361.

10. Hawthorne, *The Scarlet Letter*, 257–258. Matthew Gartner, "*The Scarlet Letter* and the Book of Esther: Scriptural Letter and Narrative Life," *Studies in American Fiction* 23.2 (1995): 131.

11. Last, "Hawthorne's Feminine Voices," 360. Nina Baym, *The Scarlet Letter: A Reading.* (New York: Twayne/London: Prentice Hall, 1986), 87.

12. Gartner, "*The Scarlet Letter* and the Book of Esther," 131, 137–138.

13. Hawthorne, *The Scarlet Letter*, 290. Schiff, "Updike's *Scarlet Letter* Trilogy," 27.

14. Hawthorne, *The Scarlet Letter*, 265, 325.

15. Adrianne Kalfopoulou, *A Discus-*

sion of the Ideology of the American Dream in the Culture's Female Discourses: The Untidy House* (Lewiston, NY: Edwin Mellen, 2000), 33.Hawthorne, *The Scarlet Letter,* 232. John Updike, *Hugging the Shore: Essays and Criticism* (1983; London: Penguin, 1985), 76.

16. Erika M. Kreger, "'Depravity Dressed Up in a Fascinating Garb': Sentimental Motifs and the Seduced Hero(ine) in *The Scarlet Letter,*" *Nineteenth-Century Literature* 54.3 (1999): 335. Kalfopoulou, *American Dream,* 21. Robert S. Levine, "Antebellum Feminists on Hawthorne: Reconsidering the Reception of *The Scarlet Letter,*" in *The Scarlet Letter and Other Writings,* ed. Leland S. Person (New York: W. W. Norton, 2005), 278.

17. Last, "Hawthorne's Feminine Voices," 353, 349, 358.

18. Portions of this chapter were originally published in M. Carmen Gomez-Galisteo, "A Month of Sundays," *The Literary Encyclopedia,* 28 September 2009, http://litencyc.com/php/sworks.php?rec=true&UID=7050 (accessed 29 September 2009).

19. John Updike, *A Month of Sundays* (New York: Alfred A. Knopf, 1985), 10.

20. James A. Schiff, *Updike's Version: Rewriting* The Scarlet Letter (Columbia: University of Missouri Press, 1992), 41–42.

21. Updike, *A Month of Sundays,* 154–155.Quoted in Greiner, "Body and Soul," 484.

22. Schiff, "Updike's *Scarlet Letter* Trilogy," 23. Quoted in Greiner, "Body and Soul," 483–484. Greiner, "Body and Soul," 486. Bernard A. Schopen, "Faith, Morality, and the Novels of John Updike," *Twentieth-Century Literature* 24.4 (1978): 526.

23. Hawthorne, *The Scarlet Letter,* 182, 270. Mervyn Rothstein, "In *S.,* Updike Tries the Woman's Viewpoint," *The New York Times,* 2 March 1988, www.nytimes.com/1988/03/02/books/in-s-updike-tries-the-woman-s-viewpoint.html?pagewanted=print(accessed 28 May 2009). Updike, *A Month of Sundays,* 44–45, 71.

24. Rothstein, "In *S.,* Updike Tries the Woman's Viewpoint," 66, 112. Schopen, "Faith, Morality, and Updike," 527.

25. Updike, *A Month of Sundays,* 136–137, 174, 170.

26. Portions of this chapter were originally published in M. Carmen Gomez-Galisteo, "Roger's Version," *The Literary Encyclopedia,* 18 November 2009, http://litencyc.com/php/sworks.php?rec=true&UID=12961 (accessed 19 November 2009).

27. John Updike, *Roger's Version* (1986; London: Penguin, 2006), 8, 29.

28. Updike, *Roger's Version,* 3, 14.

29. Updike, *Roger's Version,* 21, 24, 32.

30. Updike, *Roger's Version,* 73. Raymond J. Wilson III, "*Roger's Version*: Updike's Negative-Solid Model of *The Scarlet Letter,*" *Modern Fiction Studies* 35.2 (1989): 245.

31. Schiff, *Updike's Version,* 69–70. Updike, *Roger's Version,* 107, 35, 274.

32. Updike, *Roger's Version,* 57.

33. David Wisehart, "Review of *Roger's Version* by John Updike," http://knol.google.com/k/david-wisehart/rogers-version-by-john-updike/33mpj3qvhycam/9# (accessed 13 May 2009). Hawthorne, *The Scarlet Letter,* 227. John N. Duvall, "The Pleasure of Textual/Sexual Wrestling: Pornography and Heresy in *Roger's Version,*" *Modern Fiction Studies* 37.1 (1991): 83.

34. David Lodge, "Chasing After God and Sex," *The New York Times,* 31 August 1986, www.nytimes.com/1986/08/31/books/chasing-after-god-and-sex.html (accessed 25 June 2009). Quoted in Schiff, *Updike's Version,* 131.

35. Portions of this chapter originally appeared in M. Carmen Gomez-Galisteo, "S," *The Literary Encyclopedia.* 30 October 2009, http://litencyc.com/php/sworks.php?rec=true&UID=12963 (accessed 2 November 2009).

36. John Updike, *S.: A Novel* (1988; London: Penguin, 2006), 6, 12.

37. Updike, *S.,* 244.

38. Updike, *S.,* 156–157.

39. Updike, *S.,* 153.

40. Updike, *S.,* 87, 91, 171–172.

41. Updike, *S.,* 114.

42. Marshall Boswell, "John Updike," *The Literary Encyclopedia,* 18 March 2004, www.litencyc.com/php/speople.php?rec=true&UID=4502 (accessed 13 May 2009). Christopher Lehmann-Haupt, "In John Updike's Latest, The Woman

Called 'S,'" *The New York Times*. 7 March 1988, http://www.nytimes.com/1988/03/07/books/books-of-the-times-in-john-updike-s-latest-the-woman-called-s.html (accessed 13 May 2009). Schiff, "Updike's *Scarlet Letter*," 27.Updike, *S.*, 236. Gorton, "Unitary Self and Conflicting Voices," 32.

43. Updike, S., 102–103.

44. Quoted in Michiko Kakutani, "Updike's Long Struggle To Portray Women," *The New York Times*, 5 May 1988, http://www.nytimes.com/1988/05/05/books/critic-s-notebook-updike-s-long-struggle-to-portray-women.html (accessed 28 May 2009). Quoted in Rothstein, "Updike Tries the Woman's Viewpoint."

45. Updike, *S.*, 5, 62, 8.

46. Updike, *S.*,105, 115. Schiff, *Updike's Version*, 121.

47. Still, Sarah sees traces of Puritanism in herself—"your own genteel atrocities of coldness and blindness toward me were not by themselves enough. I was too stoical, too Puritan, too much a creature of my society for solitary rebellion," "my Puritan conscience, it must be, won't let me send it [the tape] off to you until I've filled every inch," "it was on my old-fashioned Puritan conscience and now I'm finally cleansed of my last, last iota of guilt toward Charles," "all that bourgeois repression and watered-down Puritanism." Updike, *S.*, 12, 56, 99, 136.

48. Updike, *S.*, 8–9. Schiff, *Updike's Version*, 121.

49. Schiff, "Updike's *Scarlet Letter*," 17, 29. Greiner, "Body and Soul," 495. Schiff, *Updike's Version*, 122.

50. Greiner, "Body and Soul," 495.

Chapter 6

1. Elizabeth Young, "A Wound of One's Own: Louisa May Alcott's Civil War Fiction," *American Quarterly* 48.3 (1996): 439. Alice Fahs, "The Feminized Civil War: Gender, Northern Popular Literature, and the Memory of the War, 1861–1900," *The Journal of American History* 85.4 (1999): 1461, 1463.

2. More often than not, both parts are now printed together under the title *Little Women*.

3. Its success restricted Alcott's later literary production. The expectations on the author of *Little Women* confined her to writing youth/children's books, ending her career as a sensational stories writer, a genre she came to scorn in her writings: "[Jo] took to writing sensation stories, for in those dark ages, even all-perfect America read rubbish." Her dreams of writing a serious novel never materialized and she was labeled, to her dismay, as "the Children's Friend." Judith Fetterley, "*Little Women*: Alcott's Civil War," *Feminist Studies* 5.2 (1979): 369–370. Louisa May Alcott, *Little Women*, 1868, Oxford Text Archive, University of Virginia Library, Electronic Text Center, 2003, http://etext.lib.virginia.edu/modengA.browse.html (accessed 4 June 2009), 386. Eugenia Kaledin, "Louisa May Alcott: Success and the Sorrow of Self-Denial," *Women's Studies* 5 (1978): 254. Helena Maragou, "Louisa May Alcott," *The Literary Encyclopedia*, 2004, www.litencyc.com/php/speople.php?rec=true&UID=62 (accessed 1 September 2009). Louisa Jayne Hodgson, "Transatlantic Little Women: Louisa May Alcott, the Woman Writer and Literary Community," *49th Parallel: An Interdisciplinary Journal of North American Studies* 23 (2009): 3.

4. Despite its immense popularity, critical neglect has followed because of a number of reasons: "a misreading that reduced *Little Women*, a text that mixes genres and messages, to but one genre, an ideologically purified and strained realism; next, a misreading of Alcott that reduced her to that deflated *Little Women*; next, a belittling of its vision of women and women's culture; next, the shelving of *Little Women* as children's literature ... finally, ... a snubbing of popular texts," Catherine R. Stimpson, "Reading for Love: Canons, Paracanons, and Whistling Jo March," *New Literary History* 21.4 (1990): 967.

5. Alexandra Mullen, "Father/Daughter Match: Bronson and Louisa May Alcott," *The Hudson Review*, 23 September 2009, FindArticles.comhttp://findarticles.com/p/articles/mi_qa4021/is_200904/ai_n31667268/ (accessed 8 September 2009). Quoted in Margaret Crompton, "*Little Women*: The Making of a Classic," *Con-*

temporary Review 218.1261 (1971): 99. Judith E. Harper, "Alcott, Louisa May (1832–1888)," in *Women During the Civil War: An Encyclopedia* (New York: Routledge, 2003), 17. Bethany B. Wester, "'At Home We Work Together': Domestic Feminism and Patriarchy in *Little Women*" (M.A. Thesis, Florida State University, September 2005), 7, 42. Geraldine Brooks, "Orpheus at the Plough: The Father of *Little Women*," *The New Yorker*, 10 January 2005, www.geraldinebrooks.com/docs/NYer_Alcott_article.pdf (accessed 2 September 2009). Stacy Carson Hubbard, "The Understory of *Little Women*," *Michigan Quarterly Review* 45.4 (2006): 722.

6. Elaine Showalter, *Sister's Choice: Tradition and Change in American Women's Writing* (Oxford: Clarendon Press, 1991), 50. Quoted in Crompton, "The Making of a Classic," 104. Louisa May Alcott, *Hospital Sketches*, 1863, http://digital.library.upenn.edu/women/alcott/sketches/sketches.html (accessed 11 July 2012).

7. This identification between Alcott and Jo is made even more explicit in the 1994 *Little Women* film adaptation—"in a climatic moment in the film, the camera moves from the proud young author, Jo (Winona Ryder), excitedly ripping open the brown paper on the proofs of her first major publication, to a close-up of the novel's substantial title page: 'LITTLE WOMEN / A NOVEL / BY / JOSEPHINE MARCH.'" Sheryl A. Englund, "Reading the Author in *Little Women*: A Biography of the Book," *American Transcendental Quarterly (ATQ)* 12.3 (1998): 199.

8. Quoted in Elizabeth Lennox Keyser, "*A Bloodsmoor Romance:* Joyce Carol Oates's Little Women," *Women's Studies* 14 (1988): 211. O'Faolain quoted in Keyser, "Oates's Little Women," 211–212. Young, "A Wound of One's Own," 441.

9. Elaine Showalter, ed., *Alternative Alcott.* (New Brunswick: Rutgers University Press, 1988), xi. Alcott, *Little Women*, 480.

10. Quoted in Ed Symkus, "Geraldine Brooks's *March* to a Pulitzer," *Wicked Local, Watertown*, 25 April 2007, www.wickedlocal.com/watertown/fun/entertainment/arts/x980683632?view=print (accessed 16 September 2009).

11. Louise Tucker, "A Colonized Imagination: Louise Tucker talks to Geraldine Brooks," in Geraldine Brooks, *March* (London: Perennial, 2006), 4. Trisha Ping, "An Idealist at War: Geraldine Brooks Fills in the Blanks of Alcott's *Little Women*," *Book Page*, 2005, www.bookpage.com/0503bp/geraldine_brooks.html (accessed 16 September 2009). Showalter, *Sister's Choice*, 54–55. Englund, "Reading the Author," 217. Wester, "At Home We Work Together," 5. Quoted in Mullen, "Father/Daughter Match." Quoted in Showalter, *Alternative Alcott*, xi. Sharon L. Dean, "Geraldine Brooks's *March*," *Rivier Academic Journal* 3.2 (2007), www.rivier.edu/journal/ROAJ-Fall-2007/J113-Dean.pdf (accessed 3 September 2009), 2. Maragou, "Louisa May Alcott."

12. Brooks, "Orpheus at the Plough," 2. Quoted in Showalter, *Sister's Choice*, 44.

13. Caryn James, "Amy Had Golden Curls; Jo Had A Rat. Who Would You Rather Be?" *The New York Times*, 25 December 1994, www.nytimes.com/1994/12/25/books/amy-had-golden-curls-jo-had-a-rat-who-would-you-rather-be.html?pagewanted=all (accessed 29 September 2009). Maragou, "Louisa May Alcott." Brooks, "Orpheus at the Plough," 1. Harper, "Alcott, Louisa May (1832–1888)," 14–15. Young, "A Wound of One's Own," 469. Fahs, *"The Feminized Civil War,"* 1464, 1493.

14. Hubbard, "The Understory of *Little Women*," 722. Alcott, *Little Women*, 97. Sandra M. Gilbert, "Plain Jane's Progress," *Signs* 2.4 (1977): 781. Greta Gaard, "'Self-Denial Was All The Fashion': Repressing Anger in *Little Women*," *Papers on Language and Literature* 27 (1992): 3, 11.

15. Gaard, "Repressing Anger in *Little Women*," 3. Stephanie Foote, "Resentful *Little Women*: Gender and Class Feeling in Louisa May Alcott," *College Literature* 32.1 (2005): 65. Showalter, *Alternative Alcott*, xi–xii. Crompton, "The Making of a Classic," 100. Fetterley, "Alcott's Civil War," 380.

16. Geraldine Brooks, *March* (2005; London: Perennial, 2006), 64, 121, 118–119, 128–131, 115. Quoted in Wester, "At Home We Work Together," 7.

17. Thomas Mallon, "*March:* Pictures from a Peculiar Institution," *The New York*

Times, 27 March 2005, www.nytimes.com/2005/03/27/books/review/027MALLON.html?_r=1&pagewanted=print&position= (accessed 2 December 2008). Brooks, *March*, 222. Symkus, "*March* to a Pulitzer."

18. Alcott, *Little Women*, 184. Crompton, "The Making of a Classic," 103. Foote, "Resentful *Little Women*," 83.

19. Fetterley, "Alcott's Civil War," 379. Brooks, *March*, 222.

20. Alcott, *Little Women*, 184, 304, 386. Quoted in Showalter, *Alternative Alcott*, xv.

21. Alcott, *Little Women*, 390–391, 396–397.

22. Alcott, *Little Women*, 33, 37, 32. Showalter, *Alternative Alcott*, xi. Kaledin, "Success and the Sorrow of Self-Denial," 256–257. Alcott, *Little Women*, 301, 444.

23. Alcott, *Little Women*, 469.

24. Joanne Dobson, "Portraits of the Lady: Imagining Women in Nineteenth-Century America," *American Literary History* 3.2 (1991): 399. Alcott, *Little Women*, 466.

25. Brooks, *March*, 113, 117. M. Carmen Gomez-Galisteo, *The Wind Is Never Gone: Sequels, Parodies and Rewritings of* Gone with the Wind (Jefferson, NC: McFarland, 2011), 85–86.

26. Gomez-Galisteo, *The Wind Is Never Gone*, 28. Young, "A Wound of One's Own," 463. Barbara Sicherman, "Reading *Little Women*: The Many Lives of a Text," in U.S. *History as Women's History: New Feminist Essays*, ed. Linda K. Kerber, Alice Kessler-Harris, and Kathryn Kish Sklar (Chapel Hill: University of North Carolina Press, 1995), 266. Alcott, *Little Women*, 20.

27. Brooks, *March*, 146, 38–39, 210.

28. Harper, "Alcott, Louisa May (1832–1888)," 15. Alcott, *Little Women*, 49. Brooks, *March*, 131.

29. Donna-Marie Tuck, "Blurring the Boundaries: The Sexuality of *Little Women*," *Working with English: Medieval and Modern Language, Literature and Drama* 2.1 (2006): 82–88, www.nottingham.ac.uk/english/working_with_english/special_issues/literary_fads_and_Fahsions/Tuck_31_07_06.pdf (accessed 26 May 2009). Wester, "At Home We Work Together," 1. Carroll Smith-Rosenberg, "The Female World of Love and Ritual: Relations between Women in Nineteenth-Century America," *Signs* 1.1 (1975): 20–21. Alcott, *Little Women*, 42.

30. Quoted in Tucker, "A Colonized Imagination," 4. Quoted in "A Conversation with Geraldine Brooks," Geraldinebrooks.com, 5 December 2007, http://geraldinebrooks.com/march_reading.html (accessed 2 September 2009). Brooks, *March*, 211.

31. Alcott, *Little Women*, 236, 269. Ken Parille, "'Wake Up, and Be a Man': *Little Women*, Laurie, and the Ethic of Submission," *Children's Literature* 29 (2001): 49. Brooks, "Orpheus at the Plough," 2.

32. Alcott, *Little Women*, 209, 269–270, 436, 299.

33. Dean, "Brooks's *March*," 2. Keyser, "Oates's Little Women," 222. Alcott, *Little Women*, 511, 513, 85.

34. Fetterley, "Alcott's Civil War," 370. Harper, "Alcott, Louisa May (1832–1888)," 16. Young, "A Wound of One's Own," 463. Fahs, "The Feminized Civil War," 1487, 1464, 1462, 1461.

35. Alcott, *Little Women*, 19, 14, 12. Quoted in Young, "A Wound of One's Own," 448. Harper, "Alcott, Louisa May (1832–1888)," 14. Kaledin, "Success and the Sorrow of Self-Denial," 252.

36. Young, "A Wound of One's Own," 466.

Chapter 7

1. Nicola J. Watson, *The Popular and the Canonical: Debating Twentieth-Century Literature, 1940–2000* (London: Routledge, 2005), 13. Daphne du Maurier, *Rebecca* (1938; New York: Doubleday, n.d.), 9. Val Hennessy, "Manderley Revisited," *Daily Mail*, 14 September 2001. Alan Howard website, www.alanhoward.org.uk/rebrevs.htm (accessed 9 January 2009).

2. Alfred Hitchcock, who directed the cinematographic version, cast Vivien Leigh as Rebecca. Leigh was then married to Laurence Olivier, who played Maxim. However, Hitchcock eventually decided not to show Rebecca. In *Mrs. De Winter* the second wife comes across a photograph of Rebecca in an old magazine.

3. Peter J. Rabinowitz, "The Turn of the Glass Key: Popular Fiction as Reading

Strategy," *Critical Inquiry* 11.3 (1985): 420. Watson, *Popular and Canonical*, 20. Janet Harbord, "Between Identification and Desire: Rereading *Rebecca*," *Feminist Review* 53 (1996): 101. Alison Light, "'Returning to Manderley': Romance Fiction, Female Sexuality and Class," *Feminist Review* 16 (1984): 18.

4. Du Maurier, *Rebecca*, 131, 9–10, 221. Allan Lloyd Smith, "The Phantoms of Droof and *Rebecca*: The Uncanny Reencountered through Abraham and Torok's 'Cryptonymy,'" *Poetics Today* 13.2 (1992): 304. Kathleen Brogan, *Cultural Haunting: Ghosts and Ethnicity in Recent American Literature* (Charlottesville: University Press of Virginia, 1998), 19–20.

5. Harbord, "Between Identification and Desire," 95–96. Watson, *Popular and Canonical*, 14.

6. Daphne du Maurier, *The Rebecca Notebook and Other Memories* (London: Pan Books, 1981), 10.

7. Du Maurier, *Rebecca*, 225, 41.

8. Lindley N. Swift, "Lesbian Texts and Subtexts: [De]Constructing the Lesbian Subject in Charlotte Brontë's *Villette* and Daphne du Maurier's *Rebecca*" (M.A. Thesis, North Carolina State University, 2006), 42.

9. Even though there is no true romance in the novel, du Maurier saw with frustration how *Rebecca* was labeled as a romance, and complained that "*Rebecca* isn't romantic. It is a study in jealousy and murder, not romantic at all," Du Maurier had already warned her publisher, Gollancz, prior to publication, that "the psycological [sic] side of it may not be understood." Quoted in Martyn Shallcross, *The Private World of Daphne du Maurier* (London: Robson Books, 1991), 83. Quoted in Sue Zlosnik and Avril Horner, "Dame Daphne du Maurier," *The Literary Encyclopedia*, 20 October 2001, www.litencyc.com/php/speople.php?rec=true&UID=1325 (accessed 28 May 2009).

10. Du Maurier, *Rebecca*, 19, 219.

11. Du Maurier, *Rebecca*, 52–54, 57, 139.

12. Light, "Returning to Manderley," 17. Avril Horner and Sue Zlosnik, "'Moving Pictures': Family Portraits, Gothic Anxieties and Daphne du Maurier's *Rebecca*," in *Fictions of Unease: The Gothic from* Otranto *to* The X-Files, ed. Andrew Smith, Diane Mason, and William Hughes (Newton Park, Bath: Sulis Press, 2002), 172–173.

13. Du Maurier later changed his first name to Maxim: "perhaps I thought Henry sounded dull." Du Maurier, *Rebecca Notebook*, 11.

14. Du Maurier, *Rebecca Notebook*, 32. J. B. Jackson, "Dreaming of Manderley," Writing.com, 2004, www.writing.com/main/view_item/item_id/835292/printit/1 (accessed 9 June 2009).

15. Swift, "Lesbian Texts and Subtexts," 46, 50. Anne Williams, "Why is Rose Madder? Feminism in Contemporary Gothic," in *Fictions of Unease: The Gothic from* Otranto *to* The X-Files, ed. Andrew Smith, Diane Mason, And William Hughes. (Newton Park, Bath: Sulis Press, 2002), 198.

16. Du Maurier, *Rebecca*, 127, 251–252, 249, 268.

17. Swift, "Lesbian Texts and Subtexts," 44. Du Maurier, *Rebecca*, 43, 99, 333. Harbord, "Between Identification and Desire," 101.

18. Watson, *Popular and Canonical*, 25. Light, "Returning to Manderley," 11. Horner and Zlosnik, "Moving Pictures," 176. Harriett Hawkins, *Classics and Trash: Traditions and Taboos in High Literature and Popular Modern Genres* (Toronto: University of Toronto Press, 1990), 148.

19. Watson, *Popular and Canonical*, 45–46.

20. Susan Hill, "Mrs. de Winter," Susanhill.com, www.susan-hill.com/pages/books/the_books/mrs_de_winter.asp (accessed 12 January 2009).

21. Du Maurier, *Rebecca Notebook*, 36–37, 41.

22. Watson, *Popular and Canonical*, 46. Susan Hill, *La señora de Winter* [*Mrs. De Winter*], trans. Montserrat Serra] (Barcelona: Ediciones B, 1993), 11–12, 23–24, 45–46, 48.

23. Hill, *La señora de Winter*, 75, 78, 101, 104, 317.

24. Watson, *Popular and Canonical*, 46. Hill, "Mrs. De Winter."

25. Benedicte Page, "Returning to Manderley," *The Bookseller*, 15 June 2001. Alan Howard website, www.alanhoward.

org.uk/rebecca.htm (accessed 9 January 2009). Sally Beauman, *Rebecca's Tale* (2001; London: Sphere, 2007), 3.

26. Harbord, "Between Identification and Desire," 100. Quoted in "Review of *Rebecca's Tale* by Sally Beauman," TW Books, 17 September 2001, www.twbooks.co.uk/authors/sallybeauman.html (accessed 9 January 2009). Sally Beauman, "Living with Rebecca," *The Guardian*, 12 September 2001. Alan Howard website, www.alanhoward.org.uk/living.htm (accessed 9 January 2009).

27. *Ibid.* Quoted in Page, "Returning to Manderley."

28. *Glasgow Sunday Herald* review; quoted in Beauman, *Rebecca's Tale*, i. Watson, *Popular and Canonical*, 47.

29. Beauman, *Rebecca's Tale*, 6–7.

30. Beauman, *Rebecca's Tale*, 575. 435, 415, 441–443.

31. Beauman, *Rebecca's Tale*, 586–587.

32. Beauman, *Rebecca's Tale*, 596,621, 624. Holly Blackford, "Haunted Housekeeping: Fatal Attractions of Servant and Mistress in Twentieth-Century Female Gothic Literature," *Literature Interpretation Theory* 16 (2005): 234. Lisa L. Moore, "Guilty Pleasures," *The Women's Review of Books* XVIII.1 (2000): 13.

33. Quoted in Beauman, *Rebecca's Tale*, back cover. Helen Taylor quoted in Beauman, *Rebecca's Tale*, i. Zlosnik and Horner, "Dame Daphne du Maurier."

34. Smith, "Droof and Rebecca," 304, 303. Du Maurier, *Rebecca*, 320. Preus quoted in Melissa Mazmanian, "Reviving *Emma* in a *Clueless* World: The Current Attraction to a Classic Structure," *Persuasions On-Line* 3 (1999), www.jasna.org/persuasions/on-line/opno3/mazmanian.html (accessed 17 June 2009). Hennessy, "Manderley Revisited."

35. Rebecca, until *Rebecca's Tale*, was generally interpreted by critics as being upper class although nothing in the text supports this. Horner and Zlosnik, "Moving Pictures," 177.

36. Light, "Returning to Manderley," 10. Blackford, "Haunted Housekeeping," 236.

37. Quoted in Swift, "Lesbian Texts and Subtexts," 1. Rhona J. Berenstein, "Adaptation, Censorship, and Audiences of Questionable Type: Lesbian Sightings in *Rebecca* (1940) and *The Uninvited* (1944)," *Cinema Journal* 37.3 (1998): 22. Castle quoted in Berenstein, "Adaptation, Censorship, and Audiences," 16.

38. Shallcross, *Private World of du Maurier*, 115, 30. Moore, "Guilty Pleasures," 13.

39. Nicky Hallett, "Did Mrs. Danvers Warm Rebecca's Pearls? Significant Exchanges and the Extension of Lesbian Space and Time in Literature," *Feminist Review* 74 (2003): 38, 43, 40.

40. Blackford, "Haunted Housekeeping," 236. Light, "Returning to Manderley," 9. Watson, *Popular and Canonical*, 40.

41. Watson, *Popular and Canonical*, 40. Du Maurier, *Rebecca*, 138, 140–141.

42. That even though the romance in the novel is overshadowed by the crime section, since "the girl's romance and whirlwind marriage, ... only occupy about one eighth of *Rebecca*." Light, "Returning to Manderley," 9.

43. Du Maurier, *Rebecca*, flap cover. Harbord, "Between Identification and Desire," 95.

44. Beauman, *Rebecca's Tale*, 96, 612.

45. Du Maurier, *Rebecca*, 23, 2. Quoted in Shallcross, *Private World of du Maurier*, 68.

46. Du Maurier, *Rebecca*, 24, 55. Smith, "Droof and Rebecca," 304.

47. Du Maurier, *Rebecca*, 54, 185.

48. Du Maurier, *Rebecca*, 69.

49. Watson, *Popular and Canonical*, 21. Du Maurier, *Rebecca*, 45.

50. Du Maurier, *Rebecca* 40. Watson, *Popular and Canonical*, 23.

51. Light, "Returning to Manderley," 12. Swift, "Lesbian Texts and Subtexts," 41–42. Du Maurier, *Rebecca*, 31.

52. Shallcross, *Private World of du Maurier*, 62. Zlosnik and Horner, "Dame Daphne du Maurier."

53. Supporting this view, "Rebecca, like any stepmother figure ... knows much more about sex than her childish successor." Watson, *Popular and Canonical*, 22.

54. The Hayes Code imposed a number of restrictions on movies if they were to be authorized for release, one of them being that wrongdoers had to be punished at the end of the movie. Letting Mrs. Dan-

vers go away safely after having burned the house to ashes would have been a serious infraction of the code and thence the change between the movie and the novel, where Mrs. Danvers had left the house hours before the fire was discovered.

55. Du Maurier, *Rebecca*, 185, 139. Shallcross, *Private World of du Maurier*, 13. Light, "Returning to Manderley," 24. Smith, "Droof and Rebecca," 300–301.

56. Beauman, *Rebecca's Tale*, 348.

57. "Until very recently cancer had peculiarly horrible and sexist connotations —'according to popular myth, [it] preys on spinster and nymphomaniac alike.'" Yet, "Rebecca remains one of the most enviable women in fiction for the obvious reason that she is one of the few women in all the annals of literature who controls her own life and death in the way male heroes often do. Max killed her because she wanted him to. She chose not to die an agonising death from an incurable disease," Watson, *Popular and Canonical*, 25. Hawkins, *Classics and Trash*, 149.

58. Laura Shapiro, "Manderley Confidential," *The New York Times*, 14 October 2001, www.nytimes.com/2001/10/14/books/manderley-confidential.html?page wanted=print (accessed 25 May 2009).

59. Hill, "Mrs. De Winter." Celia Brayfield, "Now discontent is our de Winter: *Mrs. De Winter*—Susan Hill," *The Independent*, 10 October 1993, www.independent.co.uk/arts-entertainment/book-review—now-discontent-is-our-de-winter-mrs-de-winter—susan-hill-sinclairstevenson-1299-pounds-1509933.html (accessed 25 May 2009).

Conclusion: The End?

1. David Lodge, *Working with Structuralism: Essays and Reviews on Nineteenth- and Twentieth-Century Literature* (London: Routledge & Kegan Paul, 1981), 153–154.

2. Quoted in Louise Tucker, "A Colonized Imagination: Louise Tucker talks to Geraldine Brooks, " in Geraldine Brooks, *March* (London: Perennial, 2006), 4.

3. Maryann Yin, "J. D. Salinger Estate Settles Suit with Fredrik Colting," 12 January 2011, http://www.mediabistro.com/galleycat/j-d-salinger-estate-settles-suit-with-fredrik-colting_b21063 (accessed 22 June 2012).

4. M. Carmen Gomez-Galisteo, *The Wind Is Never Gone: Sequels, Parodies and Rewritings of* Gone with the Wind (Jefferson, NC: McFarland, 2011), 63–69. Quoted in Andy Pemberton, "Lite imitating art?" *The National*, 19 June 2009, http://www.thenational.ae/arts-culture/books/lite-imitating-art (accessed 23 July 2012).

5. Quoted in Ralph Blumenthal, "Nabokov Son Files Suit to Block a Retold *Lolita*," *The New York Times*, 10 October 1998, http://www.nytimes.com/1998/10/10/books/nabokov-son-files-suit-to-block-a-retold-lolita.html?pagewanted=1(accessed 9 February 2010).

6. Jeannie Suk, "Originality," *Harvard Law Review* 115 (2002), http://papers.ssrn.com/sol3/papers.cfm?abstract_id=1136322(accessed 1 March 2010). Natasha Walter, "Works in Progress," *The Guardian*, 27 October 2004, http://www.guardian.co.uk/books/2004/oct/27/technology.news (accessed 7 July 2009).

7. For a discussion of the rewriting of *Gone with the Wind* in fan fiction, see Gómez-Galisteo, *The Wind Is Never Gone.*

8. Walter, "Works in Progress." Eleanor Robinson, "Once Upon a Time ... a Happy Ending for the Unauthorised Sequel?" *The New Zealand Law e-Journal* 4 (2006): 12–13.

Bibliography

Primary Sources

Alcott, Louisa May. *Hospital Sketches.* 1863. digital.library.upenn.edu/women/alcott/sketches/sketches.html (accessed 11 July 2012).

_____. *Little Women.* 1868. Oxford Text Archive. University of Virginia Library, Electronic Text Center. 2003. etext.lib.virginia.edu/modengA.browse.html (accessed 4 June 2009).

Austen, Jane. *Mansfield Park.* 1814. Project Gutenberg. 22 January 2010. www.gutenberg.org/ebooks/141(accessed 14 July 2012).

_____. *Pride and Prejudice.* 1813. Project Gutenberg. 26 August 2008. www.gutenberg.org/ebooks/1342 (accessed 11 July 2012).

_____. *Sense and Sensibility.* 1811. Project Gutenberg. 25 May 2008. www.gutenberg.org/ebooks/161(accessed 11 July 2012).

_____, and Seth Grahame-Smith. *Pride and Prejudice and Zombies.* Philadelphia: Quirk Books, 2009.

Beauman, Sally. *Rebecca's Tale.* 2001. London: Sphere, 2007.

Brontë, Charlotte. *Jane Eyre.* 1847. London: Penguin, 1994.

Brontë, Emily. *Wuthering Heights.* 1847. London: Penguin, 1994.

Brooks, Geraldine. *March.* 2005. London: Perennial, 2006.

Condé, Maryse. *Windward Heights [La migration des coeurs].* Trans. Richard Philcox. 1995. London: Faber & Faber, 1998.

Cready, Gwyn. *Seducing Mr. Darcy.* New York: Pocket Books, 2008.

Du Maurier, Daphne. *Rebecca.* 1938. New York: Doubleday, n.d.

_____. *The Rebecca Notebook and Other Memories.* London: Pan Books, 1981.

Grange, Amanda. *Mr. Darcy's Diary.* 2005. Naperville, IL: Sourcebooks, 2007.

Haire-Sargeant, Lin. *Heathcliff: The Return to Wuthering Heights.* London: Century, 1992.

Hawthorne, Nathaniel. *The Scarlet Letter.* In *Novels.* New York: The Library of America, 1983. 115–343.

Hill, Susan. *La señora de Winter [Mrs. De Winter].* Trans. Montserrat Serra. Barcelona: Ediciones B, 1993.

James, Henry. "Eugene Pickering." 1874. Project Gutenberg. 8 May 2005 www.gutenberg.org/files/2534/2534-h/2534-h.htm (accessed 2 September 2012).

Rhys, Jean. *Wide Sargasso Sea.* Ed. Hilary Jenkins. 1966. London: Penguin, 2001.

Tennant, Emma. *Elinor and Marianne.* London: Simon & Schuster, 1996.

_____. *The French Dancer's Bastard.* London: Maia Press, 2006.

_____. *Pemberley.* London: Hodder & Stoughton, 1993.

Updike, John. *A Month of Sundays*. New York: Alfred A. Knopf, 1985.

_____. *Roger's Version*. 1986. London: Penguin, 2006.

_____. *S.: A Novel*. 1988. London: Penguin, 2006.

Vonnegut, Kurt, Jr. *Slaughterhouse-Five; Or The Children's Crusade*. 1969. New York: Delacorte Press/Seymour Lawrence, 1994.

Webster, Emma Campbell. *Being Elizabeth Bennet: Create Your Own Jane Austen Adventure*. London: Atlantic Books, 2007.

Secondary Sources

Adler, Barbara Laughlin. "'A disagreement between us': Gendered Argument in Austen's Novels." *Persuasions On-Line* 24 (2002). Retrieved from FindArticles.com. findarticles.com/p/articles/mi_6747/is_24/ai_n28132583/ (accessed 18 December 2009).

Allen, Brooke. "Jane Austen for the Nineties." *New Criterion* 14.1 (1995). Retrieved from Academic Search Premier (accessed 30 June 2009).

Allott, Miriam, ed. *Emily Brontë:* Wuthering Heights*: A Casebook*. 1970. Rev. ed. Basingstoke: Macmillan, 1992.

Amis, Martin. "Jane's World." *The New Yorker*. 8 January 1996: 31–35. www.newyorker.com/archive/1996/01/08/1996_01_08_031_TNY_CARDS_000374562?currentPage=all (accessed 22 June 2009).

Arnold, Martin. "After that Night in the Airport." *The New York Times*. 22 October 1998. www.nytimes.com/1998/10/22/movies/making-books-after-that-night-at-the-airport.html (accessed 25 May 2009).

Austen-Leigh, James Edward. *A Memoir of Jane Austen*. 1870. 2d ed. London: Richard Bentley and Son, 1871. Project Gutenberg. 2006. www.gutenberg.org/files/17797/17797-h/17797-h.htm (accessed 4 December 2009).

Barthes, Roland. "The Death of the Author." Trans. Richard Howard. *Aspen* 5–6. www.ubu.com/aspen/aspen5and6/threeEssays.html (accessed 9 February 2009).

Baym, Nina. *The Scarlet Letter: A Reading*. New York: Twayne/London: Prentice Hall, 1986.

Beattie, Valerie. "The Mystery at Thornfield: Representations of Madness in *Jane Eyre*." *Studies in the Novel* 28.4 (1996): 493–505.

Beauman, Sally. "Living with *Rebecca*." *The Guardian*. 12 September 2001. Alan Howard website, www.alanhoward.org.uk/living.htm (accessed 9 January 2009).

Benedict, Barbara M. "Jane Austen's *Sense and Sensibility*: The Politics of Point of View." *Philological Quarterly* 69.4 (1990): 453–470.

Benvenuto, Richard. "The Child of Nature, the Child of Grace, and the Unresolved Conflict of *Jane Eyre*." *ELH* 39.4 (1972): 620–638.

Berenstein, Rhona J. "Adaptation, Censorship, and Audiences of Questionable Type: Lesbian Sightings in *Rebecca* (1940) and *The Uninvited* (1944)." *Cinema Journal* 37.3 (1998): 16–37.

Blackford, Holly. "Haunted Housekeeping: Fatal Attractions of Servant and Mistress in Twentieth-Century Female Gothic Literature." *Literature Interpretation Theory* 16 (2005): 233–261.

Blom, Margaret Howard. *Charlotte Brontë*. London: George Prior/Boston: Twayne, 1977.

Blumenthal, Ralph. "Nabokov Son Files Suit to Block a Retold *Lolita*." *The New York Times*. 10 October 1998. www.nytimes.com/1998/10/10/books/nabokov-son-files-suit-to-block-a-retold-lolita.html?pagewanted=1 (accessed 9 February 2010).

Boswell, Marshall. "John Updike." *The Literary Encyclopedia*. 18 March 2004. www.litencyc.com/php/speople.php?rec=true&UID=4502 (accessed 13 May 2009).

Bowman, James. "The Inexhaustible Adaptability of Jane Austen." *The New York Sun*. 11 February 2005. www.jamesbowman.net/articleDetail.asp?pubID=1595 (accessed 15 May 2007).

Brace, Marianne. "'Last Night I Dreamt I Went to Manderley Again…' and Again and Again." *The Independent*. 29 September 2001. www.independent.co.uk/arts-entertainment/books/reviews/

rebeccas-tale-by-sally-beauman-752125.html (accessed 9 January 2009).

Brayfield, Celia. "Now discontent is our de Winter: *Mrs. De Winter*—Susan Hill." *The Independent.* 10 October 1993. www.independent.co.uk/arts-entertainment/book-review—now-discontent-is-our-de-winter-mrs-de-winter—susan-hill-sinclairstevenson-1299-pounds-1509933.html (accessed 25 May 2009).

Brogan, Kathleen. *Cultural Haunting: Ghosts and Ethnicity in Recent American Literature.* Charlottesville: University Press of Virginia, 1998.

Brontë, Charlotte. "Biographical Notice of Ellis and Acton Bell," in *Wuthering Heights,* 5–11. London: Penguin, 1994.

_____. "Editor's Preface to the New Edition of *Wuthering Heights,*" in *Wuthering Heights,* 13–17. London and others: Penguin, 1994.

Brooks, Geraldine. "Orpheus at the Plough: The Father of *Little Women.*" *The New Yorker.* 10 January 2005. www.geraldinebrooks.com/docs/NYer_Alcott_article.pdf (accessed 2 September 2009).

Brown, Julia Prewitt. "The Feminist Depreciation of Austen: A Polemical Reading." *Novel* (1990): 303–313.

Buchan, John. "'Jane's All White': An Examination of Victorian Chromatic Anxiety in Brontë's *Jane Eyre.*" 8 May 2001. Queen's University of Belfast. www.qub.ac.uk/schools/SchoolofEnglish/imperial/carib/chromatic-anxiety.htm (accessed 29 June 2009).

Butler, Marilyn. "Sensibility and Jacobinism." In Sense and Sensibility *and* Pride and Prejudice*: New Casebooks,* ed. Robert Clark, 38–52. Basingstoke: Macmillan, 1994.

Cano López, Marina. "Looking Back in Desire: or, How Jane Austen Rewrites Chick Lit in Alexandra Potter's *Me and Mr. Darcy.*" *Persuasions On-Line* 31.1 (2010). www.jasna.org/persuasions/on-line/vol31no1/cano-lopez.html (accessed 28 July 2012).

_____, and Rosa María García-Periego. "Becoming Shakespeare and Jane Austen in Love: An Intertextual Dialogue between Two Biopics." *Persuasions On-Line* 29.1 (2008). jasna.org/persuasions/on-line/vol29no1/cano-garcia.html (accessed 30 July 2012).

Carroll, Laura. "Jane Austen's Abandoned Romances." *Meanjin* 67.2 (June 2008). meanjin.com.au/editions/volume-67-number-2-2008/article/jane-austen-s-abandoned-romances/ (accessed 1 August 2012).

Chretien, Elisabeth. "Gentility and the Canon Under Siege: *Pride and Prejudice and Zombies,* Violence, and Contemporary Adaptations of Jane Austen." M.A. Thesis, University of Nebraska–Lincoln, 2011.

Clark, Robert. "Jane Austen." *The Literary Encyclopedia.* 8 January 2001. www.litencyc.com/php/speople.php?rec=true&UID=5167 (accessed 12 May 2008).

Clarke, Micael M. "Brontë's *Jane Eyre* and the Grimms' Cinderella." *Studies in English Literature, 1500–1900* 40.4 (2000): 695–710.

"A Conversation with Geraldine Brooks." Geraldinebrooks.com. 5 December 2007. geraldinebrooks.com/march_reading.html (accessed 2 September 2009).

Crompton, Margaret. "*Little Women*: The Making of a Classic." *Contemporary Review* 218.1261 (1971): 99–104.

Dean, Sharon L. "Geraldine Brooks's *March.*" *Rivier Academic Journal* 3.2 (2007) www.rivier.edu/journal/ROAJ-Fall-2007/J113-Dean.pdf (accessed 3 September 2009).

D'haen, Theo. "Space as Live Experience in Postcolonial Literature: Retellings of the Caribbean." *Esercizi Filosofici* 7 (2012): 5–19.

Dobson, Joanne. "Portraits of the Lady: Imagining Women in Nineteenth-Century America." *American Literary History* 3.2 (1991): 396–404.

Dole, Carol M. "Jane Austen and Mud: *Pride & Prejudice* (2005), British Realism, and the Heritage Film." *Persuasions On-Line* 27.2 (2007). www.jasna.org/persuasions/on-line/vol27no2/dole.htm (accessed 30 July 2012).

Drew, Philip. "Charlotte Brontë as a Critic of *Wuthering Heights.*" *Nineteenth-Century Fiction* 18.4 (1964): 365–381.

_____. "Charlotte Brontë's Insight into *Wuthering Heights,*" in *Emily Brontë:* Wuthering Heights*: A Casebook,* ed.

Miriam Allott. 197–209. 1970. Rev. ed. Basingstoke: Macmillan, 1992.

Duckworth, Alastair. "Improving on Sensibility." In Sense and Sensibility *and* Pride and Prejudice: *New Casebooks,* ed. Robert Clark, 26–37. Basingstoke: Macmillan, 1994.

Duvall, John N. "The Pleasure of Textual/Sexual Wrestling: Pornography and Heresy in *Roger's Version.*" *Modern Fiction Studies* 37.1 (1991): 81–95.

Englund, Sheryl A. "Reading the Author in *Little Women*: A Biography of the Book." *American Transcendental Quarterly* 12.3 (1998): 199–220.

Fahs, Alice. "The Feminized Civil War: Gender, Northern Popular Literature, and the Memory of the War, 1861–1900." *The Journal of American* History 85.4 (1999): 1461–1494.

Fayad, Mona. "Unquiet Ghosts: The Struggle for Representation in Jean Rhys's *Wide Sargasso Sea.*" *Modern Fiction Studies* 34.3 (1988): 437–452.

Fetterley, Judith. "*Little Women*: Alcott's Civil War." *Feminist Studies* 5.2 (1979): 369–383.

Fike, Francis. "Bitter Herbs and Wholesome Medicines: Love as Theological Affirmation in *Wuthering Heights.*" *Nineteenth-Century Fiction* 23.2 (1968): 127–149.

Foote, Stephanie. "Resentful *Little Women*: Gender and Class Feeling in Louisa May Alcott." *College Literature* 32.1 (2005): 63–85.

Foster, Brandy. "Pimp My Austen: The Commodification and Customization of Jane Austen." *Persuasions On-Line* 29.1 (2008). www.jasna.org/persuasions/on-line/vol29no1/foster.html (accessed 10 June 2009).

Fowler, Karen Joy. "What Would Jane Cut?" *Persuasions On-Line* 29 (2007): 169–173. www.jasna.org/persuasions/printed/number29/fowler.pdf (accessed 31 July 2012).

Francus, Marilyn. "Austen Therapy: *Pride and Prejudice* and Popular Culture." *Persuasions On-Line* 30.2 (2010). www.jasna.org/persuasions/on-line/vol30no2/francus.html (accessed 1 August 2012).

Frey, Jennifer. "The Patron Saint of Chick Lit." *Los Angeles Times.* 1 September 2004. articles.latimes.com/2004/sep/01/entertainment/et-frey1?pg=1 (accessed 30 June 2009).

Gaard, Greta. "'Self-Denial Was All The Fashion': Repressing Anger in *Little Women.*" *Papers on Language and Literature* 27 (1992): 3–19.

Garber, Marjorie. "'I'll Be Back': Review of *Part Two: Reflections on the Sequel.*" *London Review of Books* 21.16 (1999). www.lrb.co.uk/v21/n16/marjorie-garber/ill-be-back/print (accessed 19 January 2010).

García Rayego, Rosa María. "Apuntes sobre la evolución del punto de vista en la ficción de Jean Rhys: *Wide Sargasso Sea.*" *Revista Alicantina de Estudios Ingleses* 3 (1990): 49–55.

Gartner, Matthew. "*The Scarlet Letter* and the Book of Esther: Scriptural Letter and Narrative Life." *Studies in American Fiction* 23.2 (1995): 131–151.

Gay, Penny. "Book Review of *Becoming Jane Austen* by Jon Spence." 14 February 2004. The Jane Austen Society of Australia. www.jasa.net.au/books/spence2.htm (accessed 4 December 2009).

_____. "Pictures of Perfection? Filming Jane Austen." *Sydney Studies in English* 23 (1997): 41–57. ojs-prod.library.usyd.edu.au/index.php/SSE/article/download/520/492 (accessed 28 July 2012).

Gérin, Winifred. *Emily Brontë: A Biography*. Oxford: Clarendon Press, 1971.

Gilbert, Sandra M. "*Jane Eyre* and the Secrets of Furious Lovemaking." *Novel* 31.3 (1998): 351–372.

_____. "Plain Jane's Progress." *Signs* 2.4 (1977): 779–804.

_____, and Susan Gubar. *The Madwoman in the Attic: The Woman Writer and the Nineteenth-Century Literary Imagination.* 1979. New Haven: Yale University Press, 1984.

Giles, Judy. "Jane Eyre." *The Literary Encyclopedia.* 2001. www.litencyc.com/php/sworks.php?rec=true&UID=4360 (accessed 10 July 2009).

Gómez Blanco, Carlos J. "Story and History: Jane Austen and the Politics of Fiction." *BABEL AFIAL* 2 (1993): 19–40.

Gomez-Galisteo, M. Carmen. "A Damsel in Distress: Jane Austen's *Emma* Goes

Clueless," In *Current Trends in Anglophone Studies: Cultural, Linguistic and Literary Research*, ed. Javier Ruano García et al., 234–243. Salamanca, Spain: Ediciones Universidad de Salamanca, 2011.

_____. "A Month of Sundays." *The Literary Encyclopedia*. 28 September 2009. litencyc.com/php/sworks.php?rec=true&UID=7050 (accessed 29 September 2009).

_____. "Roger's Version." *The Literary Encyclopedia*. 18 November 2009. The Literary Dictionary Company. litencyc.com/php/sworks.php?rec=true&UID=12961 (accessed 19 November 2009).

_____. "S." *The Literary Encyclopedia*. 30 October 2009. The Literary Dictionary Company. litencyc.com/php/sworks.php?rec=true&UID=12963 (accessed 2 November 2009).

_____. *The Wind Is Never Gone: Sequels, Parodies and Rewritings of* Gone with the Wind. Jefferson, NC: McFarland, 2011.

Gooneratne, Yasmine. *Jane Austen*. Cambridge: Cambridge University Press, 1970.

Gorton, Ceri. "The Unitary Self and Conflicting Voices in John Updike's *S*." *Working with English: Medieval and Modern Language, Literature and Drama* 2.1 (2006): 30–36.

Govender, Dyalan. "*Becoming Jane:* Adapting Female Authority." *Sydney Studies* 34 (2008): 86–108.

Greiner, Donald J. "Body and Soul: John Updike and *The Scarlet Letter*." *Journal of Modern Literature* XV.4 (1989): 475–495.

Grossett, Jeffrey D. "*The Wind Done Gone*: Transforming Tara Into a Plantation Parody." *Case Western Reserve Law Review* 52.4 (2002): 1113–1130.

Grudin, Peter. "Jane and the Other Mrs. Rochester: Excess and Restraint in *Jane Eyre*." *Novel* 10.2 (1977): 145–157.

Hagan, John. "Control of Sympathy in *Wuthering Heights*." *Nineteenth-Century Fiction* 21.4 (1967): 305–323.

Halford, Macy. "Jane Austen Does the Monster Mash." *The New Yorker*. 8 April 2009. www.newyorker.com/online/blogs/books/2009/04/jane-austen-doe.html (accessed 28 July 2012).

Hallett, Nicky. "Did Mrs. Danvers Warm Rebecca's Pearls? Significant Exchanges and the Extension of Lesbian Space and Time in Literature." *Feminist Review* 74 (2003): 35–49.

Hannon, Patrice. "Austen Novels and Austen Films: Incompatible Worlds?" *Persuasions On-Line* 18 (1996): 24–32. www.jasna.org/persuasions/printed/number18/hannon.htm (accessed 4 August 2012).

Hansen, Serena. "Rhetorical Dynamics in Jane Austen's Treatment of Marriage Proposals." *Persuasions On-Line* 21.2 (2000). www.jasna.org/persuasions/online/vol21no2/hansen.html (accessed 4 December 2009).

Harbord, Janet. "Between Identification and Desire: Rereading *Rebecca*." *Feminist Review* 53 (1996): 95–107.

Harper, Judith E. "Alcott, Louisa May (1832–1888)," in *Women During the Civil War: An Encyclopedia*, 14–17. New York: Routledge, 2003.

Harris, Anne Leslie. "Psychological Time in *Wuthering Heights*." *The International Fiction Review* 7.2 (1980): 112–117.

Hawkins, Harriett. *Classics and Trash: Traditions and Taboos in High Literature and Popular Modern Genres*. Toronto: University of Toronto Press, 1990.

Hennessy, Val. "Manderley Revisited." *Daily Mail*. 14 September 2001. Alan Howard website, www.alanhoward.org.uk/rebrevs.htm (accessed 9 January 2009).

Hensher, Philip. "What Rebecca Did Next, If You Care." *The Observer*. 23 September 2001. www.guardian.co.uk/books/2001/sep/23/fiction.features (accessed 9 January 2009).

Hill, Susan. "Mrs. de Winter." Susanhill.com, www.susan-hill.com/pages/books/the_books/mrs_de_winter.asp (accessed 12 January 2009).

Hinnant, Charles H. "Jane Austen's 'Wild Imagination': Romance and the Courtship Plot in the Six Canonical Novels." *Narrative* 14.3 (2006): 294–310.

Hodgson, Louisa Jayne. "Transatlantic Little Women: Louisa May Alcott, the Woman Writer and Literary Community." *49th Parallel: An Interdisciplinary Journal of North American Studies* 23 (2009): 1–14.

Horner, Avril, and Sue Zlosnik. "'Moving Pictures': Family Portraits, Gothic Anxieties and Daphne du Maurier's *Rebecca*." In *Fictions of Unease: The Gothic from* Otranto *to* The X-Files, ed. Andrew Smith, Diane Mason, and William Hughes, 170–182. Newton Park, Bath: Sulis Press, 2002.

"How to Find a Modern Day Mr. Darcy." Wikihow. www.wikihow.com/Find-a-Modern-Day-Mr.-Darcy (accessed 24 July 2012).

Hubbard, Stacy Carson. "The Understory of *Little Women*." *Michigan Quarterly Review* 45.4 (2006): 722–726.

Hudson, Glenda A. "'Precious Remains of the Earliest Attachment': Sibling Love in Jane Austen's *Pride and Prejudice*." *Persuasions On-Line* 11 (1989): 125–131. www.jasna.org/persuasions/printed/number11/hudson.htm (accessed 6 November 2009).

Hughes, Glyn. *Brontë*. New York: St. Martin's Press, 1996.

Hulme, Peter. "Jean Rhys." *The Literary Encyclopedia*. 21 January 2001. www.litencyc.com/php/speople.php?rec=true&UID=3758 (accessed 15 October 2009).

Jackson, J. B. "Dreaming of Manderley." Writing.com. 2004. www.writing.com/main/view_item/item_id/835292/printit/1 (accessed 9 June 2009).

James, Caryn. "Amy Had Golden Curls; Jo Had a Rat. Who Would You Rather Be?" *The New York Times*. 25 December 1994. www.nytimes.com/1994/12/25/books/amy-had-golden-curls-jo-had-a-rat-who-would-you-rather-be.html?pagewanted=all (accessed 29 September 2009).

Jenkins, Henry. *Textual Poachers: Television Fans and Participatory Culture*. New York: Routledge, 1992.

Johnson, Claudia L. "The 'Twilight of Probability': Uncertainty and Hope in *Sense and Sensibility*." *Philological Quarterly* 62.2 (1983): 171–186.

Jones, Jill. "Hags and Whores: American Sin and Shaming from Salem to *Springer*." *The Journal of American Culture* 32.2 (2009): 146–154.

Jordan, John E. "The Ironic Vision of Emily Brontë." *Nineteenth-Century Fiction* 29.1 (1965): 1–18.

Joseph, Gerhard. "Prejudice in Jane Austen, Emma Tennant, Charles Dickens—and Us." *Studies in English Literature, 1500–1900* 40.4 (2000): 679–693.

Kakutani, Michiko. "Updike's Long Struggle To Portray Women." *The New York Times*. 5 May 1988. www.nytimes.com/1988/05/05/books/critic-s-notebook-updike-s-long-struggle-to-portray-women.html (accessed 28 May 2009).

Kaledin, Eugenia. "Louisa May Alcott: Success and the Sorrow of Self-Denial." *Women's Studies* 5 (1978): 251–263.

Kalfopoulou, Adrianne. *A Discussion of the Ideology of the American Dream in the Culture's Female Discourses: The Untidy House*. Lewiston, NY: Edwin Mellen, 2000.

Kamel, Rose. "'Before I Was Set Free': The Creole Wife in *Jane Eyre* and *Wide Sargasso Sea*." *Journal of Narrative Technique* 25.1 (1995): 1–22.

Kaplan, Deborah. "Mass Marketing Jane Austen: Men, Women, and Courtship in Two of the Recent Films." *Persuasions On-Line* 18 (1996): 171–181. www.jasna.org/persuasions/printed/number18/kaplan.htm (accessed 9 June 2009).

Kaufmann, David. "Law and Propriety, *Sense and Sensibility:* Austen on the Cusp of Modernity." *ELH* 59 (1992): 385–408.

Kendrick, Robert. "Edward Rochester and the Margins of Masculinity in *Jane Eyre* and *Wide Sargasso Sea*." *Papers on Language & Literature* 30.3 (1994): 235–256.

Kessler, Julia Braun. "Murdering Miss Austen." *California Literary Review*. 6 December 2007. calitreview.com/292 (accessed 30 October 2008).

Keyser, Elizabeth Lennox. "*A Bloodsmoor Romance:* Joyce Carol Oates's Little Women." *Women's Studies* 14 (1988): 211–223.

Koç, Ertugrul. "*Wuthering Heights:* A Hybrid that Rejects Classification." *Journal of Arts and Sciences* 7 (2007): 115–124.

Kramp, Michael. *Disciplining Love: Austen and the Modern Man*. Columbus: Ohio State University Press, 2007.

Kreger, Erika M. "'Depravity Dressed Up in a Fascinating Garb': Sentimental Motifs and the Seduced Hero(ine) in *The*

Scarlet Letter." *Nineteenth-Century Literature* 54.3 (1999): 308–335.

Kroeber, Karl. "Jane Austen as an Historical Novelist; *Sense and Sensibility.*" *Persuasions On-Line* 12 (1990): 10–18. www.jasna.org/persuasions/printed/number12/kroeber.htm (accessed 2 September 2012).

Krupat, Arnold. "The Strangeness of *Wuthering Heights.*" *Nineteenth-Century Literature* 25.3 (1970): 269–280.

Kucich, John. "Passionate Reserve and Reserved Passion in the Works of Charlotte Brontë." *ELH* 52.4 (1985): 913–937.

Lara Rallo, Carmen. "*Sense and Sensibility* Revisited: Emma Tennant's *Elinor and Marianne.*" *Odisea: Revista de Estudios Ingleses* 4 (2003): 85–96.

Last, Suzan. "Hawthorne's Feminine Voices: Reading *The Scarlet Letter* as a Woman." *Journal of Narrative Technique* 27.3 (1997): 349–376.

Lehmann-Haupt, Christopher. "In John Updike's Latest, The Woman Called 'S.'" *The New York Times.* 7 March 1988. www.nytimes.com/1988/03/07/books/books-of-the-times-in-john-updike-s-latest-the-woman-called-s.html (accessed 13 May 2009).

Lenckos, Elisabeth. "'...[I]nventing Elegant Letters,' Or, Why Don't Austen's Lovers Write More Often?" *Persuasions On-Line* 26.1 (2005). www.jasna.org/persuasions/on-line/vol26no1/lenckos.htm (accessed 4 December 2009).

Leverenz, David. "Mrs. Hawthorne's Headache: Reading *The Scarlet Letter.*" *Nineteenth-Century Fiction* 37.4 (1983): 552–575.

Levine, Philippa. "'So Few Prizes and So Many Blanks': Marriage and Feminism in Later 19th-Century England." *The Journal of British Studies* 28.2 (1989): 150–174.

Levine, Robert S. "Antebellum Feminists on Hawthorne: Reconsidering the Reception of *The Scarlet Letter,*" in *The Scarlet Letter and Other Writings,* ed. Leland S. Person, 274–290. New York: W. W. Norton, 2005.

Lewis, Liz. "The Representation of the Doubleness of Selfhood in Charlotte Bronte's *Jane Eyre* and Jean Rhys's *Wide Sargasso Sea.*" The London School of Journalism. 2001. www.english-literature.org/essays/bronte_rhys.html (accessed 29 June 2009).

Light, Alison. "'Returning to Manderley': Romance Fiction, Female Sexuality and Class." *Feminist Review* 16 (1984): 7–25.

Lock, F. P. "The Geology of *Sense and Sensibility.*" *Yearbook of English Studies* 9 (1979): 246–255.

Lodge, David. "Chasing After God and Sex." *The New York Times.* 31 August 1986. www.nytimes.com/1986/08/31/books/chasing-after-god-and-sex.html (accessed 25 June 2009).

_____. *Working with Structuralism: Essays and Reviews on Nineteenth- and Twentieth-Century Literature.* London: Routledge & Kegan Paul, 1981.

Looser, Devoney. "Jane Austen 'Responds' to the Men's Movement." *Persuasions On-Line* 18 (2006). www.jasna.org/persuasions/printed/number18/looser.htm (accessed 2 September 2012).

López-Varela Azcárate, Asunción. "Recepción e intertextualidad." *E-Excellence.* Biblioteca de recursos electrónicos de Humanidades. Liceus. N.d.

Lundeen, Kathleen. "A Modest Proposal? Paradise Found in Jane Austen's Betrothal Scenes." *Review of English Studies* 41.161 (1990): 65–75.

Lynch, Deidre. "See Jane Elope: What *Becoming Jane* Gets Wrong About Jane Austen's Love Life." *Slate Magazine.* 3 August 2007. www.slate.com/id/2171615/ (accessed 4 December 2009).

Madden, William A. "*Wuthering Heights:* The Binding of Passion." *Nineteenth-Century Fiction* 27.2 (1972): 127–154.

Magee, William H. "Instrument of Growth: The Courtship and Marriage Plot in Jane Austen's Novels." *Journal of Narrative Technique* 17.2 (1987): 198–208.

Mallon, Thomas. "*March:* Pictures From a Peculiar Institution." *The New York Times.* 27 March 2005. www.nytimes.com/2005/03/27/books/review/027MALLON.html?_r=1&pagewanted=print&position= (accessed 2 December 2008).

Maragou, Helena. "Louisa May Alcott." *The Literary Encyclopedia.* 2004. www.litencyc.com/php/speople.php?rec=true&UID=62 (accessed 1 September 2009).

Mardorossian, Carine Melkom. "Double (de)colonization and the Feminist Criticism of *Wide Sargasso Sea*." *College Literature* (1999). findarticles.com/p/articles/mi_qa3709/is_199904/ai_n8836640/ (accessed 13 July 2009).

Martin, Robert K. "Hester Prynne, *C'est Moi*: Nathaniel Hawthorne and the Anxieties of Gender," in *The Scarlet Letter and Other Writings*, ed. Leland S. Person, 512–522. New York: W. W. Norton, 2005.

Masters, Alison. "Heathcliff: Byronic Challenge." *Occasions*. www.colorado.edu/pwr/occasions/articles/Masters_Heathcliff.pdf (accessed 2 August 2012).

Mazmanian, Melissa. "Reviving *Emma* in a *Clueless* World: The Current Attraction to a Classic Structure." *Persuasions On-Line* 3 (1999). www.jasna.org/persuasions/on-line/opno3/mazmanian.html (accessed 17 June 2009).

McAleer, John. "The Comedy of Social Distinctions in *Pride and Prejudice*." *Persuasions On-Line* 11 (1989): 70–76. www.jasna.org/persuasions/printed/number11/mcaleer.htm (accessed 14 September 2012).

McDaid, Carol. "There's No Escaping Mr. Dacy." *The Independent*. 9 June 2000. www.spring.net/karenr/articles/independent060900.html (accessed 2 August 2012).

Mezei, Kathy. "And It Kept its Secret: Narration, Memory, and Madness in Jean Rhys' *Wide Sargasso Sea*." *Critique* 28.4 (1987): 195–209.

Moore, Grace. "Great Expectations." *The Literary Encyclopedia*. 9 December 2004. www.litencyc.com/php/sworks.php?rec=true&UID=4892 (accessed 16 May 2012).

Moore, Lisa L. "Guilty Pleasures." *The Women's Review of Books* XVIII.1 (2000): 13.

Morgan, Susan. *In the Meantime: Character and Perception in Jane Austen's Fiction*. Chicago: University of Chicago Press, 1980.

_____. "Polite Lies: The Veiled Heroine of *Sense and Sensibility*." *Nineteenth-Century Fiction* 31.2 (1976): 188–204.

Mullen, Alexandra. "Father/Daughter Match: Bronson and Louisa May Alcott." *The Hudson Review*. 23 September 2009. FindArticles.com_.findarticles.com/p/articles/mi_qa4021/is_200904/ai_n31667268/ (accessed 8 September 2009).

Newman, Karen. "Can This Marriage Be Saved: Jane Austen Makes Sense of an Ending." *ELH* 50.4 (1983): 693–710.

Newton, Judith Lowder. "*Pride and Prejudice*: Power, Fantasy, and Subversion in Jane Austen." *Feminist Studies* 4.1 (1978): 27–42.

_____. "Women, Power and Subversion." In Sense and Sensibility *and* Pride and Prejudice*: New Casebooks*, ed. Robert Clark, 119–144. Basingstoke: Macmillan, 1994.

Neylon, Virginia Lyn. "Reading and Writing the Romance Novel: An Analysis of Romance Fiction and Its Place in the Community College Classroom." n.d. www.cuyamaca.net/lyn.neylon/Romance/Reading%20and%20writing%20romance.doc (accessed 4 September 2007).

Notes on Charlotte Brontë's Jane Eyre. London: Methuen Educational, 1967.

Oates, Joyce Carol. "Romance and Anti-Romance: From Brontë's *Jane Eyre* to Rhys's *Wide Sargasso Sea*." *Virginia Quarterly Review* 61.1 (1985): 44–58.

Ogawa, Kimiyo. "Marianne's Addiction: Amorous Pleasures in *Sense and Sensibility*." *Persuasions On-Line* 32.2 (2012). www.jasna.org/persuasions/on-line/vol32no2/ogawa.html (accessed 18 July 2012).

Ojeda Alba, Julieta. "Elizabeth Bennet and Her Weaknesses." *BABEL AFIAL* 3-4-5 (1996): 57–71.

Orcutt, Leah. "How To Find Mr. Darcy." *Take Root and Write*. 17 August 2009. www.takerootandwrite.com/2009/08/how-to-find-mr-darcy.html (accessed 2 August 2012).

Page, Benedicte. "Returning to Manderley." *The Bookseller*. 15 June 2001. Alan Howard website, www.alanhoward.org.uk/rebecca.htm (accessed 9 January 2009).

Pálmadóttir, Katrín Júlia. "Heaven and Hell—a human creation: Emily Brontë's Vision of an Earthly Heaven an Hell in *Wuthering Heights* with a Miltonic Comparison." B.A. Thesis, Sigilum Universitatis Islandiae, 2012.

Parayre, Catherine. "'Madness' and Desire: *Jane Eyre* and *Wittgenstein's Nephew*." *The Brock Review* 10.2 (2009): 1–9.

Parille, Ken. "'Wake Up, and Be a Man': *Little Women*, Laurie, and the Ethic of Submission." *Children's Literature* 29 (2001): 34–51.

Parrill, Sue. *Jane Austen on Film and TV: A Critical Study of the Adaptations*. Jefferson, NC: McFarland, 2002.

Pemberton, Andy. "Lite imitating art?" *The National*. 19 June 2009. www.thenational.ae/arts-culture/books/lite-imitating-art (accessed 23 July 2012).

Perry, Ruth. "Sleeping with Mr. Collins." *Persuasions On-Line* 22 (2000): 119–135. www.jasna.org/persuasions/printed/number22/perry.htm (accessed 14 September 2012).

Peters, Joan D. "Finding a Voice: Towards a Woman's Discourse of Dialogue in the Narration of *Jane Eyre*." *Studies in the Novel* 23.2 (1991): 217–236.

Ping, Trisha. "An Idealist at War: Geraldine Brooks Fills in the Blanks of Alcott's *Little Women*." *Book Page*. 2005. www.bookpage.com/0503bp/geraldine_brooks.html (accessed 16 September 2009).

Pinion, F. B. *A Jane Austen Companion. A Critical Survey and Reference Book*. London: Macmillan, 1973.

Pollard, Arthur. *Charlotte Brontë*. London: Routledge & Kegan Paul, 1968.

Porter, Laurence M. "Maryse Condé." *The Literary Encyclopedia*. 23 March 2011. www.litencyc.com/php/speople.php?rec=true&UID=5580 (accessed 7 December 2012).

Potter, Cherry. "Why do We Still Fall for Mr. Darcy?" *The Guardian*. 29 September 2004. www.guardian.co.uk/film/2004/sep/29/books.gender (accessed 1 August 2012).

Pugh, Sheenagh. "The Democratic Genre: Fan Fiction in a Literary Context." *Refractory* 5 (2004). blogs.arts.unimelb.edu.au/refractory/2004/02/03/the-democratic-genre-fan-fiction-in-a-literary-context-sheenagh-pugh/ (accessed 19 January 2010).

Rabinowitz, Peter J. "The Turn of the Glass Key: Popular Fiction as Reading Strategy." *Critical Inquiry* 11.3 (1985): 418–431.

Radcliffe, Claire. "Updating Austen: Jane Austen's Stories in a Modern World." Earl Gregg Swem Library, College of William and Mary. dspace.swem.wm.edu/jspui/bitstream/10288/622/1/Radcliffe.pdf (accessed 16 June 2009).

Rampton, James. "Forever Darcy." *The International Express*. 26 December 2000. hem.passagen.se/lmw/articles.html (accessed 2 August 2012).

Reinstein, P. Gila. "Moral Priorities in *Sense and Sensibility*." *Renascence* 35.4 (1983): 269–283.

Reisz, Matthew. "Review of *What Matters in Jane Austen? Twenty Crucial Puzzles Solved*." *Times Higher Education*. 7 June 2012. www.timeshighereducation.co.uk/story.asp?sectioncode=26&storycode=420217&c=2 (accessed 11 June 2012).

"Review of *Rebecca's Tale* by Sally Beauman." TW Books. 17 September 2001. www.twbooks.co.uk/authors/sallybeauman.html (accessed 9 January 2009).

Rich, Adrienne. *On Lies, Secrets, and Silence: Selected Prose, 1966–1978*. 1979. London: Virago Press, 1986.

Robinson, Eleanor. "Once Upon a Time ... a Happy Ending for the Unauthorised Sequel?" *The New Zealand Law e-Journal* 4 (2006): 1–21.

Rodríguez Martín, María Elena. "La influencia de la ficción breve de Jane Austen en su obra posterior y en la adaptación al cine de su novela *Mansfield Park*." *El Cuento En Red* (2004). 148.206.107.15/biblioteca_digital/estadistica.php?id_host=6&tipo=ARTICULO&id=3281&archivo=10-242-3281pfp.pdf&titulo=La influencia de la ficción breve de Jane Austen en su obra posterior y en la adaptación al cine de su novela Mansfield Park (accessed 4 August 2012).

Roper, Valerie P. "Woman as Storyteller in *Wide Sargasso Sea*." *Caribbean Quarterly* 34.1-2 (1988): 19–36.

Rosenbloom, Stephanie. "Living Your Dreams, in a Manner of Speaking." *The New York Times*. 16 September 2007. www.nytimes.com/2007/09/16/fashion/16lucid.html?_r=1&pagewanted=print (accessed15 December 2009).

Rothstein, Mervyn. "In *S.*, Updike Tries the Woman's Viewpoint." *The New York Times*. 2 March 1988. www.nytimes.com/

1988/03/02/books/in-s-updike-tries-the-woman-s-viewpoint.html?pagewanted=print (accessed 28 May 2009).

Roy, Parama. "Unaccommodated Woman and the Poetics of Property in *Jane Eyre*." *Studies in English Literature, 1500–1900* 29.4 (1989): 713–727.

Sadoff, Dianne F. "The Father, Castration, and Female Fantasy in *Jane Eyre*." *Psychoanalytic Criticism*. www.ux1.eiu.edu/~rlbeebe/d%20sadoff%20—%20Jane%20Eyre.pdf (accessed 29 June 2009).

Salber, Cecilia. "Bridget Jones and Mark Darcy: Art Imitating Art ... Imitating Art." *Persuasions On-Line* 22.1 (2001). www.jasna.org/persuasions/on-line/vol22no1/salber.html (accessed 31 July 2012).

Schiff, James A. "Updike's *Scarlet Letter* Trilogy: Recasting an American Myth." *Studies in American Fiction* 20.1 (1992): 17–31.

_____. *Updike's Version: Rewriting* The Scarlet Letter. Columbia: University of Missouri Press, 1992.

Schneider, Ana-Karina. "Pride and Prejudice." *The Literary Encyclopedia*. 19 January 2008. www.litencyc.com/php/sworks.php?rec=true&UID=2575 (accessed 12 May 2008).

_____. "Sense and Sensibility." *The Literary Encyclopedia*. 9 January 2008. www.litencyc.com/php/sworks.php?rec=true&UID=2122 (accessed 31 July 2012).

Schopen, Bernard A. "Faith, Morality, and the Novels of John Updike." *Twentieth-Century Literature* 24.4 (1978): 523–535.

Schwarzbaum, Lisa. "Rebecca Redux." *Entertainment Weekly*. 22 October 1993. www.ew.com/ew/article/0,,308500,00.html (accessed 9 June 2009).

Seeber, Barbara K. "A Bennet Utopia: Adapting the Father in *Pride and Prejudice*." *Persuasions On-Line* 27.2 (2007). www.jasna.org/persuasions/on-line/vol27no2/seeber.htm (accessed 1 August 2012).

Shaffer, Julie A. "The Ideological Intervention of Ambiguities in the Marriage Plot: Who Fails Marianne in Austen's *Sense and Sensibility?*" in *A Dialogue of Voices: Feminist Literary Theory and Bakhtin*, ed. Karen Hohne and Helen Wussow, 128–151. Minneapolis: University of Minnesota Press, 1994.

Shallcross, Martyn. *The Private World of Daphne Du Maurier*. London: Robson Books, 1991.

Shannon, Edgar F., Jr. "Lockwood's Dreams and the Exegesis of *Wuthering Heights*." *Nineteenth-Century Literature* 14 (1959): 95–109.

Shapiro, Laura. "Manderley Confidential." *The New York Times*. 14 October 2001. www.nytimes.com/2001/10/14/books/manderley-confidential.html?pagewanted=print (accessed 25 May 2009).

Sherrod, Barbara. "*Pride and Prejudice*: A Classic Love Story." *Persuasions On-Line* 11 (1989): 66–69. www.jasna.org/persuasions/printed/number11/sherrod.htm (accessed 6 November 2009).

Shoben, Edward Joseph, Jr. "Impulse and Virtue in Jane Austen: *Sense and Sensibility* in Two Centuries." *Hudson Review* 35.4 (1982–1983): 521–539.

Showalter, Elaine. *Sister's Choice: Tradition and Change in American Women's Writing*. Oxford: Clarendon Press, 1991.

_____, ed. *Alternative Alcott*. New Brunswick: Rutgers University Press, 1988.

Shunami, Gideon. "The Unreliable Narrator in *Wuthering Heights*." *Nineteenth-Century Fiction* 27.4 (1973): 449–468.

Sicherman, Barbara. "Reading *Little Women*: The Many Lives of a Text," in *U. S. History as Women's History: New Feminist Essays*, ed. Linda K. Kerber, Alice Kessler-Harris, and Kathryn Kish Sklar, 245–266. Chapel Hill: University of North Carolina Press, 1995.

Simons, Judy. "Classics and Trash: Reading Austen in the 1990s." *Women's Writing* 5.1 (1998): 27–42.

Smith, Allan Lloyd. "The Phantoms of Droof and *Rebecca*: The Uncanny Reencountered through Abraham and Torok's 'Cryptonymy.'" *Poetics Today* 13.2 (1992): 285–308.

Smith-Rosenberg, Carroll. "The Female World of Love and Ritual: Relations between Women in Nineteenth-Century America." *Signs* 1.1 (1975): 1–29.

Solender, Elsa. "Recreating Jane Austen's World on Film." *Persuasions On-Line* 24 (2002): 102–120.

Solomon, Eric. "The Incest Theme in

Wuthering Heights." *Nineteenth-Century Literature* 14.1 (1959): 80–83.
Soukup, Charles. "Television Viewing as Vicarious Resistance: *The X-Files* and Conspiracy Discourse." *The Southern Communication Journal* 68.1 (2002): 14–26.
Stevenson, John Allen. "'Heathcliff is Me!' *Wuthering Heights* and the Question of Likeness." *Nineteenth-Century Literature* 43.1 (1988): 60–81.
Stimpson, Catherine R. "Reading for Love: Canons, Paracanons, and Whistling Jo March." *New Literary History* 21.4 (1990): 957–976.
Stout, Janis P. "Jane Austen's Proposal Scenes and the Limitations of Language." *Studies in the Novel* 14.4 (1982): 316–326.
Stovel, Bruce. "Secrets, Silence, and Surprise in *Pride and Prejudice*." *Persuasions On-Line* 11 (1989): 85–91. www.jasna.org/persuasions/printed/number 11/stovel.htm (accessed 6 November 2009).
Stovel, Nora Foster. "From Page to Screen: Emma Thompson's Film Adaptation of *Sense and Sensibility*." *Persuasions On-Line* 32.1 (2011). www.jasna.org/persua sions/on-line/vol32no1/stovel.html (accessed 19 July 2012).
"Study Guide for *Wuthering Heights* by Emily Brontë." The Glencoe Literature Library. New York: Glencoe McGraw-Hill, n.d.
Suk, Jeannie. "Originality." *Harvard Law Review* 115 (2002). papers.ssrn.com/sol3/papers.cfm?abstract_id=1136322 (accessed 1 March 2010).
Swift, Lindley N. "Lesbian Texts and Subtexts: [De]Constructing the Lesbian Subject in Charlotte Brontë's *Villette* and Daphne Du Maurier's *Rebecca*." M.A. Thesis, North Caroline State University, 2006.
Symkus, Ed. "Geraldine Brook's *March* to a Pulitzer." *Wicked Local. Watertown.* 25 April 2007. www.wickedlocal.com/water town/fun/entertainment/arts/x98068 3632?view=print (accessed 16 September 2009.
Taleb-Khyar, Mohamed B. "An Interview with Maryse Condé and Rita Dove." *Callallo* 14.2 (1991): 347–366.
Thompson, Allison. "Trinkets and Treasures: Consuming Jane Austen." *Persuasions On-Line* 28.2 (2008). www.jasna.org/persuasions/on-line/vol28no2/thompson.htm (accessed 16 June 2009).
Thorpe, Michael. "The Other Side: *Wide Sargasso Sea* and *Jane Eyre*." *Ariel* 3 (1977): 99–110.
Tierney, John. "The Big City; Fab Dads and Wanton Wives." *The New York Times Magazine.* 11 February 1996. www.ny times.com/1996/02/11/magazine/the-big-city-fab-dads-and-wanton-wives.html?pagewanted=all&src=pm (accessed 17 July 2012)."
"Time-Travel Tango." Review of *Seducing Mr. Darcy* by Gwyn Cready. *Book Page.* August 2008. www.cready.com/pics/bookpage_Aug_2008.jpg (accessed 15 December 2009.
Troost, Linda, and Sayre Greenfield. "Appropriating Austen: Localism on the Global Scene." *Persuasions On-Line* 28.2 (2008). www.jasna.org/persuasions/on-line/vol28no2/troost-greenfield.htm (accessed 1 August 2012).
Tuck, Donna-Marie. "Blurring the Boundaries: The Sexuality of *Little Women*." *Working with English: Medieval and Modern Language, Literature and Drama* 2.1 (2006): 82–88. www.nottingham.ac.uk/english/working_with_english/special_issues/literary_fads_and_Fahsions/Tuck_31_07_06.pdf (accessed 26 May 2009).
Tucker, Louise. "A Colonized Imagination: Louise Tucker talks to Geraldine Brooks," In *March*, by Geraldine Brooks, 2–7. London: Perennial, 2006.
Updike, John. *Hugging the Shore: Essays and Criticism.* 1983. London: Penguin, 1985.
Van Der Meer, Carolyne. "Interrogating Brontë Sequels: Lin Haire-Sargeant's *The Story of Heathcliff's Journey Back to Wuthering Heights*." *Brontë Studies* 29.1 (2004): 77–81.
Vine, Steven. "Wuthering Heights." *The Literary Encyclopedia.* 30 June 2002. litencyc.com/php/sworks.php?rec=true&UID=8891(accessed 12 November 2009).
Wagner, Tamara S. "Rewriting Sentimental Plots: Sequels to Novels of Sensibility

by Jane Austen and Another Lady." In *Second Thought: Updating the Eighteenth-Century Text*, ed. Elizabeth Kraft and Debra Taylor Bourdeau, 210–244. Newark: University of Delaware Press, 2007.

Walter, Natasha. "Works in Progress." *The Guardian*. 27 October 2004. www.guardian.co.uk/books/2004/oct/27/technology.news (accessed 7 July 2009).

Watson, Mary. "A Defense of Edward Ferrars: Austen's Hero as a Nexus of *Sense and Sensibility*." *Persuasions On-Line* 32.1 (2011). www.jasna.org/persuasions/on-line/vol32no1/watson.html (accessed 19 July 2012).

Watson, Melvin. "Tempest in the Soul: The Theme and Structure of *Wuthering Heights*." *Nineteenth-Century Fiction* 4, no 2. (1949): 87–100.

Watson, Nicola J. "Daphne du Maurier, *Rebecca*," in *The Popular and the Canonical: Debating Twentieth-Century Literature, 1940–2000*, 13–56. London: Routledge, 2005.

Wester, Bethany B. "'At Home We Work Together': Domestic Feminism and Patriarchy in *Little Women*." M.A. Thesis, Florida State University, September 2005.

Wiesenfarth, Joseph. "Jane Austen's Family of Fiction: From Henry and Eliza to Darcy and Eliza." *Persuasions On-Line* 22.1 (2001). www.jasna.org/persuasions/on-line/vol22no1/wiesenfarth.html (accessed 4 December 2009).

Williams, Anne. "Why is Rose Madder? Feminism in Contemporary Gothic," In *Fictions of Unease: The Gothic from* Otranto *to The X-Files*, ed. Andrew Smith, Diane Mason, and William Hughes, 193–201. Newton Park, Bath: Sulis Press, 2002.

Williams, Sally. "Not So Plain Jane." *Telegraph*. 17 February 2007. www.telegraph.co.uk/culture/3663235/Not-so-plain-Jane.html (accessed 3 December 2009).

Wilson, F. A. C. "The Primrose Wreath: The Heroes of the Brontë Novels." *Nineteenth-Century Literature* 29.1 (1974): 40–57.

Wilson, Jennifer Preston. "'One has got all the goodness, and the other all the appearance of it': The Development of Darcy in Pride and Prejudice." *Persuasions On-Line* 25.1 (2004). www.jasna.org/persuasions/on-line/vol25no1/wilson.html (accessed 3 November 2009).

Wilson, Raymond J., III. "*Roger's Version*: Updike's Negative-Solid Model of *The Scarlet Letter*." *Modern Fiction Studies* 35.2 (1989): 241–250.

Winnifrith, Tom. "Charlotte Brontë and Mr. Rochester," in *Brontë Facts and Brontë Problems*, ed. Tom Winnifrith and Edward Chitham, 1–13. London: Macmillan, 1983.

_____, and Edward Chitham. *Charlotte and Emily Brontë: Literary Lives*. Basingstoke: Macmillan, 1989.

Wisehart, David. "Review of *Roger's Version* by John Updike." knol.google.com/k/david-wisehart/rogers-version-by-john-updike/33mpj3qvhycam/9# (accessed 13 May 2009).

Wisker, Gina. "Pemberley." *The Literary Encyclopedia*. 1 November 2002. www.litencyc.com/php/sworks.php?rec=true&UID=2861 (accessed 10 October 2008).

Yang, C. M. "A Deleuzian Reading of *Wuthering Heights:* The Micropolitics of Minorization." *Arts and Social Sciences Journal* 44 (2012). astonjournals.com/manuscripts/Vol2012/ASSJ-44_Vol2012.pdf (accessed 2 August 2012).

Yeazell, Ruth. "Fictional Heroines and Feminist Critics." *Novel* 8.1 (1974): 29–38.

Yee, Danny. "Review of *Pemberley: A Sequel to Pride and Prejudice* by Emma Tennant and *Presumption: An Entertainment* by Julia Barrett." March 1997. dannyreviews.com/h/Pemberley_Presumption.html (accessed 19 May 2008).

Yin, Maryann. "J. D. Salinger Estate Settles Suit with Fredrik Colting." 12 January 2011. www.mediabistro.com/galleycat/j-d-salinger-estate-settles-suit-with-fredrik-colting_b21063 (accessed 22 June 2012).

Young, Elizabeth. "A Wound of One's Own: Louisa May Alcott's Civil War Fiction." *American Quarterly* 48.3 (1996): 439–474.

Zlosnik, Sue, and Avril Horner. "Dame Daphne Du Maurier." *The Literary Encyclopedia*. 20 October 2001. www.litencyc.com/php/speople.php?rec=true&UID=1325 (accessed 28 May 2009).

Index